HOW TO RESTORE YOUR
Volkswagen Beetle

Eric LeClair, Susan Anderson, and the Airkooled Kustoms Krew

CarTech®

CarTech®

CarTech®, Inc.
6118 Main Street
North Branch, MN 55056
Phone: 651-277-1200 or 800-551-4754
Fax: 651-277-1203
www.cartechbooks.com

© 2019 by Eric LeClair, Susan Anderson, and the Airkooled Kustoms Krew

All rights reserved. No part of this publication may be reproduced or utilized in any form or by any means, electronic or mechanical, including photocopying, recording, or by any information storage and retrieval system, without prior permission from the Publisher. All text, photographs, and artwork are the property of the Author unless otherwise noted or credited.

The information in this work is true and complete to the best of our knowledge. However, all information is presented without any guarantee on the part of the Author or Publisher, who also disclaim any liability incurred in connection with the use of the information and any implied warranties of merchantability or fitness for a particular purpose. Readers are responsible for taking suitable and appropriate safety measures when performing any of the operations or activities described in this work.

All trademarks, trade names, model names and numbers, and other product designations referred to herein are the property of their respective owners and are used solely for identification purposes. This work is a publication of CarTech, Inc., and has not been licensed, approved, sponsored, or endorsed by any other person or entity. The Publisher is not associated with any product, service, or vendor mentioned in this book, and does not endorse the products or services of any vendor mentioned in this book.

Edit by Wes Eisenschenk
Layout by Hailey Samples

ISBN 978-1-61325-896-5
Item No. SA426P

Library of Congress Cataloging-in-Publication Data Available

Written, edited, designed and printed in the U.S.A.

CarTech books may be purchased at a discounted rate in bulk for resale, events, corporate gifts, or educational purposes. Special editions may also be created to specification.
For details, contact Special Sales at 6118 Main Street, North Branch, MN 55056 or by email at sales@cartechbooks.com.

CONTENTS

Dedication 4
Foreword 4
Preface 4

Chapter 1: History of the Iconic Beetle 6
The Beetle's Origin Story 6
Standards and Supers 8
How Mass-Produced Economy Cars Became Prized Collectibles 9
Lots of Good Volks Waiting to Meet You 11

Chapter 2: Why Restore Your Beetle? 12
Restoration Options 12
Things to Consider 13
Sourcing Project Cars 15
Make a Plan 16
Upgrades to Consider 17
Happy Parts Hunting 19

Chapter 3: Let's Roll—Restoration First Steps 20
Safety First 20
BYOBC: Build Your Own Body Cart 21
Yikes! That's a Lot of Dirt 23
Disassembly 23
Interior Removal 29

Chapter 4: Beetle Bodies Start Here 37
Blast, Dip, Strip, or Sand? 37
Your Naked Beetle 39
Rust, Dents, Dings, and Damage 39
Panel Replacement 41
Finish Metal Work 43

Chapter 5: Prime, Paint, and Polish 49
Primer 49
Paint 50
Clear Coat 54
Cutting, Buffing, and Polishing ... 54
Polish It Up 56
Caring for Paint Finish 58

Chapter 6: The Beetle Pan 59
Restoring a Pan 59
Pan Reassembly 63
Wheels 65
Suspension 65

Chapter 7: Transmissions 70
VW Transaxles 70
Repair versus Replace 70
Transmission Rebuilding 71
Inspection 73
Reassembly 75
Final Assembly 81

Chapter 8: Brakes 85
Brake Replacement 85
Brake Lines 91

Chapter 9: Body Mating 92
Safety Reminder 92
Body to Pan Reassembly 92

Chapter 10: Engine 97
Engine Disassembly 98
Engine Rebuilding 102
Stock Parts versus Aftermarket Parts 109
If at First You Don't Succeed ... 109
Engine Break-In 110
Fan Belt 111
Fuel Line Safety 111

Chapter 11: The Electrical System . 112
Wiring Harnesses 112
Wiring Harness Replacement . 114
Troubleshooting 115
Fuel-Injection System 115

Chapter 12: Your Beetle's Interior .. 118
Make It 118
Buy and Bolt In 118
Installing Sound Deadener 118
Installing Headliner Padding .. 120
Installing Headliner 120
Emergency Brake Boot 122
Installing Carpet 122
Door Cards, Armrests, Door Handles, and Window Cranks . 125
Interior Items 127

Seats 129
Complete the Trunk 131
Installing the Dash Pad 131
Steering Wheel Installation 133
Emergency Brake 133

Chapter 13: Trim and Finish 135
Refurbishing Recommendations 135
Installing Chrome Trim 138
Installing Glass and Seals 138
Running Board 141
Bumpers 142
Turn Signals 142
Headlights 143
Taillights 143
Miscellaneous Shiny Bits 144

Chapter 14: Exhaust, Carburetor, and Distributor 148
Fluid Levels 148
Brake Lines 149
Exhaust System 150
Carburetor 151
Distributor 152

Chapter 15: Before the First 1,000 Miles 154
License Plate, Registration, and Insurance 154
Gently Breaking In the Beetle . 155
Troubleshooting 155
75-Point, 500-Mile Inspection Checklist 155

Chapter 16: Care and Maintenance 159
Protecting Your Baby 159
Kill Switch 160
Fuel Cutoff Switch 162
Battery Cutoff Switch 163
Keep It Shiny 163
Show and Shine 165
Maintenance 165
Transmission Troubles 166
Conclusion 167

Source Guide 168

DEDICATION

This guide is dedicated to the worldwide community of Beetle lovers. We are an odd bunch.

Today, most folks dream of driving whatever shiny, plastic, cup holder–filled model rolls off the factory floor next. It's almost like cars are disposable, really. But that's not us.

We stalk boneyards and dream of barn finds; always on the lookout for salvageable air-cooled relics.

We pour our blood and sweat into restoring sorely neglected vintage steel hulks that originally sold for pennies compared to their worth today.

May this guide help you through your first or next restoration project. You have a daunting task ahead of you; one that will be marked by sore muscles, some measure of puzzled head-scratching, and a few purchases that may make your wallet gasp. But in the end, you may very well find yourself wishing the project wasn't over.

As you toil on this labor of love, may your Volkswagen dreams and memories keep you going, and may this book keep you on track. And when your project is complete, may you drive it with pride as you inspire the next generation.

P. S. Roger "00Dub" Moore, we miss you every damn day. We think you would have smiled about this book—and then hid when it came time to take your photo.

FOREWORD by Lonny Speer of Count's Kustoms

You wouldn't be wrong to say I've got paint in my blood.

In my family, painting is more than just a profession. My father and older brother were both painters, and following in their footsteps was an easy choice for me. I'm even training my son to be a painter, which makes it three generations of painters in my family.

Although I don't carry a fancy title (I'm a painter; just a painter), I can say for certain that I know a thing or two about custom work on cars. I worked for 15 years in collision repair before spending the last 6 at Count's Kustoms.

As a longtime painter of vehicles, I can tell you that there's no feeling quite like the one you get when you're looking at the final product. All the hard work—tearing the car down and sandblasting it, bodywork and fabrication, and all the way to painting and buffing—is all worth it in the end. Seeing the customer react to the end result is easily the most gratifying part of what we do.

If you're hoping to experience that feeling for yourself, then you bought the right book.

I first met this book's author through my coworker and fellow VW enthusiast, Shannon Aikau. Sometimes when you meet a fellow painter, things just click; although it doesn't usually happen so fast for me, when I met Spook, the two of us had an instant connection. I'd even call him a brother, which isn't a distinction I'd give to just anyone. Maybe we both have the same paint in our blood.

A book is only as good as the mind that makes it, and Spook is absolutely the best man for the job. I know his background, and I know the work he does. But even if I didn't, he would still have my trust. He has the kind of passion you only ever see in real leaders, and those are the guys who put out the best builds. With Spook, it comes down to a feeling you get from the way he carries himself and the way he talks about his shop and his team. My belief in Spook, and in the wisdom that he has to offer, is why I was so honored that he asked me to write this foreword.

As a painter with more than two decades of experience in the field, you can take my word for it: "If you read this book, you're learning from one of the best."

—Lonny Speer
Count's Kustoms

PREFACE by Susan Anderson

I sometimes wonder just how high a human's eyebrows can be raised.

"You build high-end custom Volkswagens and Porsches in a shop located in Hazel Green, Alabama?"

Yes. Hazel Green, with its bustling population of about 3,111 and a whopping four traffic lights (two of which are fairly new additions), is the home of Airkooled Kustoms. In roughly 7,500 square feet of an area aptly named Mush Island, we transform rusted-out heaps into gloriously glossy marvels of German engineering. More than that, we build kinetic art in the shape of our clients' memories and dreams.

I use the word *we* loosely here. As a writer, I personally do not turn wrenches or make sparks (although I have a growing fascination for welding). My callous-free hands betray the truth: a near-complete ignorance of the nuts and bolts that go into a Beetle restoration. However, gawking at the finished product? Of that I am supremely experienced.

To tell the truth, spending so much time with the krew at the shop has ruined me a bit. When I see a standard-height VW Beetle, my nose wrinkles and the guys remind me that not everyone prefers the slammed-to-the-ground lowered stance that seems normal to me. Where others see a nice paint job, I now notice the orange peel, tiger striping, and wavy panels that are inevitable from a builder who's not quite as obsessive-compulsive as our krew. As particular as I've become, the truth remains: They build cars. I write words. We do best when everyone minds their own part of the business.

The shop has received countless awards for its work, including taking People's Choice at the Las Vegas Ultimate VW Build-Off in 2015 (for my car *Miss Mabel*). We have clients from all over the country. Sometimes krew members even get stopped for photographs and autographs.

We joke about being a decades-long overnight success. The shop started as a one-man shop when founder Eric "Spook" LeClair hung his shingle after retiring from real estate. He'd dreamed of spending his days banging metal and polishing paint and jumped on the opportunity when it arrived. This was in spite of countless raised eyebrows from people who either cautioned that "nobody would pay that kind of money for a Beetle" or expressed a measure of jealousy that he'd figured out a way to get paid to do what he loves.

After some time, the shop added an employee, who was the only person to take home a paycheck for years. Eventually, two employees became three, then four, five, and now nearly a dozen, including (of all things) a writer. Each of us works in our area of genius, we have no secrets in the shop, and nearly everyone who visits comments that somehow time seems to operate differently here. Our passion is for doing it right, whatever part of *it* we play.

The shop has its own book: *Blood, Sweat & Vintage Steel*. Writing that one was easy. I just fell in love with each car we featured, then told the story of how it came to be. It was different when we were approached by CarTech to add this volume to their incredibly broad catalog of restoration books. My own enthusiasm for this art form wasn't nearly enough. We had to figure out how to extract nearly a century's worth of combined experience restoring Volkswagen Beetles that's housed in the krew's craniums and calloused into plain English so a hobbyist could follow it through his or her own restoration project.

Cue the bright lights and straight-backed wooden chair. Eventually, each krew member submitted to my bossy interrogations. "No, wait. Tell me step by step. Explain it like I'm a toddler," was uttered daily.

They say the mark of a true expert is being able to describe complicated processes and ideas in simple ways. That the Airkooled Kustoms krew members were able to convey the information in this book to me with such simplicity that I actually began toying with the idea of swapping my keyboard for a socket set (because restoring a Beetle now seems so doable) is a testament to their enthusiasm and expertise.

This book is the result of many, many hours of interviews. Working with the fine team at CarTech to publish this book is exciting in many ways for us. First, there's the honor of being chosen to produce this how-to guide. There are many other shops out there that could have done a very fine job if they'd been asked. Second, by getting all of this information out of the krew's heads and into print, we now have a bit of required reading we can assign to new team members to help them get their feet wet. But the biggest reason we were delighted to have the opportunity to produce this book is that we can help educate and encourage the next generation of Volkswagen Beetle enthusiasts.

Planning to roll up your sleeves and restore your own Bug? What you're about to do is no small feat. It's our hope that this book will help you build the Bug you've been dreaming about and save you some of the aggravation that comes from doing it by trial and error.

Are you leaning toward committing the small fortune needed to have a pro build it? Just by reading this book, you'll feel a lot less nervous during your project because you'll understand what's going on during every phase. The more you know, the better you'll be at choosing and working with the shop you trust with your project, and that's the best way to get the Beetle you really want.

Congratulations in advance. The moment you've been imagining—cruising on a sun-dappled street with the wind in your hair, listening to the purring of your Beetle's engine—is closer than ever before. Now get to work!

CHAPTER 1

HISTORY OF THE ICONIC BEETLE

Every superhero has an origin story. Spider-Man, Batman, Superman, and Wonder Woman all came from somewhere ordinary and morphed into instantly recognizable and iconic characters that stand the test of time. The Volkswagen Beetle is no different. Originally known as the Type 1, the *Käfer*, and the Bug, the VW Beetle is a unique, iconic car. But how did it come to be?

Like many of today's economy-size cars, the Beetle was born from a need for mass-produced, inexpensive transportation. It was also born from the German love for efficiency and to allow the populace to take advantage of Germany's brand-new road systems.

The Beetle continues to hold records as the longest-running and most-manufactured car in history. In fact, it was the first car ever to reach more than 20 million units sold.

The Beetle's Origin Story

In 1934, Adolf Hitler reached out to Ferdinand Porsche to commission and design a car for German citizens. His requirements were that it needed to be cheap and simple. It needed to be so cheap that a majority of German citizens could purchase it through a government-sponsored savings booklet, or *sparkarte*. And it also needed to be air cooled.

Fast-forward four years. Porsche unveiled the original Beetle: an air-cooled, rear-engine, two-door car seating up to four people in relative comfort. However, mass production did not begin right away. It wasn't until 1945 that Germany started producing Beetles in large quantities. The wait was because of World War II, which impacted multiple industries across the country.

Marketed as "The People's Car," it got the nickname *Käfer* because of its unusual, rounded bodystyle. What is the English translation of *Käfer*? You guessed right; it means beetle. The nickname stuck and spawned a permutation or two. In France, it was referred to as *Coccinelle* (ladybug), and many people still commonly refer to them as *Bugs*.

Design Origins and Creativity

In the quest to create a cheap, simple, air-cooled car, Ferdinand Porsche settled on using a 25-hp engine. With a top speed of roughly 62 mph, it was a respectable option for the Autobahn at the time. With an oil cooler built right into the flat 4-cylinder engine, the little Beetle was a small marvel of efficiency.

Between 1941 and 1944, a limited number of Beetles were produced for select members of the German

Here's a gratuitous, mouth-watering shot of a 1975 semi-custom Super Beetle Convertible, just to show you that Fat Chicks (nickname for Supers) can be downright cool. Cherry Bomb was built as a gift for a client's wife. The build concept began with the acquisition of a set of Porsche wheels and went from there. (Bryan Bacon Photo, Courtesy Airkooled Kustoms)

elite, as well as for military purposes. The air-cooled engine turned out to be a great benefit in northern Africa's desert heat. With a few modifications, the Germans created both an amphibious vehicle (Schwimmwagen) and an all-terrain vehicle (Kommandeurswagen). The ingenuity went even further. As gasoline shortages became more and more common, the factories started turning out vehicles powered by burning wood (Holzbrenners).

Post-War Production

The iconic Bug's history may have ended with World War II if not for a few British Army officers. The officers discovered some Beetle blueprints in a bombed-out Volkswagen factory in Wolfsburg. The British Army ordered 20,000 Type 1 Beetles.

Following World War II, many buildings were destroyed, and others were littered with the remains of unexploded bombs. When the Wolfsburg Volkswagen factory restarted, it was discovered to have live ordnance wedged between several pieces of specialty equipment. One wrong move would have blown the machines to smithereens, but they got lucky.

After the factory had been deemed safe, the British Army officer in charge used what was remaining of the facility's limited materials to start producing about a thousand cars a month. This blueprint discovery and large production order saved the Beetle from becoming a historical footnote.

The Next Generation

In 1948, the Volkswagen plant came under new management. An industry veteran from Opel, Heinrich Nordhoff, took over plant operations. While he detested the original cars, he understood the industry very well. He knew that if the Beetle was going to survive, it would require significant improvements without fundamental changes to the physical design.

Under Nordhoff's guidance, Beetle production ramped up quickly. Improvements started as well, including the introduction of a convertible top, a feature with popularity that would know no bounds. As time wore on, all the specifications Hitler had for the Volkswagen (economical, friendly, and reliable) started drawing more attention.

America Meets the Beetles

In 1949, the Beetle finally landed stateside. It was delivered to Ben Pon Sr., a businessman from Holland. By taking delivery, Pon earned the title "World's First Volkswagen Importer." This Deluxe model came with a few extra bells and whistles, namely color choice (i.e., something not military khaki) and chrome plating.

Alas, the Beetle import business did not exactly get off to a roaring start. In fact, only two sold in that first year. The lackluster sales were to be expected though. Skepticism for foreign cars ran high. Questions about reliability and reparability handicapped most imports, and the Bug was no exception.

But even in the face of opposition, the Volkswagen Beetle quickly gained momentum. It became America's budget car of choice, especially for those who wanted to poke fun at the monster autos of the time. Thousands more arrived and were promptly sold. With the boom in sales, Volkswagen even went so far as to establish local offices in New Jersey.

However, these sales comprised only a small fraction of the auto market. US manufacturers still accounted for more than 95 percent of car sales in 1955. The Beetle's inroads into the US automotive market was a door opener for other auto imports, and more countries started sending cars over. Consequently, this began the decline of the US-produced automotive market.

Volkswagen's Design Evolution

The Bugs continued to get better and better as each year passed. Hydraulic brakes, a sunroof, and modified heaters arrived in 1950. The following year saw more chrome trim. For an extra $1,000 or so, you could buy the Beetle's convertible cousin: the VW Cabriolet.

In 1953, the most significant change to be seen was the replacement of the double rear window. The rear window had been two windows separated by a thin piece of steel. While not much bigger, the redesign replaced these two windows with a single small, oval-shaped pane of glass.

Though little changed during the next two years, a banner moment for Volkswagen arrived in 1955. The one millionth VW Beetle rolled off the assembly line. People praised it for the high speeds relative to engine size and fuel consumption. It was found to be more favorable than other foreign economy car models, such as the Citroën 2CV and the Austin Mini.

For the next three years, there were similar small changes. And then 1958 arrived. That year, the small rear window was replaced with a large rectangle of glass and the front windshield size was increased. These changes had trickle-down design impacts. The rear air intakes needed modification, as did the engine cover, dashboard, and gauges.

During the next decade, a series of changes were made. These included:
- Addition of windshield wipers

CHAPTER 1

- Improved horsepower
- Increased size of the side windows
- Headlight bump outs
- Addition of the semi-automatic stick shift

While these were improvements, they were not unique to the Beetle. Other imports were mastering engineering challenges as well and stepping up their game. While still viewed as reliable, the Beetle was no longer a hip car to own. But that didn't stop it from making history.

In 1972, the humble Beetle finally toppled the reigning auto production champion, the Ford Model T. When Beetle number 15,007,034 rolled off the line, it became the most-produced car in history. It has held on to that record decade after decade to top the 21 million production mark.

The Beginning of the End (Sort Of)

The 1970s were a tough decade for Volkswagen. While still the largest-selling imported car, Beetle manufacturers saw margins declining rapidly. Even as they attempted to bump up horsepower and improve engine performance, they were hit with a new challenge: emissions regulations. This forced the newer models to drop down to 48 hp. The result was lackluster performance to say the least.

The convertible held on a bit longer, being the go-to car for sorority girls in the late 1970s. But it wasn't enough. Eventually, Volkswagen shut down several plants and stopped exporting cars to the United States. While manufacture and export continued in other countries (the record-setting 21 millionth car was produced in Mexico), the Beetle's death knell began to ring.

Feast your eyes on this 1956–1957 example, classically known as an Oval. At this point, the manufacturing techniques made it possible to create and use curved glass. This eliminated the split rear glass design and increased visibility.

Beetle Revival

In the early 1990s, Volkswagen was looking to tell a story of modernization. To do so, the auto manufacturer decided to design a car that paid homage to the original but with a modern edge. And so the Concept 1 was born.

It was unveiled at the Detroit auto show in 1994, and it was met with resounding enthusiasm. However, it still had some kinks to work out. Large-scale production didn't kick off until 1998. When it finally rolled out, VW marketed the new Beetle as a fun, sexy, and stylish descendent of the original. It delivered on its performance promises.

Even though the Beetle had struggled, other Volkswagen cars had stepped in to carry the mantle of continuous improvement. As a result, the engines available under the new hood were impressive. The small car was amply powered and fun to drive.

Volkswagen also opted for bright, cheery color options that set them apart in the market. Everything about the car screamed personality. The next generation found the new model adorable and bought in big time. True to form, VW followed up with a convertible version in 2003, and it saw great success there as well.

To this day, Volkswagen continues to improve and streamline the new Beetle's design, all while continuing to focus on reliability and affordability. With its familiar profile and long-running presence inside the United States, few people can claim to be untouched by this iconic car. Whether it was games of Slug Bug on family car rides, a love for the movie *Herbie*, or as the car you used to ride around in during college, almost everyone has a Beetle story. It wouldn't be surprising if they were still being manufactured decades from now! Truly, the Beetle is the people's car.

Standards and Supers

Owing to the Beetle's unique and colorful history, there are several unusual models out there. Putting those rare and oddball versions aside, classic Beetles fall into two categories: Supers and Standards. However, it's not always easy to tell one from another.

What Is a Super Beetle?

Supers were introduced to keep pace with the technologically advanced vehicles being produced by other manufacturers. These were sold side by side with Standard cars and advertised as being built on a better-riding platform. They only sold between 1971 and 1979.

In fact, for the first two years of manufacture, the only difference was that Supers had a front suspension upgrade. Instead of the Standard's torsion-beam axle, the Supers of the

Even though some of the body panels are interchangeable, some mechanical parts can cross over between the models, and they look similar. There are two different Beetle models represented in this image: Super and Standard. Can you figure out what model each Beetle is?

Here is an example of the differences between Super and Standard Beetles. This Super Beetle features elephant's foot taillights, a vented engine lid, and a more bulbous body (hence the nickname Fat Chicks for the Supers).

early 1970s rode on MacPherson struts. Some minor adjustments were required to accommodate the struts, including different tie-rods, a revamped steering box, and the lengthening of the front hood. These changes made it hard to share front end parts with the Standards. In fact, only a few parts could be interchanged, such as the wheels, lights, and bumpers.

The Supers also had more luggage space and was more comfortable for passengers. This extra roominess could account for why Supers are often lovingly referred to as "Fat Chicks."

In 1973, Volkswagen wanted to differentiate the Supers even further. Engineers added a curved windshield and a flatter roofline along with a modified dashboard. But these subtle changes weren't enough in the increasingly competitive automotive marketplace. Manufacture of Super Beetles stopped in 1975, although Super convertibles continued production through the end of 1979.

How Can You Tell a Super from a Standard?

There are two easy ways to tell if you have a Super Beetle on your hands. First, all Super Beetles have the spare tire lying flat in the hood. You'd have to pop the hood to take a look. The tire position is one of the only differentiating factors that remain the same in all model years. By contrast, Standards have their spares in an upright position.

The second no-fail way to tell you've got a Super is by looking behind your wheels. The MacPherson struts used on these models were basically giant springs. They marked a significant deviation from the Standard torsion-beam suspension. So if you see a spring, you've got a Super!

Super Lies

Myths abound regarding how to identify a Super, but don't fall for them! If it's not mentioned in the previous section, it's not a reliable means of identifying your Beetle. To help you out, here are the five most persistent Standard versus Super myths and the truth behind them.

Myth 1: The engine on a Standard is smaller. Actually, they shared the same engine in North America. There were no unique parts or numbering systems differentiating a Super engine from a Standard for cars in the United States. For those manufactured and sold in Europe, the engines had *S* or *LS* to denote a larger engine, but the designation does not necessarily mean it's a Super Beetle.

Myth 2: It's only a Super if it has a curved windshield. Not true. The 1971 and 1972 models used the same windshield as the Standard. The curved windshield was added in 1973, along with other redesigned elements.

Myth 3: Some Supers had Standard front ends. Nope. Every Super that rolled off the line had MacPherson struts. No exceptions. Keep in mind that this was the single biggest differentiator between the two models. It was not possible to interchange.

Myth 4: All convertible Beetles are Supers. Only if they were manufactured between 1971 and 1979. There were no Standard convertibles put out during this time frame. But there were plenty of convertibles produced in the 1960s (and before) that aren't Supers.

Myth 5: If the Beetle has big bumpers or elephant's foot taillights, it's a Super. The Volkswagen factories were efficient, so they used up their stock of parts rather than abandoning them. This meant some Standard Beetles were built with Super parts.

How Mass-Produced Economy Cars Became Prized Collectibles

You might find it surprising that one of the least-rare and

The spare tire is stored underneath this tray. The gas tank is moved backward in the car, changing the weight bias of the vehicle.

Here you can see the MacPherson strut's attachment point to the upper body. This design change increased stability and created a smoother drive on American roads.

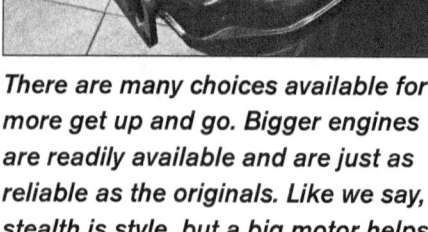

There are many choices available for more get up and go. Bigger engines are readily available and are just as reliable as the originals. Like we say, stealth is style, but a big motor helps.

There are many choices when replacing your struts. Wheel and tire combinations, performance level, and ride height dictate which spring will work best for your build. There are manufacturers providing air-over systems to choose from as well.

most-produced cars in history is still collectible, but it's true. There are several ways to help determine whether you might have a collectible on your hands (or figure out what to look for while shopping).

Original Documentation

While the paperwork is not necessarily valuable in and of itself, it can give the value of your Bug a boost. If you've got any original documentation regarding the sale of the car or its origins, it will go a long way toward establishing provenance and spark buyer interest.

Original Parts and Paint

This goes without saying, but anything original that is in good condition will always be valuable. One example of this was a 1962 Bug that sold for $11,000 at auction. Originally purchased by a pilot stationed in Hamburg, Germany, it came complete with all German and American paperwork. It also had the original paint and dual luggage racks.

Low Mileage

If the car is in good condition, low mileage can be a desirable aspect for a collector. These were the cars of the military, the working class, the college student, and the family man. They were built to be used in everyday life, and most of them were. So a low-mileage Beetle is rare. A word of caution: It's not hard to do an odometer rollback, so what you see is not necessarily what you get here.

Model Year

Any VWs from the 1950s or earlier are going to be rare. Those with the KdF designation are exceedingly so. If you're lucky enough to come across one of these, it's worth checking out.

Ragtop

The 1950s and 1960s saw a large number of Beetles imported with a ragtop feature. However, these examples are relatively scarce. If you find one, it may be worth the time and effort to restore it. A recent auction of an unrestored 1954 model with ragtop netted nearly $40,000.

Rear Windows

A split rear window automatically indicates an older model, assuming it is original. This is a great indicator of age at a glance and can be helpful when weeding through a crowd of cars.

Rust

Rust-proofing was less than stellar back in the day, and the very fact that Beetles were nearly airtight made for problems with drainage. A good rule of thumb is if you spot rust anywhere, there's going to be a lot more. It can be expensive to repair and restore, but rust remediation will be a factor in nearly any restoration project.

HISTORY OF THE ICONIC BEETLE

Supers don't actually come in all shapes and sizes, but it can be hard to differentiate them from Standards if you don't know what to look for. Don't be surprised if your Super has pieces and parts that were originally intended for the Standard Beetle. (Bryan Bacon Photo, Courtesy Airkooled Kustoms)

Don't always trust the mileage on the odometer. Look for documentation to back up a low-mileage claim. The odometer uses a mechanical gearing counter, which is easy to hack.

"Weird"

A lot of the most-valuable Beetles have some oddity. For example, a Beetle manufactured between October 1952 and March 1953 had the split window of 1952 and the redesigned dashboard that was more common in 1953. Known as the Zwitter, this is an extremely rare car only produced for a short period in VW history.

A Note about Collecting

The tips above are a loose guideline to help encourage your love for all things Beetle. At the end of the day, you need to decide why you're buying the car and what your goal is in restoring it. Do you want to sell it to the highest bidder, or do you want something fun to drive around? The answer will dramatically impact which of the above items you're most concerned with as you search. Whether you're an early-model connoisseur or a late-model modified enthusiast, there is no wrong answer. As long as you love your car, you're doing it right.

Lots of Good Volks Waiting to Meet You

If you've caught Dub Fever, restoring and driving your Beetle will become one of life's greatest pleasures. Doing so in the company of other VW enthusiasts just sweetens the pot.

Even before you loosen your first bolt, you should consider joining your local Volkswagen club. There are clubs all over the world, and you can find them with a little online research. Some are more active than others, of course.

When you join a club, you'll find yourself surrounded and supported by other VW nuts who share your passion for fine German engineering. Many will share your penchant for tackling projects that most folks would never undertake. You'll also find some of the most-generous, kind-hearted people you could ever hope to meet.

You will meet some of the nicest people in the Volkswagen community. There's a good sense of camaraderie, and they will be the first to pull over and help if you should get stuck on the side of the road.

Here is a good example of original paint on an unrestored Beetle. Generally, unrestored cars have higher resale values, unless the restoration was done well. Depending on the year, unrestored cars may fetch even higher resale prices.

Miss Mabel, a 1959 Beetle Ragtop, won People's Choice at the Las Vegas Ultimate VW Build-Off. It's a fine example of a late 1950s Ragtop, and it has loads of custom touches. (Jennifer Bagwell Culp Photo, Courtesy Airkooled Kustoms)

CHAPTER 2

WHY RESTORE YOUR BEETLE?

The definition of "labor of love" should include "car restoration" as part of the definition. This project you're considering is going to test your patience, skills, wallet, and maybe even your marriage and other personal relationships. There are a lot of other ways you can spend the next several months or years. Even if you're one of the best bargain hunters out there, you won't come out of this project without it costing an arm, a leg, and maybe a couple of other treasured body parts.

And after all the blood, sweat, and tears you pour into this labor of love, the end result will still be a VW Beetle. Before you start dreaming of jaw-dropping numbers at a classic car auction, it's important to face this reality: You may or may not ever get a return on your investment.

Still reading? Great! Because in return for all the work and money you're about to spend on this project, you're also setting out on the adventure of a lifetime. You'll be bringing a piece of history to life. You'll know your car inside out. You'll develop skills and knowledge that will serve you well for as long as you have your car. And you may also wind up with a Beetle that draws stares and drops jaws.

Let's make sure you know your options and have a few basic requirements covered so your project gets off to a good start.

Restoration Options

"I want to restore my Beetle." It sounds simple enough, but that little statement can have many different meanings. It's important to understand the nomenclature before you dig in. Here's a quick and dirty glossary for restoration types:

DIY Restoration
Overall, you're planning to do the work yourself. However, you might hire an engine shop, transmission specialist, or sandblasting service to take care of some of the tasks.

Pro Restoration
You entrust your Beetle to a professional restoration shop or even have the shop source a project car for you.

Resurrection Restoration
Your goal here is to do whatever is needed just to make sure your Beetle will run, go, and stop.

Partial Restoration
You'll do a complete restoration on just some of the subcomponents,

This 1975 Super Beetle convertible came in with a shocking surprise in the electrical system: all red wiring. It left the shop after a partial reconstruction rocking a new top, new brakes, and a refreshed engine. The electrical system was cleaned up from previous wiring hacks and contacts were cleaned, polished, and reconnected with the appropriate factory-spec wire.

A mild stock restoration was done to this 1970 Beetle. It had the stance and paint finish similar to how it rolled off the factory floor to go with its refurbished engine. The goal was to match the stock factory specifications as closely as possible.

For this 1965 Beetle's custom restoration, the chrome molding was removed and the front turn signals were shaved and incorporated into the front lower fender. The paint finish was completely custom with the one-off paint formulations (Tuxedo Black and Jolly Rancher Green) created in-house. The decklid featured one-off custom airbrushed artwork. Even the interior was custom with Italian leather upholstered seats.

leaving the rest alone. Included here is the mechanical restoration, in which you leave the body and upholstery alone but restore the mechanical systems.

Stock Restoration

The goal here is to get your Beetle as close to how it was when it rolled off the factory line.

Custom Restoration

If you've seen it done, or even just imagined it, you can probably do it to your Beetle. Remember that just because you *can* doesn't mean you *should*. Many custom touches cause a domino effect. For example, that 1,914-cc engine you've been drooling over will require an upgraded suspension, transmission, and brakes.

Body Restoration

Unless your Beetle is miraculously free of rust, you will probably want to restore the body. There are a few different options to consider:

Patina: Simply address any structural issues and then leave the paint alone to show off the ravages of time until it rusts into dust.

Candy Patina: Add a protective clear finish over that lovely patina to give it a bit of shine. That clear coat will slow the progress of the rust from the outside, but the body will still rust from the back side of the panels.

Shiny: There's a lot of work that goes into shiny. You'll want to get your panels as straight as possible, replace any areas that are rusty, and then paint and polish to show off your work. This restoration and finish is the best way to slow the rusting process significantly. You can't stop rust because it's a natural electrochemical process, but you can sure slow it down.

Things to Consider

There are a few things to consider when deciding which type of restoration you want to do.

Tetanus is a 1956 patina Beetle that by all rights should not be on the road anymore. Held together by goodwill and positive thoughts, the rust particles of this patina Beetle cheat death on a regular basis.

CHAPTER 2

Boasting custom paint created in-house and countless hours of polishing and perfecting, Miss Mabel *won People's Choice at the 2015 Ultimate VW Build-Off in Las Vegas.*

While having an enormous workshop for your restoration project would be a dream come true for most hobbyists, all you really need is a one-car garage. It's important to have enough room to move around and work without bumping into your project or the walls.

How Long Will It Take?

Asking how long your Beetle restoration will take is a bit like asking how long a piece of rope is. It all depends. A professional restoration shop can finish a fairly stock restoration in as little as three to six months, assuming the client's cash keeps flowing and the build plan doesn't get changed dramatically during the process. For a hobbyist, the same restoration might take as little as 18 months, or it could take decades. It all depends on how much time and money you can devote to your project and whether you're going for a stock look or a full custom restoration.

Do You Have the Space You Need?

It's best if you have at least a one-car garage you can use for this project. More space is nice of course. You need enough room to move around, store tools, and keep parts corralled and accessible.

How Handy Do You Need to Be?

The skills you have when you begin your project will pale in comparison to the skills you'll have when you finish it. Probably the most important skill you'll need is the ability to follow directions. While the aim of this book is to take you step by step through your restoration, you may have questions along the way. There are tutorials for nearly every task under the sun online. Go to enthusiast forums, live video tutorials, and social media to answer questions you have.

At least once during your restoration project, you're going to be stumped, frustrated, or feel clueless. The best advice we can give is, "Don't give up!" Restoration is just as much art as it is science. If you stick with the project and keep looking for solutions when you hit bumps in the road, you'll figure out how to solve any problem you encounter.

What Tools Do You Need?

Having the right tool makes doing a job right a whole lot easier. Stock your work area as well as you can. Use the right tool instead of brute force and you'll get better results and less muscle fatigue. As Spook says, "Finesse, not force."

You could spend a small fortune outfitting your toolbox, but here are the basics you really need for your restoration:

Air compressor: This is a must-have item. Buy the best, most-powerful air compressor you can afford. You want one that can handle the workload ahead.

Air files: You'll connect this to your air compressor and use it on your initial pass to file away any body filler material you use, even in tight spots. It's a lot faster than sanding by hand.

Air lines: If you're using air tools and compressed air, you've got to have a way to connect them to each other.

Body hammers and dollies: If your project car has dents (and that's nearly guaranteed), using a combination of hammer and dolly to move the steel back into place will give you the power to push low spots up and flatten high areas.

Breaker bar: You'll need a 1/2 inch and a 3/8 inch, as well as sockets to use with them. Remember, the longer the breaker bar, the more leverage you'll get.

Die grinder: This tool is an absolute must if you have rust or dents that require cutting out the area to fix the problem. They can reach areas

WHY RESTORE YOUR BEETLE?

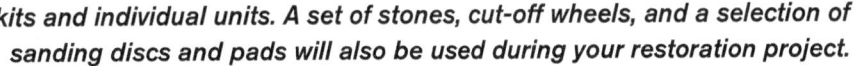

An air line connects your air tools to the compressor. Spend a bit more on a good air line; a cheap one will break down and allow contamination in your project's finish. Be sure to inspect your air line monthly.

Hammers and dollies can be purchased in a basic kit, which will give you a range of sizes, shapes, and faces. You will also need die grinders and angle grinders, which are also available in kits and individual units. A set of stones, cut-off wheels, and a selection of sanding discs and pads will also be used during your restoration project.

a sander can't, so they're also useful for stripping painted surfaces to get to the bare metal.

Long-handle file boards: You'll get better results when you shape by hand rather than using air files. The boards give you a flat, rigid surface so you can level surfaces more easily.

MIG welder: This is another must-have item, and you'll want to invest in a good welder from a reputable manufacturer. A metal inert gas (MIG) welder creates an arc between the wire electrode and the metal you're welding. The arc heats the surface, melting them enough to join them together.

Paint guns: You'll be spraying sealer, primer, paint, and clear, so there will be a lot of opportunities to practice your paint skills. While you can buy inexpensive guns, it's nearly guaranteed you will be disappointed with your results. Buy the best you can get. You won't regret it.

Pry bars: Get a full set. They are excellent for pulling parts apart rather than trying to use brute strength, which is more likely to damage the surface and send you flying across the garage.

Ratchets and sockets: Get a full set of metric ratchets and sockets.

Screwdrivers: A full set is needed. It's a lot easier to use a screwdriver that's the right size for the task at hand than trying to make one work that's too big or too small.

Wrenches: Get a full set of metric open-end wrenches. You need metric because you're working on a German-built car.

Drop light (optional): You don't absolutely need this, but it will sure make your work easier. There's a lot of work in tight spots and dark corners ahead. The light's protective cage makes it nearly indestructible, and the hook allows you to get the light you need without having to hold it.

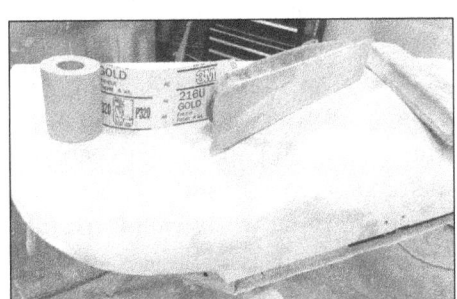

Long-blocks are available by special order from local auto parts stores or online. You will use them to straighten panels that should be straight and curve panels that should be curved. Get an assortment of sizes; kits are available.

Uni-spotter nail welder (optional): Using this tool to pull dents out from the outside is much more effective than trying to punch a hole in the metal. A good brand to look at is Stinger.

This isn't an exhaustive list of the tools that you will need, but it should get you well on your way to getting the job done in an efficient manner. Keep tools organized, clean, and ready to use so you don't have to hunt for them every time you need them.

How Much Will Your Restoration Cost?

Again, this is a question that's hard to answer. It all depends on choices you make during the project. Beetle restoration at a high-end shop could cost a small fortune because you're entrusting your ride to specialists who won't settle for anything less than near-perfect work. That level of work is pricey.

If you're doing the restoration yourself, you will save a bundle on labor costs, of course. Using your own labor means all you really need to budget for is parts. The great news is you don't need to buy everything at once. Your project will take a while, so you can spread your parts purchases out along the way.

Sourcing Project Cars

If you don't have a Beetle to work on, where can you find a project car to restore? That used to be a small challenge. Now, it's much easier to find project cars.

CHAPTER 2

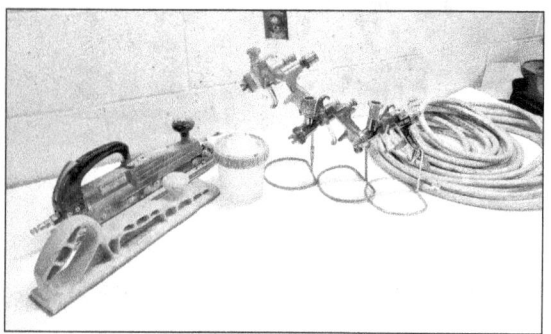

Professional-grade paint guns and an air file are shown. The air file connects to a compressor and is used to level and straighten panels. Essentially, it is a pneumatic-powered long-block.

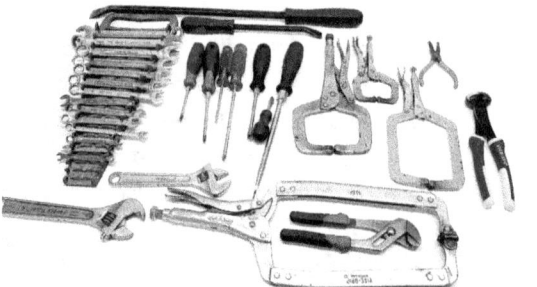

Here is a set of open-ended wrenches and sockets (metric), screwdrivers, clamps, and pry bars. This is an extended set of homeowner tools, giving you almost every size you will need.

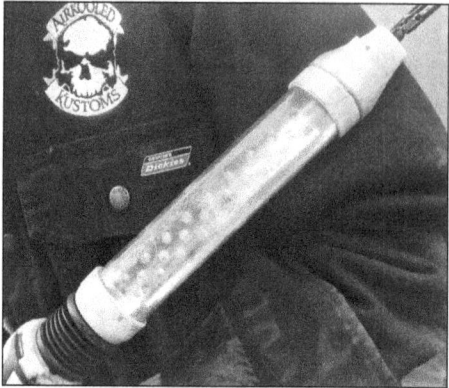

Droplights similar to this cordless LED model are preferred. They are available online and from big-box retailers. Look for a model that is rechargeable and has a magnetic base so you can attach it to the car's surface and have plenty of light as you work.

Visit enthusiast web forums, such as TheSamba.com, to start your search. This website has been around forever and will become one of your favorite online haunts from here on out. There are always vehicles for sale, but you'll also find advice and tons of parts and accessories.

Online classified advertisement sites may turn up a great project car for you. Do your due diligence to make sure you're dealing with a reputable seller. Your local newspaper's classified advertisement listings may be online these days, or you could break down and buy a print copy. It's not all that likely that you'll find a Beetle in these listings, but if you're in or near a city, especially in areas where classic cars are popular, you might find one.

Some auto restoration companies will help you source a project car. For a fee, they'll handle locating a car, inspecting it, and reporting back to you. Some will even transport the car from the seller to you.

Another option is to attend car shows and look at what's for sale. Many hobbyists find their cars at shows sponsored by local clubs. You'll find cars that people bought with every intention of doing a restoration but never got around to. You'll find cars that have been partially restored or even just disassembled. You might even find cars that have undergone restoration already, which could decrease or even eliminate your restoration work completely.

Visit local scrap yards and wrecking companies. Most of the time, the cars they buy sit until someone buys it for replacement parts.

Finally, ask your friends. If you join a local VW club (and many hobbyists do), you'll find a whole crowd of people who share your passion. They may know someone who's selling a project car and will probably be willing to keep an eye out for a car you could buy.

Make a Plan

You've determined what type of restoration you want to do, you've gathered your tools, and you have your project car. Before you get started on that project, you have some planning to do. It's time to put those ideas on paper so you can plan before you dive into the work of restoration. What works well is to create three different lists:

Got to Have: This list includes the repairs, replacements, and upgrades your Beetle absolutely must have so it's safe, reliable, and no longer in danger of rusting into dust.

Nice to Have: This list includes the items from the Got to Have list and includes some extras. Add items it will take to make it more comfortable, faster, safer, and even better looking.

Money's No Object: This list includes the first two lists, but then it

Parts Selection

There's a tip that we hope you'll hear loud and clear: buy the best parts and tools you can possibly afford. It's always better to buy once rather than to buy cheaply and have to buy again. In some cases, it's a matter of safety. In other cases, it's more about durability. You'll never regret buying well.

goes a little crazy. Do you want to add air-conditioning, a custom interior, go-fast goodies, or an ear-splitting sound system? Whatever tickles your fancy, add it to this list. You never know when you might find a way to include some of these in your build. Including them on this list keeps them on your radar so you'll remember to jump on the opportunity to get them.

When it comes to your project, for sure you'll tackle all the tasks on the Got to Have list. You'll pick through the items on the Nice to Have list and add whatever makes sense for your budget and skill set. Then, pick one or two items from the Money's No Object list to add to your ride's cool factor. The rest of the items may never make their way into the current restoration, but maybe someday you'll do it all again, and it's good to have a dream to chase.

Upgrades to Consider

When Beetles rolled off the VW factory lines, they were fine for their time. Today is another story. Surrounded by faster, bigger vehicles on the road, it's a good idea to update a few items to make sure driving your Beetle isn't ridiculously dangerous.

Switch Drum Brakes to Disc Brakes

Disc brakes weren't available on Beetles until the early 1970s, although this was standard on Karmann Ghias a bit earlier. Reliable stopping power is not a luxury. With disc brakes, you'll be able to stop with confidence.

Install a New Wiring Harness

Your original wiring harness has endured thousands of use cycles during its life. The insulation gets

Evaluating Project Cars

The better the condition of your project car is from the start, the easier, faster, and less expensive your restoration will be. In other words, if you start with a rusting hunk of junk, you're in for a bumpy and expensive ride. There comes a time when a classic car's condition gets too rough to make restoration feasible. If you're planning to restore a Beetle you already own, you'll do whatever it takes to make it right. But if you're sourcing a project car, you don't have any emotional investment in the vehicle yet, so make sure you get the most solid project car you can.

If you know a lot about cars and automotive restoration already, you'll probably feel comfortable evaluating a potential project car on your own. But if you're new to the hobby or not sure what you're looking at, you might want to get a second opinion before you buy.

Questions to Ask
- How complete is the car? Are all the parts there?
- How much rust does the car have?
- How many small, furry creatures have lived and died in that car? (They chew through the wiring, and you can get sick if you come in contact with their droppings during your restoration work.)
- How much damage has the car suffered? There are almost always dents, dings, and creases in cars this old.
- How well were those dents and dings repaired? You may run into some surprises along the way as you discover the many creative repair techniques that were used over the years. What's important is to determine how hard or expensive it will be to fix those past repairs.
- What modifications have been made to this car? Do you like the mods? The more you have to correct, the longer and more expensive your restoration process will be.

As you hunt, keep in mind that nearly any vehicle that's been around for decades is going to require a lot of work to restore. The ultimate creampuff (the car that someone's grandmother bought and drove only to church, then parked in the garage for the next 40 years) is a myth.

How Much Rust Is Too Much Rust?

As relentless and powerful as it is, rust may be the ninth wonder of the world. No matter what preventative measure we take to protect steel, nature has its way. The chemical process of oxidization is unstoppable. The odds are slim that your project car will begin the restoration process completely rust-free.

When evaluating potential project cars, pay attention to the rust. Even extensive rust does not disqualify a car from being a good restoration candidate. Most enthusiasts would agree that rare models deserve restoration no matter what condition they are found in to start.

Don't be scared off by rust, but take it seriously. That said, don't bite off more than you can chew in the rust department. The more time and effort you need to put into the rust remediation process, the longer it will take to finish the restoration and hit the road.

CHAPTER 2

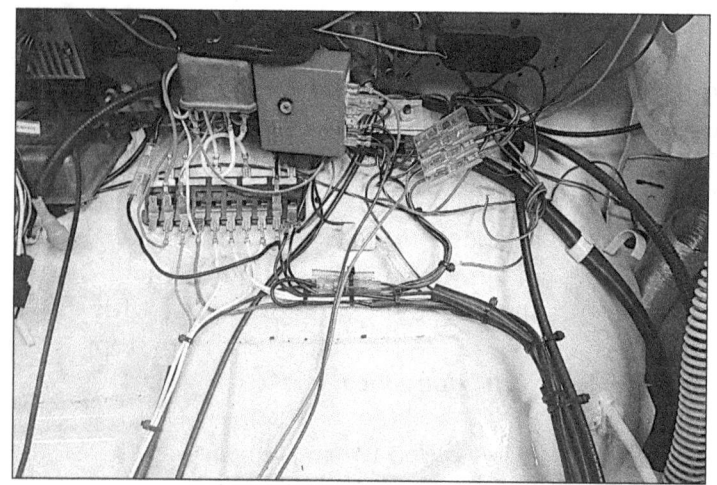

A wiring harness was only meant to last 20 to 30 years. Push it too far and you'll face electrical gremlins or worse. While you're doing a restoration, it makes good sense to replace your harness both for safety reasons and to eliminate any incorrect fixes that have been done along the way.

brittle with age, heat, and exposure to ultraviolet (UV) light, environmental toxins, and chemicals. Ultimately, when two 12-volt circuits connect because the wiring insulation has failed, you wind up with a short and have to replace fuses constantly, or worse, have to put out a fire.

Swap Incandescent for Halogen Lighting

Half of the secret of avoiding a nighttime collision is visibility. By upgrading your headlights to halogen, you'll find it easier to see and be seen.

The original incandescent headlights produce a yellowish light that many drivers find too dim, either to see the road or to be seen by other drivers.

Add a Fire Extinguisher

With good maintenance, your restored Beetle is highly unlikely to catch on fire. That's typically only an issue for people who have poorly maintained their engine or fuel delivery system. However, carrying a fire extinguisher is a smart idea in any vehicle. Be sure to get a carbon dioxide extinguisher available at any local auto parts store. A standard extinguisher will put out a fire, but the chemicals will eat your paint.

Install Ethanol-Rated Fuel Line and Components

Older rubber hoses will break down from the alcohol in ethanol, causing problems for your carburetor and engine.

Upgrade Anything Below a 1,600-cc Engine

In normal driving conditions, you'll want an engine that can keep up with the other vehicles on the road. The little engines that came standard in Beetles were fine for their time and

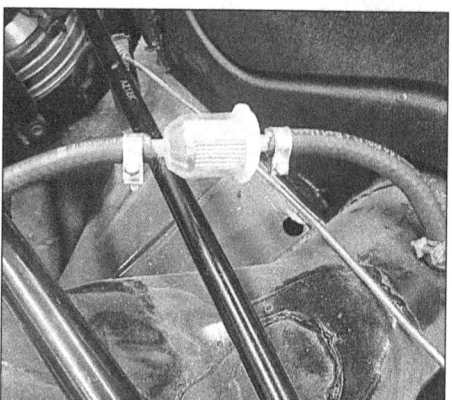

Ethanol eats rubber hoses. If you'd rather not have highly flammable fuel leaking through your fuel line in close proximity to a running engine, swap them for ethanol-rated hoses.

Check your friendly local auto parts store for a carbon dioxide fire extinguisher rather than a standard household version. Keep it in the front cabin of your Beetle so you can reach it if you need it.

Today's vehicles are built to go faster than they were several decades ago. While you're on the road in your Beetle, safety means being able to keep up in traffic. Now's a good time to look at getting a bigger engine.

will probably serve you well if you only drive your car on special occasions. But if you plan to drive your Beetle regularly, a bigger engine is a safety must.

Install Three-Point Seat Belts

Most Beetles produced in the United States after 1969 include provisions for swapping in three-point seat belts for the original lap belts. Besides, do you trust 30-, 40-, or 50-year-old lap belts?

Happy Parts Hunting

You have a project car and you've made a plan, so now it's time to find missing parts or upgrade parts. Whether it's a door handle or a hood, you have a hunting adventure ahead as you gather all the parts your Beetle needs.

If you want original equipment manufacturer (OEM) parts, check forums and online groups. Just be prepared to restore and possibly retrofit these parts. There's some variation in production runs, so it's no shock to find they don't fit perfectly out of the box.

There are hobbyists who restore individual subcomponents to a detailed level. Search them out. They are great at what they do, and it will be well worth the price.

There's also a large aftermarket parts industry. You can find a lot of what you need through aftermarket vendors. Purchase the highest quality you can manage.

If you aren't set on a stock custom restoration, you might also consider repurposing parts from other vehicles for your project. There's usually more than one way to use any object, and you can create a completely custom element for your project this way.

It's worthwhile to check out small specialty parts retailers as well. Not all of them have websites, so you may need to visit in person. It is worth the trip if they have the parts you need, and even better if they have a VW parts manager who enjoys passing wisdom and lore along to other enthusiasts. You may find they've forgotten more VW knowledge than many folks ever know.

This banjo-style steering wheel is an example of a repurposed part. It was taken from an early 1960s Triumph and heavily modified to work in the Beetle. This is just one of the custom touches you'll find in **Miss Mabel.**

Miss Mabel's gauges are another example of creative recycling and repurposing. They are now housed in a set of 1950s Japanese microphones that were bought online, gutted, and repainted. They were a lot of work to refurbish, but it was well worth it.

CHAPTER 3

Let's Roll—Restoration First Steps

There's a whole lot of work ahead to restore a vintage vehicle back to factory condition or better. Before we get started, there are a couple items to address. Then, we will jump into disassembly.

Safety First

Some of the tools, equipment, and processes you'll use during this restoration project can be dangerous if you don't follow reasonable safety recommendations. Goggles, gloves, and good face masks are a must. Get a good pair of safety glasses and wear them like your vision depends on it. You'll also want to use hearing protection when operating noisy equipment.

Some additional safety measures you'll want to put in place before you get going include:

Fire extinguisher(s): Fire extinguishers should be charged and stored where you can access them easily. Get carbon dioxide models if possible because they won't damage your engine or paint like a standard fire extinguisher would.

Floor jacks and jack stands: Place floor jacks and jack stands properly on a solid, level surface or metal substrate. Never crawl under a car that's only supported by a jack; it's dangerous because it can tip and drop your car on you. It's the same concept as using cinder blocks; they tend to crumble under the weight of a car. The safest way to work under your car is to use your floor jack to lift it and then use jack stands to stabilize it.

Wheel chocks: Wheel chock both sides of the wheel on the floor to keep your car from rolling away. Chocks can be purchased at local automotive supply stores.

Good ventilation: You'll be using some processes and chemicals that create fumes and dust that you don't want to breathe. It is important to protect your lungs with proper ventilation and use of a face mask or respirator.

Here you see a 53-year-old Beetle that has seen better days and is starting to show its wear. A shiny set of rims does not make a restoration complete.

LET'S ROLL—RESTORATION FIRST STEPS

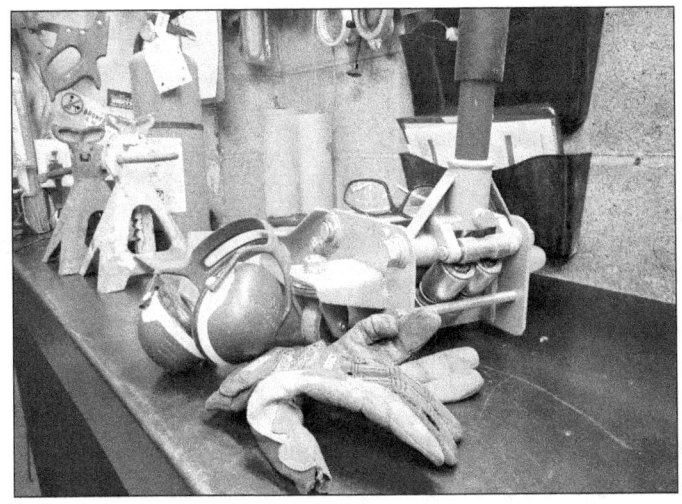

Here you'll find a basic set of safety equipment for working around automobiles. Be sure to get a quality jack, a set of wheel stands, and a chock. They are invaluable. Gloves, hearing protection, and eye protection are a must while working in the shop.

Safety Habits

Now is also the best time to start building good safety habits, both for you and your project car. One habit to have is to keep your shop and workspace clean. Put your tools away every time you finish for the day, and sweep up after each work session. When you have a storage space for each item and put each item in its space, you won't waste time searching for tools. You'll also prevent tripping, dropping tools and other objects on your car, and being injured by objects falling on your head as you work.

Another habit to develop is to unplug tools that are not in use. Some of the equipment you'll be using can generate some serious heat, and you don't want to leave them unattended. This is common sense but needs to be said. The last sight you want to see is your garage and Beetle engulfed in flames because you left some piece of equipment on and smoldering to the point where it ignites.

It is important to wear your personal safety equipment every single time. Nothing hurts quite like getting metal fragments in your eye. Protect any body part you'd like to keep functioning properly. Don't forget about guarding your lungs, ears, and eyes as well.

Finally, read, understand, and follow all safety instructions and manufacturer guidelines that accompany your equipment.

BYOBC: Build Your Own Body Cart

Before you start your Beetle restoration, let's build a body cart so you can move your car around easily even after the wheels come off. The easiest dolly you can make uses pallets and caster wheels so it can roll in any direction. If you're into heavy metal, you can get some welding practice in by building a metal body cart instead. We'll walk you through both processes.

Wood Body Cart

For a wood body cart, you'll need:

- A Beetle-sized pallet that's in good condition (Note: If you can't find one, you could make your own by constructing a frame and adding supports across the top.)
- Four large metal caster wheels, 250-pound rating minimum
- Bolts, washers, and nuts

Bolt the wheels to each corner of the pallet, about 5 inches from the edges. Be sure to test your cart before using it. Beetles can be deceptively heavy, and you probably don't want to drop one on your foot.

Steel Body Cart

Wood is easier and less expensive to use for your cart; just a quick trip to a home-improvement store will get you all the materials you need. However, wood is not nearly as strong as steel, and because the entire weight of your Beetle's body will rest on the cart, stronger is better. A steel body cart will hold up better than wood and is the best choice if you plan to undertake more than one restoration project.

For a steel body cart, you'll need:

- Four large metal caster wheels, 250-pound rating minimum
- Assorted tubing or angle iron
- 1/4-inch steel plate
- Welder
- Grinder with cutoff wheel, or a pneumatic cutoff wheel
- Drill and bits

When creating the cart, first determine the size of it. Once the measurements are in hand, cut the tubing pieces. Cut sections of steel plating to create the four mounting plates. The legs to hold the car up will needed to be cut to size here as well. Make sure they're all cut to the same size so the car sits balanced atop them.

Once the pieces are cut, use a drill press to create the holes to mount the plates onto the body. Next, the legs are welded to the casters vertically. The supports can then be welded to the legs and casters. Lastly, we'll weld the body plates to the body.

Creating a Steel Body Cart

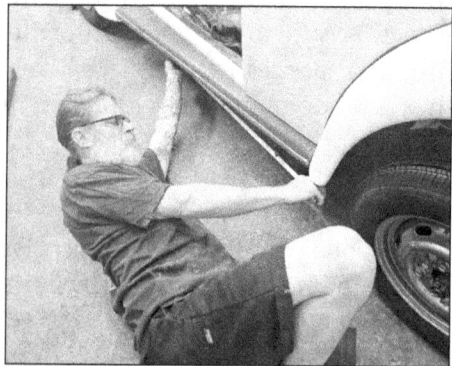

1 Measure your Bug from front to back and side to side for the attachment points of the pan to the body. You can use the measurements we'll provide, but taking them yourself will give peace of mind. You never know what kinds of damage your Beetle may have sustained to take it out of square.

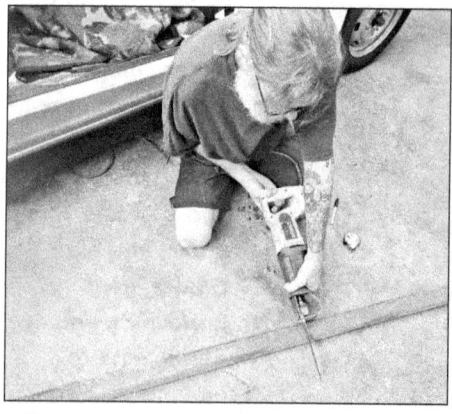

2 Cut the tubing or angle iron to the proper size for the cart. We recommend cutting three pieces at 48 inches long and one piece at 42 inches long to form a trapezoid. The front width of the Beetle mounting points are slightly narrower than the rear.

3 Cut four wheel supports from 1/4-inch steel tubing at 12x2. Then cut 1/4- to 3/8-inch plate steel into four 3x3-inch square mounting plates. These do not have to be perfect. You can use a Sawzall, a right-angle grinder with cutting disks, or a band saw (shown). Remember to wear eye protection.

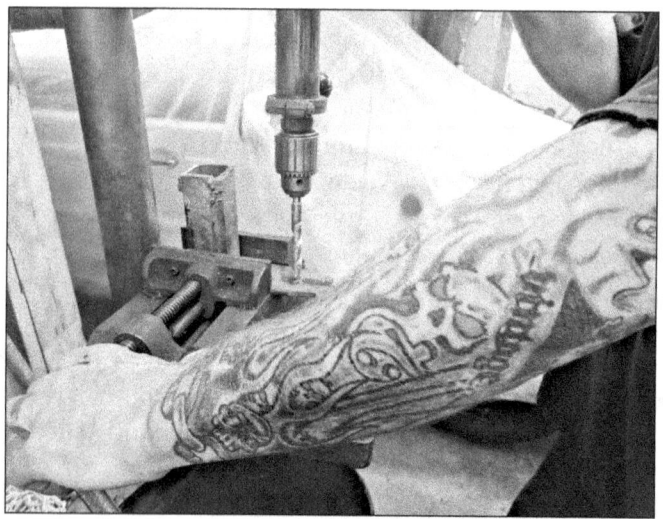

4 Use a 3/8- or 1/2-inch drill bit and drill two holes 7-7/8 inches on center to each wheel support. We prefer using a drill press to keep the bit from moving as we drill, but you can use an electric drill if you don't have a drill press.

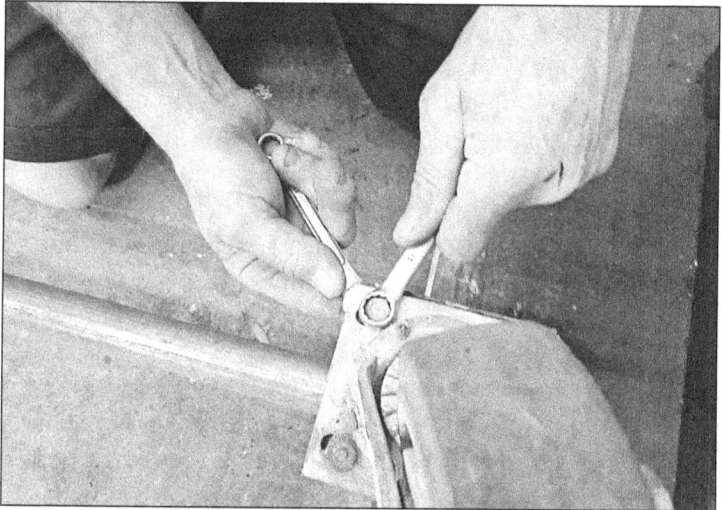

5 Line up the casters and mounting plates, mark where to drill holes, then drill four holes to fit the bolts. Bolt or weld the four plates to the casters.

6 Determine the height that will be comfortable for you to work on; you want to be able to work without straining. We suggest cutting legs to be 4 to 8 inches if you're from 5 foot, 8 inches to 6 foot, 4 inches tall. Cut four legs to your desired height out of 1/4-inch steel tubing.

7 Weld the legs to the casters vertically. Here we're using a MIG welder with an 0.032 wire at a fairly slow speed. Make sure you've got good penetration so your welds don't fail when you roll the loaded cart around.

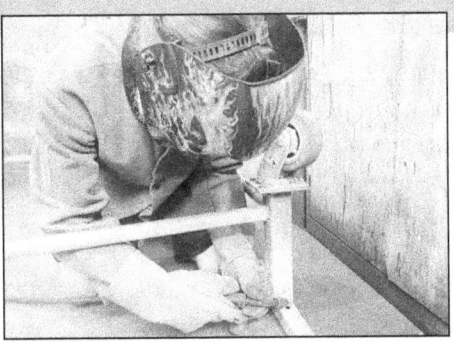

8 Weld horizontal supports to the legs and casters following the same process as in the prior step. Be sure to work safe. It doesn't need to be a perfect weld, but it is a great opportunity to practice your welding skills.

9 Weld the body plates in place to bolt to the body, again using the same process as above. Front to rear, your uprights will measure 37.5 inches front to back, 43.75 inches on center on the rear, and 40 inches on center on the front of the post. Double-check your bolts to make sure they line up with the attachment points on your Beetle body.

Body Cart Safety

A couple of safety notes about your body cart:
Never crawl under a car body while it's up on the dolly.
Don't roll your homemade body cart around more than needed.

Yikes! That's a Lot of Dirt

Now that you're sold on safety and you've got your handy-dandy body cart, it's time to roll up your sleeves. It's a good idea to give your car a good, thorough wash before you start. This is especially true if you bought your project car from a junkyard or if it has been stored for a long time. Spiders, wasps, and rodents adore classic cars, and some may have called your vehicle home for a while. It's better to find this out with the end of a water hose than with your hands or face while you're working.

Use a good degreaser and a scrub brush to loosen accumulated debris. Your shop vacuum will come in handy for clearing critters and cobwebs from the interior. Brace yourself and take photos before you go any further.

If you are doing a complete restoration, the next step is taking your Beetle apart, piece by piece. This stage is where all its past sins are revealed. If nothing else, during cleanup you'll gain a bit of compassion for that poor old Beetle and the fact that nobody before you bothered to treat it right.

Disassembly

The information in this book is based on a 1968 Euro Beetle project car. Your Beetle will most likely have small differences, even if it is a 1968. But you should be able to spot the differences as you work, and while you may have an extra bolt or screw to deal with, the process is the same.

First, a tip that will save your sanity: your camera is your friend. We always think we'll remember what we see until it's time to put parts back together. You can't possibly take too many pictures. Take pictures from multiple angles and distances so you have a visual reference of all the parts and systems you're about to disassemble. Also, take pictures before and after you disassemble each component. You'll thank yourself when it's time to reassemble.

The more organized and systematic you are during the disassembly, the less aggravation you'll have later. Clearly tag and bag each component as you go to avoid the headaches that come from misplacing parts. Grab a few permanent markers, a couple of boxes of plastic bags with slider seals, and large moving boxes. The name of the game is keeping components together even if they're no longer usable. Make notes on the bags to help keep track of what you have and what you need.

Old Battery, Fuel, and Oil

Before you start disassembling your Beetle, be sure to disconnect and remove the battery if your car still has one. Dispose of the battery properly according to your local requirements.

CHAPTER 3

A Beetle Is a Beetle Except When . . .

One reason we love Beetles is their brutally efficient German engineering. That efficiency showed up in all its glory on the assembly line. Beetles vary from year to year and from Standards to Supers, but there are also differences within a single year's production line. In some cases, the factory ran out of a specific part. In other cases, the engineers came up with mid-year modifications. The long and short of it is, you never know exactly what you'll find in your Beetle's construction.

If your car has been restored, repaired, or modified before, you may discover even more mysterious pieces and parts as you work. Some of these surprises will leave you shaking your head, wondering what on earth a prior owner was thinking. Finding cement, newspapers, zip ties, and other interesting body repair tactics is not uncommon.

Include Dates

As you tag, bag, and take photos throughout the disassembly process, note the current date on each bag. It will be easier to search through your photo record to find specific photos as you need them.

Next, turn your attention to any fuel still in your Beetle's tank and drain it into an approved container. There are three ways to drain fuel: crawl under your car, cut the gas line, and drain; run a flexible fuel extension line from the engine on the driver's side and drain; or unbolt the tank and lift it a bit, then clamp and cut the line. Remember, fuel is heavy and dangerous.

Drain your oil too. Pull the drain plug, which is a large bolt in the middle of the oil strainer. The more thoroughly you let your oil drain out, the less messy the next steps will be.

Engine

Whether you plan to rebuild or replace your engine, it's a good idea to remove it before disassembling the rest of the car. It's a lot lighter without the engine, and you'll have better access to the engine compartment.

It's important to clean your engine before removing it. A clean(ish) engine is less likely to slip or cause your tools to slip, and you'll be able to see what you're doing better. You can steam clean it, use a spray degreaser (it's best if you can do this at a commercial car wash because it will make a mess on your garage floor), or even use a blasting solvent.

If you plan to rebuild the engine, be sure to cover the carburetor, coil, and distributor with aluminum foil or plastic bags before you clean it. You don't want those parts to get wet. Always follow all manufacturer's instructions, whichever process you choose.

Now that your engine is clean, get your floor jacks, jack stands,

A dirty, greasy engine is hard to remove because it's slippery. Whether you steam clean, use spray degreaser, or use a blasting solvent, be sure to read and follow the manufacturer's instructions.

some plywood, zippered bags and other containers, and your marker and camera ready. If at all possible, remove the engine on a hard-paved surface. If that's not possible, get a second sheet of plywood for the floor

Removing the Engine

1 *Ensure that your jack stands are under solid framework. Soft metal can fail, so it's imperative that you have the car securely in place.*

24   HOW TO RESTORE YOUR VOLKSWAGEN BEETLE

Removing the Engine Continued

2 Disconnect the air filter hose and any other cables connected to the air filter inlet. Unscrew the air filter housing base clamp and remove the air filter. Keep it upright to prevent any remaining oil from spilling out.

3 Remove the heater choke element, throttle cable, and idle cutoff switch (if you have one), then remove the carburetor. The carburetor is held on the intake manifold by two 13-mm nuts holding the studs.

4 The stock fuel line comes in from the gas tank through a series of soft and hard lines. The intake is on the fuel pump. The output is also on the fuel pump and goes out to the carburetor. For safety, make sure all fuel is drained before you perform this step.

5 In order to remove the engine, the rear engine tin must first be removed. Depending on the year and model, it may be held on by four or six cheese-head screws.

6 When removing the control functions of your engine, keep in mind that there are cables, fuel lines, and electrical connections to remove. Take care so the wires don't snag.

Removing the Engine Continued

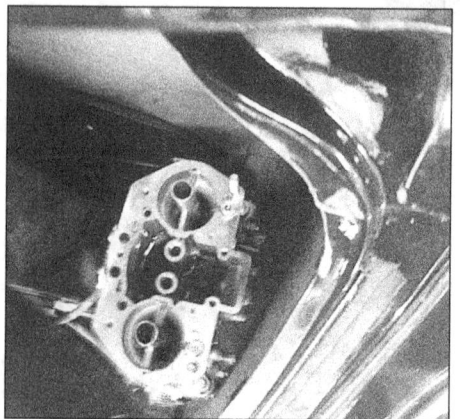

7 Reach around the carburetors and find two 17-mm nuts that serve as the upper mounting points for the upper transmission to engine bolts. Remove these bolts.

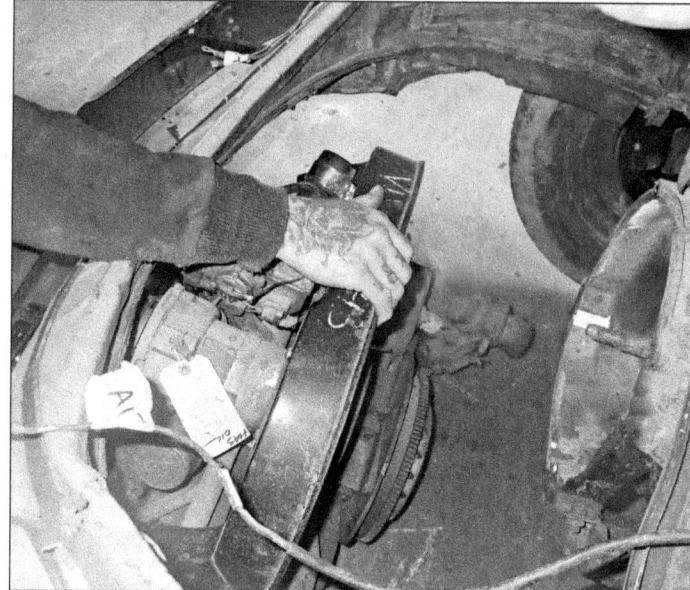

8 After the engine is free of the car, double-check to make sure all wires, hoses, and cables are disconnected. If not, you will have a hard time completing the engine removal.

so your surface is clean and even. Make sure to photograph, tag, and bag each component.

Place wheel chocks under the front wheels on both sides of the wheels. Jack up the rear of the car by about 3 feet. Place the car on jack stands. Label all wires and hoses on the engine prior to removal. Take pictures too.

Engine removal begins obviously at the rear of the car. At this point, the hood can be removed for clear access. Starting from the top down, we'll be removing attached items to the engine.

Remove the choke heating element and the wires that control the fuel cutoff. Then, remove the throttle cable and fuel line, and finally, the front engine tin hoses. Remove the carburetor. Under the distributor you will see the oil-pressure unit. Disconnect all the electrical wires connected to it. Also remove the wires on the coil. The generator has three wires that are usually attached with slip-on connectors. Remove them.

If your Beetle has an alternator, detach the multiple wire connector and voltage regulator. If your Beetle is post-1972, remove the fuel injection system wiring, which is in a harness. You can trace its path around the engine, disconnecting as you go. Remove the fuel line.

Go to the back of the engine to remove the rear engine cover plate. Depending on the year of your car, it may be a matter of removing four screws or removing hoses and gaskets. Find the intake manifold. There are two heater tubes with covers that are attached by four bolts each. Remove the eight bolts, and you'll be able to unscrew the rear engine cover plate and remove it.

Maneuver the jack just in front of the transaxle, *not* directly under the engine. Find the heater control valves along the front and sides of your engine. Release their cables from their connectors by removing the bolt. A cylinder will come loose as you remove the cables. You may need to use penetrating oil and two wrenches to do this step.

The bellhousing nuts are next. Important: Look for upper bolts and make sure they're still in place. Then, find the two 17-mm hex nuts threaded onto studs that go into the transaxle. The nuts and washers are on the bellhousing's bottom corners. Remove them.

This is not applicable to a 1968 Beetle, but if your Beetle has an auto-stick, disconnect its lines. One goes to the automatic transmission fluid tank, and the other goes to the oil pump. Transmission fluid may gush out as you remove that line.

Slide the engine toward the rear of the car while it's on the floor. Jack it up enough to clear the transaxle mainshaft. Put your plywood on top of the jack saddle, then maneuver the jack so the plywood is under the engine. Remove the bolts and nuts that connect the upper engine to the transaxle. Lower your engine. If possible, get a buddy to help you keep an eye on the engine compartment to make sure you don't have any remain-

LET'S ROLL—RESTORATION FIRST STEPS

> ### Removing Wires
>
> If you'll be rebuilding your engine, avoid pulling wires as you work. Instead, pull connectors in order to keep more of the wiring intact. This will make the rebuilding process easier (and less mysterious because you'll be able to see what goes where better). ■

ing connections, hoses, or wires that will get snagged along the way.

Body Panels

Disassembling the body panels can be fairly straightforward. If some of the components are rusted into place, it's wise to have a can of WD-40 near you. You'll need to remove the doors and lids that attach to the main body of the Beetle. This includes the doors themselves, the hinges and connectors, and the glass windows.

All Beetles came with door panels, door handles, and working glass. Door panels were made of thin cardboard and held in place by small metal upholstery clips. Your first task is to determine if the panel is salvageable or if it needs to be replaced. Remove the panel and examine its condition.

Your door is made up of the materials attaching it to the body and the components inside of it used for the window. If your project is missing some of these components, take note of what is missing.

It's best to work on the doors and mechanisms while they're still on the car and supported by the door hinges. You'll have an easier time with this step with them in place. Label the door shells "driver" and "passenger." In this section, we'll remove the door windows, including the wing window and the one you roll up and down, the winder mechanism, tracks, latch assemblies, and rubber door seals. The specific configuration differs by year, so your car may be a little different, but the following is the general process.

Typically, the door latch mechanism is attached to the door shell with two or three bolts. Unbolt the mechanism, tag them, and store them in a zippered bag.

The Beetle door shell should be stripped of its door cards, windows, latches, and seals. By dismantling the door while it's still on its hinges, you will be able to hold the door steady enough to work. Some of the screws and bolts you will need to remove are not easily visible and may be covered by the weatherstripping. The attachments for the quarter window include one bolt or screw right in the track; the other one is directly down from that point.

Remove the window that rolls up and down by rolling it all the way down, removing the glass from the track mechanism, and then stripping the window seals and chrome trim. Make sure to save the original interior scraper clips because the aftermarket ones are junk.

Remove the wing or quarter window. You'll see a small screw or bolt right inside the track for the quarter window. Remove it. Go straight down from that screw point and you'll find another bolt or two in the door shell. Remove them. Slide the window

Overall, it's easier to disassemble the components and assemblies within the door shell while the door is still on the car. However, it can be done with the door removed from the car as well.

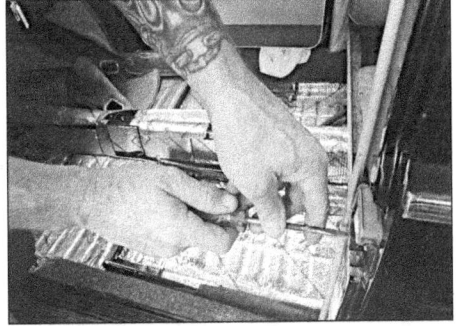

There are several variations among strike plate mechanisms. Some have three flat-head screws; some have four. Some have three or four Phillips-head screws. No matter what your configuration, be sure to bag and tag whatever you remove.

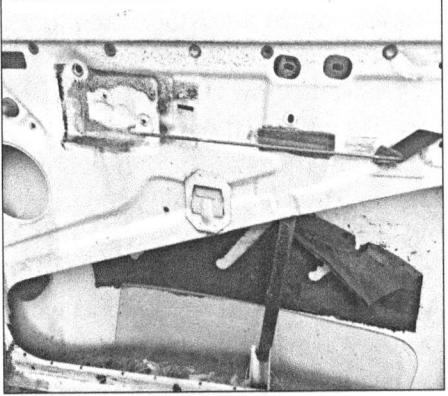

Here is a Beetle door shell stripped of its door cards, windows, latches, and seals. By dismantling the door while it's still on its hinges, you will be able to hold the door steady enough to work.

HOW TO RESTORE YOUR VOLKSWAGEN BEETLE

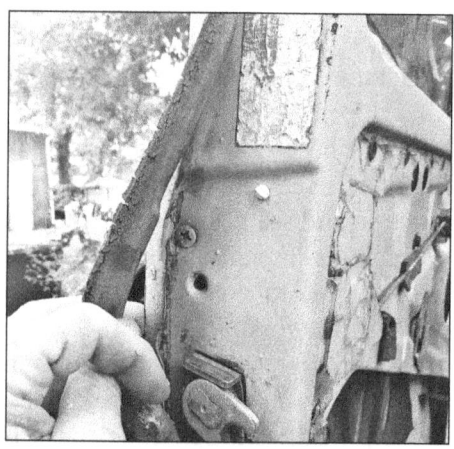

Some of the screws and bolts you will need to remove are not easily visible. The attachments for the quarter window include one bolt or screw right in the track, and the other one is directly down from that point.

With the rolling window in its lowered position, unscrew the Phillips-head screw in the doorjamb. You may need to dig the seal out to reach the screw, especially if the seals and other rubber components on your Beetle have dry rotted.

Open the door all the way. Depending on the year of your Beetle, you will either have a door check rod or a strap. If you have a rod, there's a pin with a C-clip on the bottom that you need to remove. Do not lose the C-clip.

Start at the bottom of the door. You will find three or four Phillips-head screws along the bottom. Remove all but one. Just loosen the last screw. Support the door or get a buddy to help because the door is heavy and awkward to support as you work.

toward the back of the door and maneuver the quarter window out. Be sure to put all nuts and bolts either back into their original holes or tag and bag them.

Remove the window track from the door shell, leaving the glass in place (rolled down, detached, and floating).

Remove the door latch. There's one Phillips-head screw in the inner doorjamb behind the seal. Remove the door handle. Push one end in toward the door while pulling the other end out at the same time, moving laterally toward the back of the car. Then rotate it out.

Push the glass up through the opening where you took out the scrapers. Remove the glass carefully. Make sure to put all nuts and bolts back into the track for safekeeping. Label which window is which by writing the label on painter's tape and sticking it to the glass. Do not use a permanent marker directly on the glass; it will stain the glass and you will have to replace it.

Remove the window winder mechanism from the back side of the door. The interior latch mechanism should now slide right out.

Doors

Some Beetles have a check rod rather than a strap. When you remove the rod, be sure to save the C-clip holding it in place. If you have the strap, unbolt both locations where it ties into the door and body. As usual, take photos, then bag and tag so you will know where that clip goes when it's time to reassemble the car.

A number-3 Phillips screwdriver, an impact screwdriver, and some penetrating oil will be helpful. All fasteners should be coated in penetrating oil before you get started so they'll come off more easily.

There are four screws attaching the car door to the Beetle's A-pillar. Remove three of the four screws. Loosen the fourth screw but do not

Remove all four screws at the top that attach the door to the A-pillar. Remove the fourth screw from the bottom of the door. The door will now slide out with its hinges intact. Set the door aside to send it out for sandblasting.

remove it. This will help you keep control of the car door until you are ready to lift it off the body. If you're not comfortable unbolting the door and holding it at the same time, it would be a good idea to have someone assist you for this process.

The door is now a bare shell. You can either leave the shells on the body or take them off, which makes it easier to work on the body. If you leave the doors in place, you still need to remove all the components on the inside of the door.

Front Seat Removal

Again, the details vary according to the year of manufacture, but the mechanisms are similar. The driver- and passenger-seat mechanisms are built the same way. Look under the driver's seat and remove any wiring that may be attached to the seat.

Locate the large return spring between the seat and the track. A Standard Beetle has a two-track system. Slide the seat all the way forward, find the metal tab, push it down, and continue sliding the seat all the way forward to make it come off the tracks. The Super Beetle has a three-track system. There's a center pin on the track with a metal tab stop mechanism. Push the seat all the way forward, push the tab down, and lift the seat off the tracks.

Backseat Removal

The lower section of the backseat will lift right out. The upper section is held on by two bolts, one on each side going into the body. If your Beetle came equipped with seat belts, remove them by unbolting from the body. Save the bolts to use in reassembly. However, it would be crazy to trust your life to old belts, so don't even think about using them; they go in the trash.

Interior Removal

With the seats removed, you'll have more room to work on extracting parts ranging from cards to carpet and seals to straps. The components you'll be removing change from model to model and year to year. How you'll remove them remains the same, though.

Cards and Carpeting

To remove your interior trim panel (also called cards), simply remove the metal pushpins that hold them in place. When you remove the cards, the pins come out with them. Unclip and you're good to go.

Your carpeting may be glued in. The only attachment points on the body would be on the door sills on both the driver's side and passenger's side. The rear carpet is tucked into the luggage tray behind the back seat. Once you free the carpet from the door sills, yank it all out.

Front and Back Windshields

Start by removing the rubber seal on the front windshield. To do this, take a knife to the seal and cut it out. Remove the front windshield carefully. It's easy to replace if needed,

The seat adjusters differ slightly from year to year. However, the basic mechanisms are similar, and the driver-side and passenger-side seats use the same track and spring system.

Without the driver and passenger seats, your Beetle is starting to look rather empty. As a bonus, you get to keep all the pennies you find as you remove the seats. You may even find other treasures prior owners and passengers have lost or unintentionally stuffed into the seats.

CHAPTER 3

Be careful as you remove your front windshield. It's easy to get carried away and use too much force. While replacing the windshield is easy enough to do, if it's needed, you don't want to have to stop your work to clean up shattered glass.

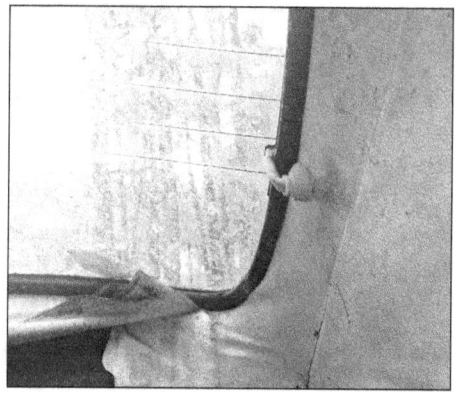

This Beetle came equipped with a rear defrost mechanism. That means there were wiring connections we needed to remove before lifting the back glass off the car.

Here is an interior view of the pop-out window mechanism, including the rear attachment points for the latch. As you remove the hardware from your Beetle, be sure to take photos first, then tag each part (including which side of the car it came from) before bagging and storing.

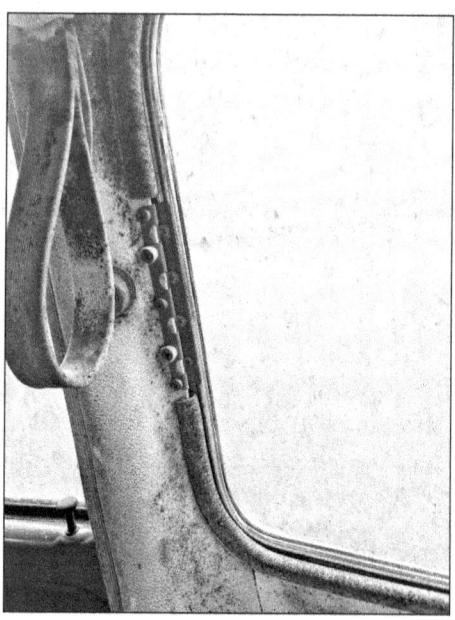

The pop-out windows need to come out too. Removing them is usually a matter of removing the screws at the hinge and into the body. Discard the rubber seals. All of the seals will be replaced during the reassembly process.

but if you can clean it up and reuse it, you will save some money and hassle.

Do the same with the back windshield. If the Bug has a defrost mechanism, be sure to remove the electrical hookups before you remove the glass.

Pop Outs

If the car has pop outs, remove them now. There may be a series of five screws at the hinge point and three at the rear body. If not, you can cut the rubber like you did on the windshield and back glass. The rear latch has three screws attached to the body; remove these as well.

Visors, Straps, Mirror, Courtesy Light, and Headliner

Remove the visors and their latch. Then, remove the courtesy straps from the B-pillars. The rearview mirror is next; twist 90 degrees to pull it out. Remove the interior courtesy light next.

Cut the headliner out, cutting close to the outside of the body. Leave it intact. Leave the rods in place (they go in a specific order). Just roll it up and store for later. Most of the headliners are one-piece, although there are some multi-piece units out there. For the one-piece units, after you cut out the upper section, remove the remainder of the headliner, which is glued to the body and tucked over the pinch welds where the windows go. An adhesive remover such as Goo-Gone will help you.

Front Hood (Trunk)

Remove the handle first by removing the two bolts on the inside of the hood. Then, remove the hood latch mechanism; there will either be four bolts or four rivets on the front upper apron. If there are rivets, you'll need to drill them out. Carefully unscrew the cable that is in the mechanism. Tag and bag the mechanism.

There are two bolts on each side of the back side of the hood. Lift the hood and you will see four bolts attaching the hinges to the hood. Remove the first three. Get a buddy to help as you remove the final bolt and carefully lift the hood from the car.

LET'S ROLL—RESTORATION FIRST STEPS

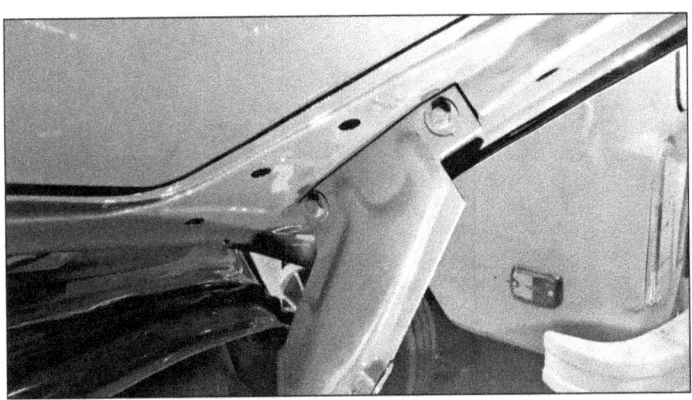

These are two of the four bolts you will be unbolting to remove the hood. Do not lose the washers behind the bolts. You will need them for reinstallation, so take photos, bag, and tag them.

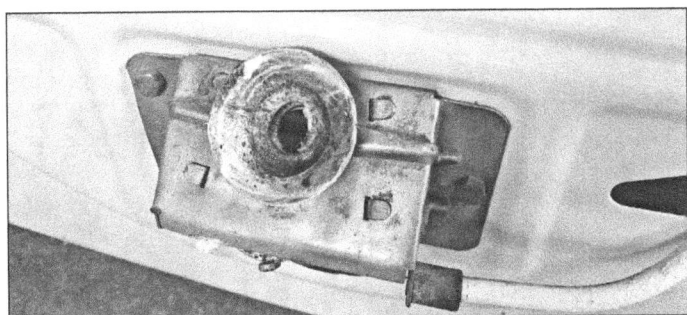

This locking mechanism for the hood latch on the front valance is a piece of a two-part safety system that keeps the hood from flying off while the car is driven. Be sure to note where the cable attaches to this mechanism. Make a mark at the attachment point for the length of the cable. This will help during the reassembly and adjustment phase.

Electrical System

Be sure to take pictures of your wiring and connections. You'll want to replace the wiring harness because the original wiring is likely to be worn out and unsafe. This makes removing the wiring easy because you don't need to be especially careful.

Early Beetles (pre-1965 in the US market) used a 6-volt system with four basic circuits running everything in the car. Post-1965, a 12-volt system with eight circuits was used. As these cars evolved, their electrical system became more complicated and used relays, double-action switches, and piggybacked electrical connections. The nice thing is that we're not dealing with a computerized system. Analog systems are much easier for hobbyists to work with.

First, disconnect the electrical system from the back of the dash. Then, carefully cut out all remaining connections.

Dashboard

Beetle dashboards vary widely depending on the year of manufacture. There are padded dashes and unpadded steel dashes, and Super Beetle dashes are completely different. But you'll follow the same basic process of unscrewing, bagging, and tagging.

Safety regulations in the United States required padded dashboards as of 1968. The 1968 featured in this book was built for the European market, so we have a mix of US and European design specifications.

Removal of the Dashboard Components

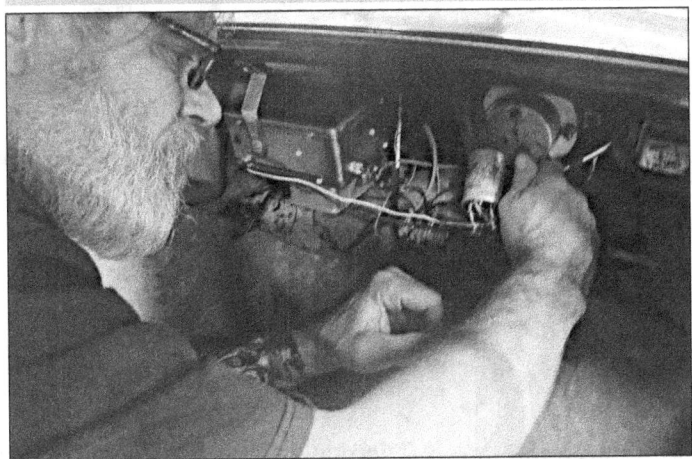

1 Unhook the speedometer and all electrical and mechanical connections. Unscrew everything, bag them, and tag them. Pull the speedometer out from the back side.

2 With an unpadded (steel) dash, work from the inside of the car. Unscrew the radio faceplate. There are two bolts under the volume and station knobs. Unbolt them. Then, go back to the trunk and pull the radio out.

HOW TO RESTORE YOUR VOLKSWAGEN BEETLE

CHAPTER 3

Removal of the Dashboard Components *Continued*

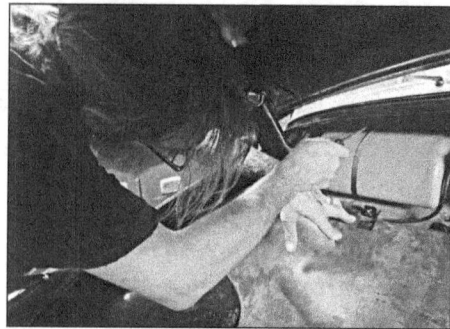

3 In the trunk is a strap on the back side of the glove box that is held in with a bolt or a screw. Remove the glove box. Save the pennies you find because you'll need every cent to put toward your project.

4 It's difficult to see, but you will find the four tabs underneath a white, goopy seam sealer. Carefully scrape the goo away, and you will find the four tabs. They will need to be straightened before you can remove them.

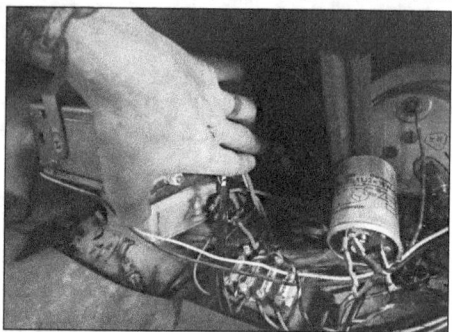

5 Go back to the driver's side. You'll see two trim grilles on either side of where the speedometer was. There are four goo-covered tabs on these grilles. Scrape off the goo and straighten the tabs, being careful not to break them. Push the trim plates out toward the inside of the car.

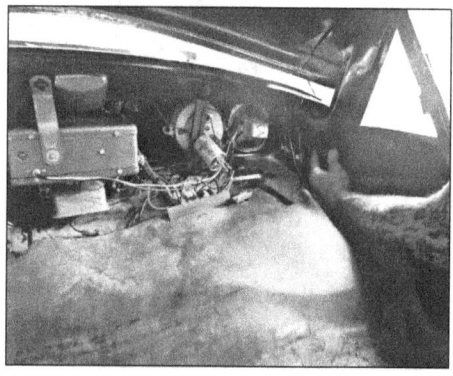

6 Remove all switches and knobs in the dash. Unscrew the trim rings from the inside, and the switches will come off on the trunk side. Remove the fresh air and heater tubes.

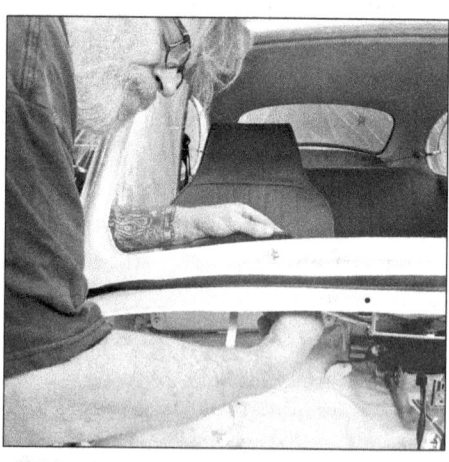

7 Remove the two bolts on the strap on the passenger's side of the dash.

8 Remove the glove box door from your bare dashboard. Don't lose the hinges. They will work themselves loose if you're not careful.

9 Remove the windshield wiper motor and arms. The first step is to remove the windshield wipers. Then, remove the nuts on the outer shafts, go underneath the cowl to the third attachment point (attaching the motor to the body), and slide it right out.

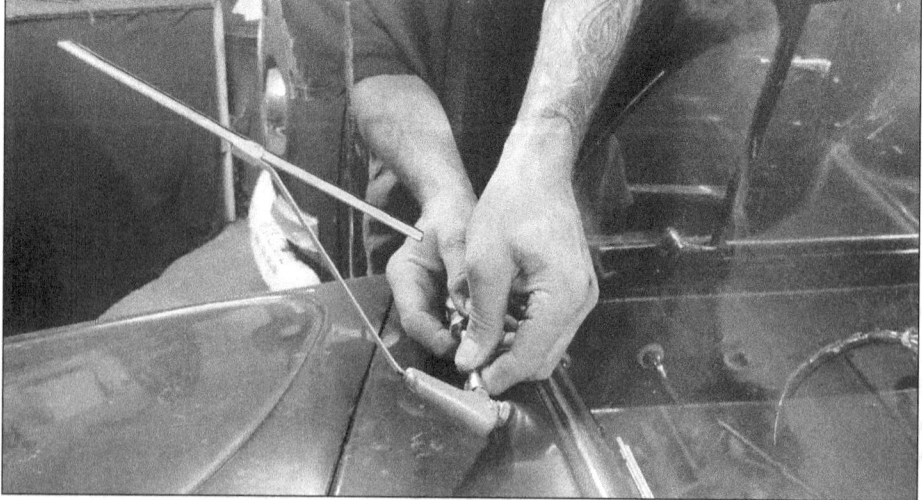

LET'S ROLL—RESTORATION FIRST STEPS

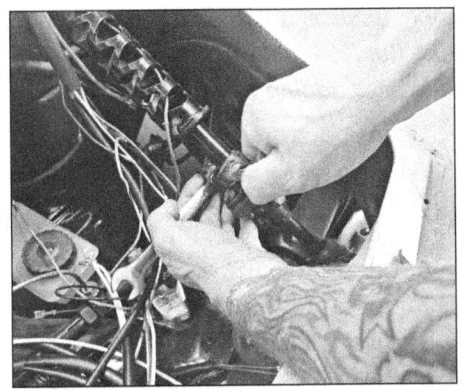

Label all wires going to the fuse block and wiring harness. Unbolt the pinch clamp at the steering box, which is located under the gas tank.

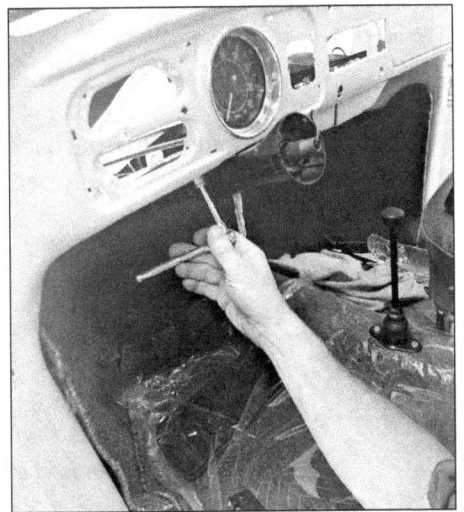

Unbolt the two bolts under the dashboard.

Remove the necessary wires and leave the labels intact for reassembly. Pull the steering column out toward the inside of the car. The steering column and its wires should come out as one assembly.

Steering Column

Pre-1965, the steering wheel featured a solid shaft running from the steering coupler up to the steering wheel. It was encased in a tube with bearings to help center it on the steering-wheel side only. Post-1968, per US safety regulations, the steering wheel was required to include a collapsible section with upper and lower bearings to keep it from impaling a driver in the event of a collision.

Every few years, Volkswagen changed the style of the steering wheel itself. The steering wheels are largely interchangeable. Your Beetle may have its original steering wheel, or a prior owner may have changed it.

Fuel Tank

Remove the electrical wires going to the top of the tank. There are four bolts securing the gas tank with retainer plates. Remove the bolts and retainer plates, then tag and bag. Lift

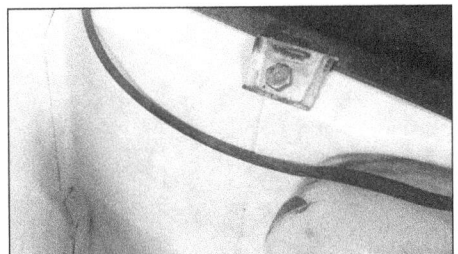

the tank out carefully. It will stop because the line is only so long. Since it's empty, it's safe to cut the fuel line and remove the tank.

Brake Reservoir

In 1967–1968, there was a transition from a single-feed brake master cylinder (where the reservoir was in front of the gas tank, behind the spare tire) to a dual-feed brake master

With your gas tank empty, it is safe to cut the fuel line with wire cutters or a razor. Then, remove the gas tank. If your tank does not have holes in it, you can refurbish and reinstall it later.

There are four bolts and retaining plates holding your gas tank in place. There is also a foam seal underneath your tank. Do not lose them; photograph, bag, and tag them.

Your Beetle's gas tank is up front. The front hood is the trunk. If your car has been sitting for years, the fuel is degraded and unsafe to use or even keep. Drain the fuel into an approved container before you go any further in the project.

HOW TO RESTORE YOUR VOLKSWAGEN BEETLE

CHAPTER 3

These are the lower hoses that connect the brake fluid reservoir to the master cylinder. There are companies making reservoirs that fit directly on top of the master cylinder, which eliminates the extra piping and hosing.

The brake master cylinder reservoir is easy to access, but you might find a bit more rust in this area. That's because brake fluid is highly corrosive on paint, and most people do not clean up their spills after adding fluid to the reservoir or bleeding the brakes.

cylinder. At that time, Volkswagen relocated the reservoir to the inner upper wheelwell. Although there are dual reservoirs available that can be fitted directly on top of the master cylinder, they were primarily designed for the Mexican market. With the addition of disc brakes on Karmann Ghia models in 1969, the master cylinder changed again to accommodate the line pressure required for disc brakes.

At the master cylinder, you'll see two blue flex hoses connected to aluminum hoses. They are connected to two more blue hoses that are connected to the brake reservoir.

Cut the lower blue hoses. Let fluid drain out into a coffee can or a similar container. Dispose of it properly. Cut the upper lines.

Remove the aluminum hoses. They go through the body. Don't bend them. Just wiggle and wrangle them out. There's a screw holding the tabs on the reservoir. Remove the screw. The reservoir pulls out through the top side.

Back Decklid

Since the engine is in the back, the terminology is a bit different

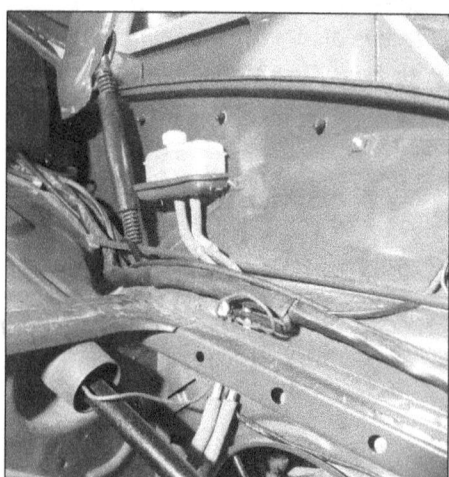

The aluminum tubes for the brake reservoir pass through the body to get to the master cylinder. Do not be surprised if there is goo around the tubes where it passes through the body.

Two wires go to the license plate light. You will need to remove them before unbolting the four bolts that hold the decklid in place.

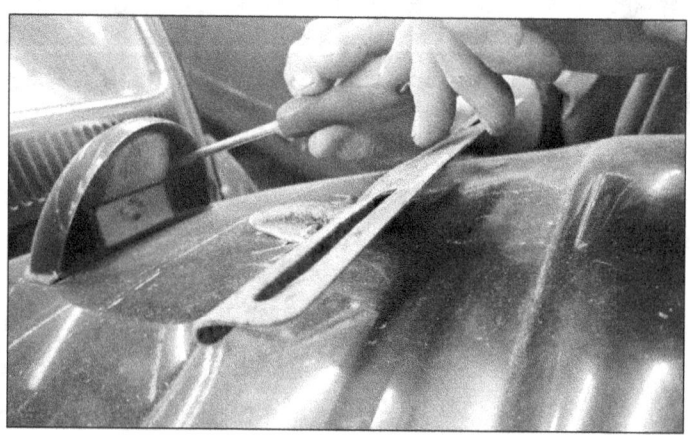

Remove the electrical connection that powers the taillight. Remove the license plate light housing by removing the three or four small nuts and washers that hold it on. Set them aside.

HOW TO RESTORE YOUR VOLKSWAGEN BEETLE

LET'S ROLL—RESTORATION FIRST STEPS

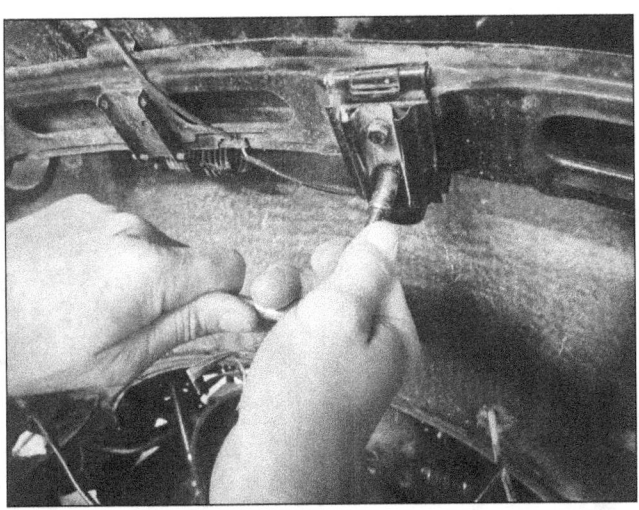

Remove the rear decklid from its hinge point by removing the four bolts that hold it on.

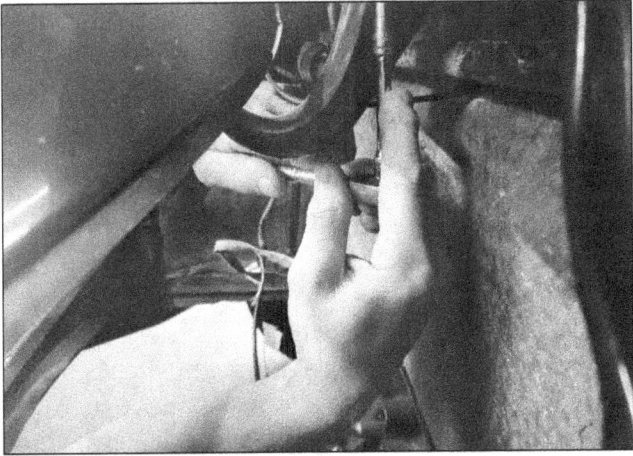

Remove the three bolts holding each hinge on. Watch for the spring.

Save yourself time and headaches by removing the headlight and its bracket all in one piece rather than trying to disassemble it while it's still on the car. It is held in place by three screws on an inner retaining ring. Once those screws come out, the entire assembly lifts out easily.

from front-engine vehicles. The back decklid is the engine's hood. As bodystyles changed, the shape of the back decklid and latching mechanism changed to accommodate the body changes. How the decklid attached to the body never changed, though. The hinge and springs are as they always were.

Bumpers and Running Boards

Your bumpers will protect your Beetle in a crash as long as you're only going about 5 mph at the time of impact. That met the US safety requirements at the time. The running boards are more of a nod to the style of the late 1930s and early 1940s.

The front and rear bumpers are held on with four bolts. Remove the bolts, and the whole bumper slides out of the body. Then, remove the taillights, housings, and any remaining electrical connections.

The running boards are held onto the body with four bolts and onto each fender with nuts. You'll find a rubber washer between the fender and running board. Remove all and bag and tag them.

Remove the headlight trim rings next. Leave the light in the headlight bracket to make sure you keep the parts together. Disconnect the three-prong switch. Remove the rubber grommet between the body and the headlight bucket.

Remove the other rubber grommet, which goes to the turn signal. Then, remove the upper turn signals.

Unbolt the fenders. There is a C-clip in the driver-side front wheel

The turn signal is removed by unbolting the nuts from the underside. If you already cut the wires, you can lift it out as a unit. Reproduction parts are available, but you should save the components just in case. You never know what you might need.

HOW TO RESTORE YOUR VOLKSWAGEN BEETLE

The project 1968 Euro Beetle's body has been lifted off its chassis, or pan. It is now resting on a body cart and is ready to go out to blast.

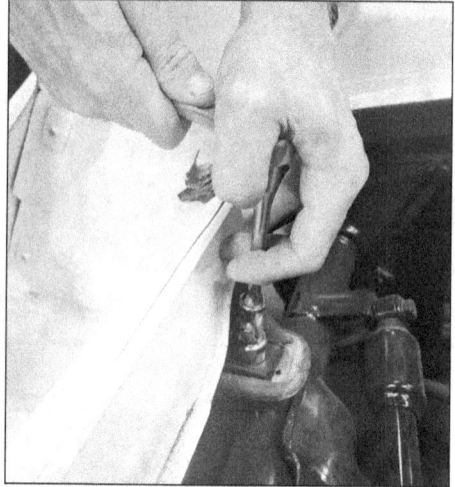

The majority of the bolts are 13 mm with a retaining washer. Don't forget the 17-mm bolts that are in the front pan head and attached to the rear suspension.

bearing cover. The cable the clip is on goes through the spindle under the car; you'll see it when you pull the hubcap. Unhook the speedometer cable and draw it back through the chassis. Remove all electrical connections and fuel lines from the engine. Remove the heater control cables from the heat exchangers.

Body from Pan

If you are performing a complete restoration, you need to remove the body from the pan. Taking the body off the pan also allows you to clean everything thoroughly and inspect for structural damage. If you are sending your car out to be media blasted, it's a lot easier to work with if the body is off the pan.

While there are tales aplenty of folks doing this step solo, the safe and smart plan is to use pizza and beer to lure four of your closest friends over to your shop for an hour or so. You might want a fifth friend to video the process; choose one who can hold the camera steady while laughing. Also, you will need a set of sawhorses or your handy-dandy body cart.

Begin by removing the bolts. There are 2 under the gas tank, 13 running down each side of the pan, 2 in the front fire wall, 2 on each side of the backseat (sometimes 3), and 1 above the rear passenger tire on the outside of the body.

Lift the body slowly off the pan. You'll hear a pop as the seal separates from the body and pan. You might need to do some scraping. Take care when lifting, and check to make sure that you didn't forget any other connections.

Remove the main electrical wiring harness. Keep all switches, relays, and the main fuse panel. The rest of the wiring can be thrown away. Now that you can see everything, do a final check for any rubber, bump stops, grommets, or grounding screws you might have missed.

Even if you're putting a new wiring harness in, it's advisable to tag where your connections go. Yellow painter's tape and a ballpoint pen are your friends in this process.

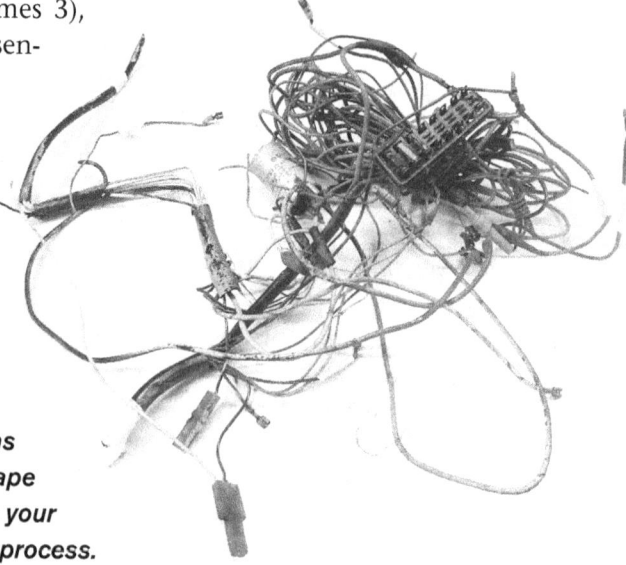

CHAPTER 4

BEETLE BODIES START HERE

Strolling through a Volkswagen car show, you'll see a little of everything: smooth, glassy finishes; patina rides that show their age; rusty hunks of metal barely holding themselves together; and everything in between. There is no bigger decision you'll make in restoring your Beetle than what you want the body and finish to look like. That decision will determine how much your restoration will cost, how much work it will require, and even how long you will extend the life of your Bug. It's all a matter of personal taste, budget, and patience.

If you want a patina ride, you can either leave your Beetle body as is or give it a clear coat and skip this chapter entirely. If you want a strong, smooth Beetle body, you'll probably refer to this chapter so often that you may memorize it word for word.

If you are prone to perfectionism and obsessive compulsion, this phase of your restoration is likely to give you fits. There is always room for improvement. Even in the highest-level restorations done by Airkooled Kustoms, we can point out tiny flaws no normal human being would ever notice but that drive us nuts. We only release a car when we can stand for people to lay eyes on them. You will likely learn a lesson in how good enough is good enough as you work on your Beetle's body.

Blast, Dip, Strip, or Sand?

You have four main options for taking your Beetle down to bare metal. They vary in cost, time, mess, and elbow grease requirements. While there are pros and cons with each method, our shop nearly always chooses to send disassembled project cars out to blast. It's the most cost-efficient, thorough method; and by sending cars out rather than blasting them in-house, we can keep the shop from looking like a dust storm rolled through.

Blast

Nothing strips paint, grease, grime, and filler off a car body faster and more thoroughly than shooting it with a high-speed stream of blast medium. As exciting as all that sounds, there are some drawbacks to this method. First, you absolutely must disassemble your Beetle and remove the body from the chassis.

Safety for You and for Your Beetle

As you work on your Beetle's body, you will likely be amazed by how much dust you create: piles of dust, dust in the air, dust in your hair, and dust coating your body. That's all part of the job, but you do not want this dust in your lungs or eyes. A mask and safety glasses are a must. ■

Standard safety equipment is an absolute must for protecting your eyes and lungs from the dust storm you're about to create.

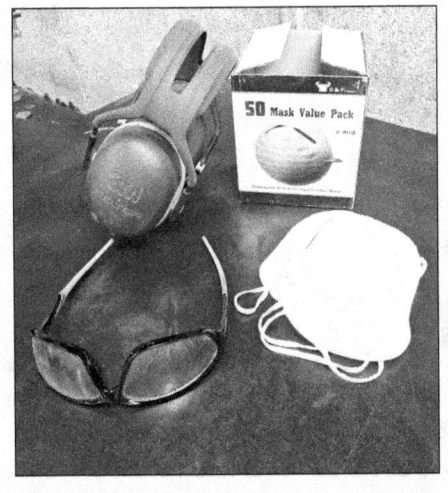

HOW TO RESTORE YOUR VOLKSWAGEN BEETLE 37

CHAPTER 4

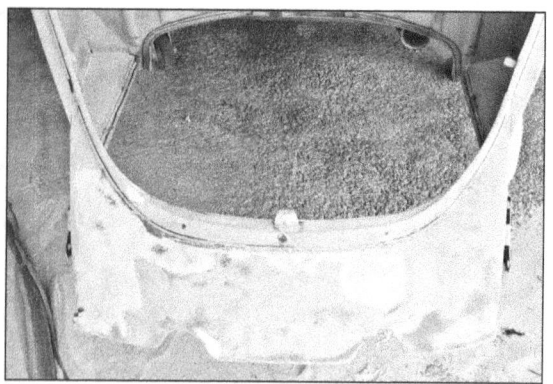

More than 30 years of driving takes its toll on a Beetle's body. Usually the front and rear sections are damaged quite badly and are often poorly repaired.

good investment. Between the mess blast creates and the possibility you could damage your Beetle, blasting is a great task to outsource. Prices vary widely depending on where you live. In many places, there's also the option of having a dustless blast service come to your location.

Chemical Dipping and Stripping

This method is as effective as it is old school and dangerous. If you are considering chemically stripping your Beetle, be sure you understand the risks of using a concoction so caustic and harsh that it can strip paint from steel. You will need a respirator, appropriate safety gloves, a protective apron, and safety glasses or goggles. Another option is to find a company that does chemical dipping and stripping and send the body off to them.

Sanding, Sanding, Sanding

We could probably add a few more "sanding" words in this subhead because if you choose this method, that's exactly what you

Some tools needed are an air file, file paper, dual-action sander, and the sandpaper that goes with it. Also shown are the glass mixing board and metal spatulas.

will be doing for what feels like forever. You should invest in a pneumatic or electric sander and the proper-grit disks for each phase of this never-ending project.

Unless you've been lost in a desert during a sand storm, you will never see dust like you'll see if you go this route. Be sure to wear the appropriate safety gear. You will also go through a ton of filters for the respirator you'll need.

Second, you will gain new respect for your air hose and shop vacuum because your car will be full of blast medium when it comes back to you. You'll find heaps of sand in every nook and cranny. Third (and this is a pro and a con), every secret that was hidden by paint will now be revealed, including rust and horrible repairs. You'll see it all: the good, the bad, and the ugly.

You could buy blasting equipment and turn this phase into a DIY project, but you will probably find that paying a professional is a

This looks to be the result of a low-speed parking lot collision. Matters were complicated by a poor attempt at repairs. You never know what you are dealing with until it's all stripped down.

All sins are revealed by blasting. No more paint, no more filler, no more rust. Now it's time to get this bare metal sealed and healed.

Your Naked Beetle

Once you've got your Bug down to bare steel, the oxidation process will begin immediately. Naked steel is surprisingly vulnerable, and you could pretty much watch it rust right before your eyes if you don't protect it.

If your car went to blast, it will have a bit of protection because the blast media is formulated with a protectant. But you now need to remove as much media as you can with compressed air and your shop vac. If you used another method to strip your Beetle, it will be completely unprotected. Either way, you will need to seal it quickly. But before you get rolling with sealer, we need to have a quick discussion about working clean from here on out.

Working Clean!

Do not touch the bare metal with your ungloved hands because the oils from your skin will transfer to the metal. You want to avoid a situation where each stage of your work is contaminated by residue from the prior one. You won't be able to see that residue until you've painted your car. Then you'd either need to live with that unforced and very visible error or strip it back and start again. Play it safe; don't touch it with your bare skin.

When you work clean, you get much better results. Working clean means using new microfiber towels, not making do with old ones or a cheaper substitute. Keep a spray bottle filled with a mixture of water and isopropyl alcohol on hand to use for cleaning.

Now that your car's body parts are intact and you understand about working clean, you need to seal all that metal. Etch with a two-part epoxy sealer, spraying it as soon as possible so you don't get flash rust as ambient moisture evaporates. The first part is a sealer that bonds to the steel, helping to prevent rust while protecting and sealing. The second part is a good coat of sealer sprayed on every single surface and crease of your Beetle.

Rust, Dents, Dings, and Damage

One of the biggest reasons Beetle owners decide to undertake a restoration project is that their beloved ride has accumulated the usual dents, dings, and body damage you'd expect on a decades-old automobile. Depending on where your Beetle had been driven and stored, you may also have significant rust that needs attention.

There is no four-letter word more dreaded among classic car enthusiasts than R-U-S-T. It sends shivers down our spines—and not in a good way. We've all seen it. We know the devastation it causes; it is a cancer that eats through our beloved rides and leaves nothing but heartbreak in its path.

It's time to protect your freshly blasted shell with some good 2K epoxy etching primer. Never touch bare steel with your fingers. The oil in your skin will leave a residue on the metal that will cause contamination issues when you paint.

There is no need to blast spots that will be repaired or replaced. In fact, it's a good idea not to shoot epoxy primer over the damaged areas you know you will need to weld in later.

It's not uncommon, after stripping your Beetle down to bare steel, to discover that entire swaths of steel are just plain gone, devoured by rust. Certain areas are especially likely to disintegrate during the blast process because the rust was so advanced. They include the bottom of the heater channels, the area by the wheelwells on the inner fenderwells, floorpans, and the battery tray (if any overcharging led to an acid leak).

If you want a sleek, glossy finish, you must fix the damage. But this is more than just a cosmetic issue. In many cases, the car's structural integrity is at stake. If you skip the necessary metalwork, your car could fall apart while you're driving it; if you were to wreck, there's no telling how the car would hold up. In general, you either need to remove the damaged areas completely or repair them.

About Welding

If you are new to welding, you can get a lot of pointers by purchasing CarTech's book *Weld Like A Pro*. The only way you will improve your skills is by practicing on scrap metal. Remember to keep your surface clean and free of paint, oil, and dirt. The cleaner the metal, the better your welds will be.

It sure is nice if you have a friend who's got a good welder and knows how to use it. But if you decide to buy your own, be prepared to spend several hundred dollars to get a decent one. If you buy a cheap welder, it won't last. Even if you have professional welding skills, a cheap welder won't produce good welds.

Welding Safety

Welding is dangerously hot and bright work, and you can seriously hurt yourself if you are not careful. Always wear a helmet, leather gloves, and a leather jacket or arm protection. You're dealing with red, hot molten metal that can easily burn through regular clothes.

No matter how tempting it is, do not look at the welding arc. You will burn your retinas. Make sure you use a high-quality welding helmet. The best masks are auto-darkening, which means you can see normally through the mask until the light hits, and then the mask turns to black. When activated, your mask will essentially give you night vision, casting a green tint on everything. With your mask activated, you can look directly at the weld without going blind.

Here's a list of the equipment and tools you will need in addition to safety gear (mask, gloves, and safety glasses):

- Grinder
- Cutoff wheel
- Sanding disk
- Welder
- Protective clothing for welding, including leather gloves, leather jacket, and welding helmet
- Hammer and dolly
- Sheet metal screws

A Sawzall and a right-angle grinder are the basic tools you'll need to do the rough metal removal and prep for the new panels.

Taking care of all the rust can be tricky because there is always more rust than meets the eye. You can count on there being 30 to 50 percent more rust present than what you can detect. So, if you see a rust spot the size of a quarter, it's really the size of a baseball.

Assess the extent of rust and damage before you go any further. You'll need to decide how to handle the metalwork that is needed. There are two types of metalwork ahead: rough metal and finish metal. Rough metal is about replacing and repairing the damaged areas. Finish metal is about repairing much smaller flaws in the steel. You can take either or both on by yourself or outsource the work to a professional or even to an experienced hobbyist.

Panel Replacement

In areas completely devoured by rust, you'll need to replace them or even the entire panel. When cutting out your panel, be sure to use your repair panel as a cutting guide. Mark it with a permanent marker or grease pencil. Cut just shy of the line, about 1/16 inch, so you can grind or sand both panels. This is important for getting a proper fit. Ideally, you want about a 1/16-inch gap between panels for good penetration of the weld. Be sure to address all areas with a chemical rust treatment, otherwise the rust will creep back in.

Aftermarket panels will not be 100 percent perfect from the suppliers. You will need to test fit and grind away a little here and a little there. After you have the panel in good shape, you'll want to use zip screws to temporarily secure it in place. As you start, remove them and weld in the holes for plug welds.

Set your welder up to the proper setting for the gauge of metal you are using. Each welder is different, so check the inside flap on the machine to get a good wire speed and heat setting to start with.

Replacing the Package Tray

1 *Years of leaky windows, damaged seals, and old carpet can definitely leave a mess. You will find rust in some very strange places as you disassemble your Beetle.*

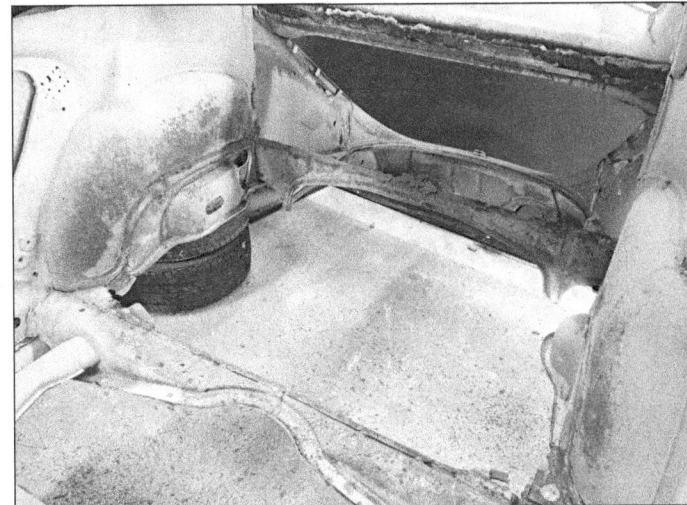

2 *Take care when removing old damaged panels. Always cut back to a spot where the metal is solid and sound. If you want, you can get a few pennies from the recycling company by selling them scrap steel.*

3 *Now that all of the rusty sections are removed, it's time to clean up where you will be attaching the new steel replacement panels. Use a grinder to get down to bright, shiny steel so you have a good attachment point.*

CHAPTER 4

Replacing the Package Tray *Continued*

4 Using zip screws, fit the replacement panel into place. Measure twice and cut once to save yourself some aggravation. It's a good idea to do a rough fit of the panel, then make slight adjustments to get it the way you want it.

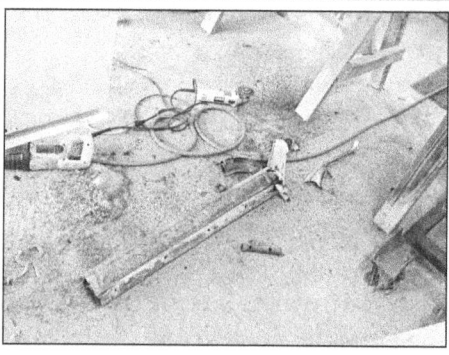

5 These channels are a structural component of the body and a common spot for rust damage. They also carry heat to the front of the car, so they are kind of important.

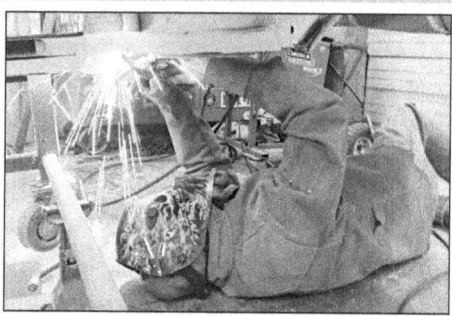

6 Next, suit up. It might look awkward, hot, and uncomfortable to suit up before welding. But the whole welding getup is much less uncomfortable than dealing with welding injuries on your skin or eyes.

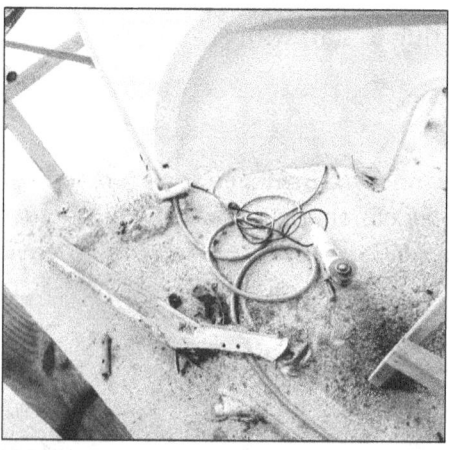

7 The old channel has been removed. There's still more work to do to get the body ready to accept the new channel.

8 Here's a good example of stitch welding, which is the best way to minimize distortion on your metal panels. It takes practice and patience, but by the end of your Beetle restoration, you will be amazed by your newly honed welding skills.

9 It's a good idea to mark your replacement panel to show the area you will use and the area you will cut away. Mark it so it is perfectly clear where to cut. It can be hard to remember when you are in the heat of cutting.

10 Now is the time to address any hidden rust behind the panels. A wire brush with some phosphoric acid will generally take care of these issues.

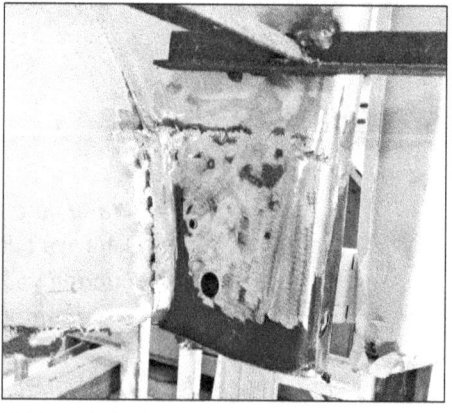

11 Grind down the excess welding material to get the panel ready for more advanced bodywork.

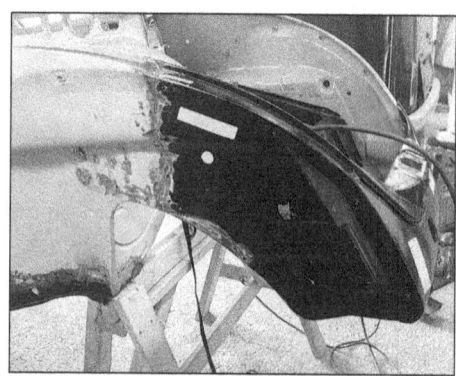

12 After you grind down the weld, you will be left with results that look something like this. This panel is now ready to go into the body shop.

HOW TO RESTORE YOUR VOLKSWAGEN BEETLE

Weld and Grind

Work across the panel with short dots of weld to keep the heat area to a minimum. Applying too much heat to one area will warp the panel, and that takes a whole lot of time and a different technique to fix.

Once the panel is fit and welded, you can grind down the area with an electric grinder, air grinder, or sander. Keep it moving as to not build up heat. Once you are satisfied with the results, treat the area with metal etch, apply an epoxy sealer, and then apply filler.

Assess and Replace

If needed, order replacement panels. Quality parts are worth spending the money on. Replacement steel varies both in its thicknesses and in the actual metal composition. Always go with the same thickness that the original manufacturer used if possible.

You can buy panels that are already stamped into the shape you need, whether it's for a quarter panel, door, fender, bottom of the fender, bottom of the hood, pillar, or even a whole side. You can buy panels from metal fabricators. You might even find what they call new old stock (NOS), which is leftover stock parts from when the car was originally produced.

Remove the Rust

Cut all remaining rust out of the panel. You'll want to cut outside the rust line because you want a solid edge rather than an edge that includes any rust. The more solid the new edge, the better.

Prep the Panel

Etch and prep the steel with phosphoric acid. This will neutralize any invisible oxidation in progress. Repeat this wipe down on every panel you

---

Tools Needed for Finish Metal Work

- Air nozzle for your compressed air line
- Basic set of body dollies
- Dual-action sander and an assortment of grits: 40, 80, 120, 220, 320/400, 600
- Fillers: Kevlar-infused epoxy and Evercoat's Extreme Gold
- Latex gloves
- Primer and gun
- Red Scotch-Brite pads
- Selection of body hammers
- Shrinking disk
- Slapping spoons
- A whole lot of patience

---

work on. This will protect the panel without affecting how the body filler and paint adhere to the steel. You should also spray it on the underside and inside any cavities to help prevent rust from coming back.

Mind the Gap and Thickness

Fit the new panel to the spot where it's going. The more precise the fit, the better your results. Any gap larger than 1/8 inch is too big of a gap. You can use clamps to hold the new panel in place before you start welding.

Take your time welding and follow a stitch-welding pattern: do a dot of weld, skip an inch, do a dot of weld. Let it cool. Then, go back to where you started and fill in the gaps. Welding this way helps keep your panel from warping. If your panel does warp, you can save it while it's still warm by using a hammer and dolly to straighten it back out.

Grind the weld down to match the thickness of the panel. Don't grind on the panel itself because that will thin the panel out. You are looking for a smooth finish. Don't linger in any area too long because the grinder will heat the panel too much and warp it. It's also possible to grind right through the metal itself if you're not careful.

While grinding, keep your hands away from the disk. Always wear gloves and eye protection; the grinder throws little bits of the grinding disk, and it hurts if it hits you.

Finish Metal Work

Next, it's time for finish metal, where you'll move steel with a hammer and dolly combination to get it where it's supposed to be. If you have any Jedi mind-tricks up your sleeve, now is the time to use them. This is a physically demanding process that will make muscles hurt that you didn't even remember you had. CarTech offers a book called *Automotive Sheet Metal Forming and Fabrication* that will get you up to speed quickly on this process.

Working with a hammer and a dolly is an advanced technique that is time consuming and difficult, but it is also the best way to get the smoothest, straightest panels possible. Essentially, this is how you coax the steel back into the form it was pressed into originally.

Then, you're going to use the shrinking disk to heat the top layer of steel, then cool the steel. Repeat this process until the metal is back where it belongs. The shrinking disk uses friction to heat the upper layer of crinkled steel. Water quenches the heat and cools the metal. Using this process of heating and quenching steel, you can get metal to do just about anything you want it to. By doing this work, you can remove parking-lot dings and any shrinking or stretching resulting from welding by hand.

Some shops slather filler onto their project cars like they're icing a cake to fix damage. Most Beetles have suffered from poor body repairs. Industry norms allow for up to 1/8 inch of filler, but at our shop, our standards are 1/32 inch to 1/16 inch. We know we are ridiculously particular.

Ultimately, you could skip this step, do it yourself, or hire a professional. In the end, it really depends on your skill level and what you find acceptable.

Evaluate the panels to see

Shrinking and Stretching Metal

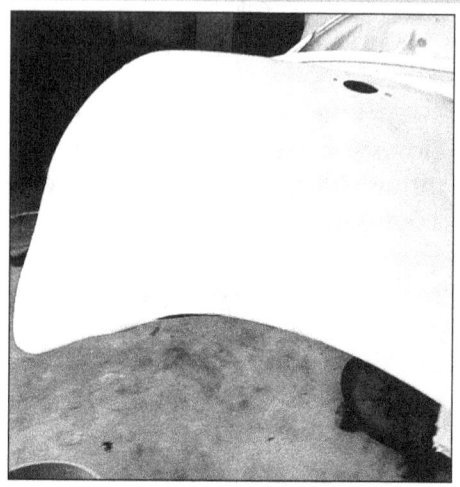

1 After all the old body work is removed post-blast, you will end up with some panels that are extremely lumpy. Now is the time to straighten them out and start fresh.

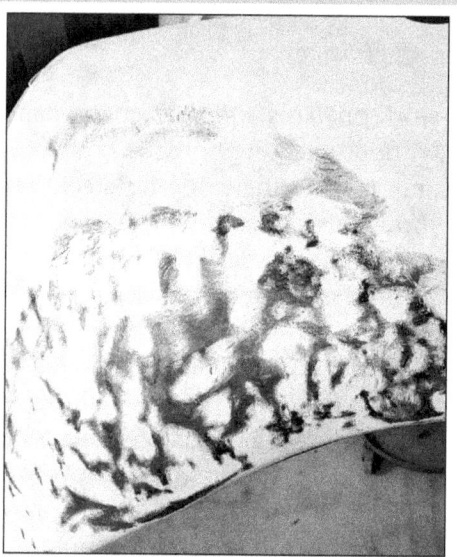

2 Use a dolly that corresponds to the size and shape for the panel to pound out any damage.

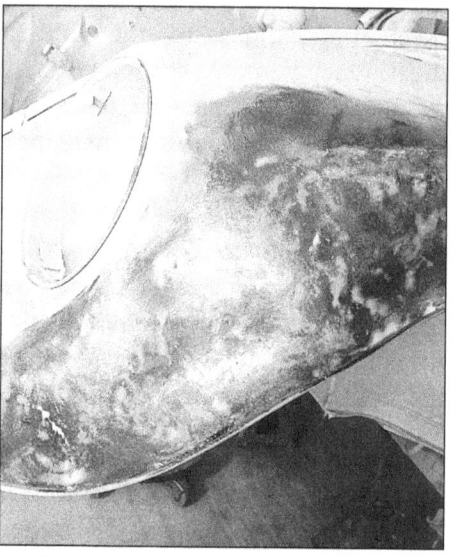

3 Next, use a shrinking disk to recurve and straighten the panel. This is about an hour into our session with the shrinking disk. At this point we could stop, hit it with some 40-grit sandpaper, and put some filler on it. But with another hour or so, we could get it smooth enough not to need filler.

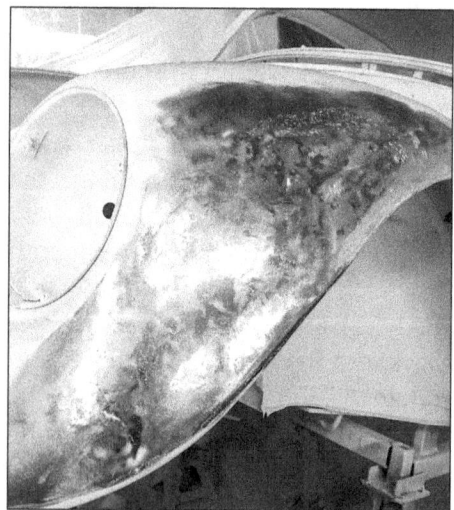

4 Here is the finished product; the result of beating, shrinking, and cussing at steel. We could have slathered it with filler, but doing it right will pay off.

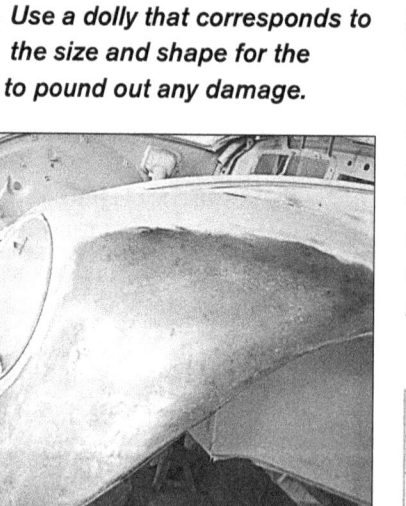

5 With the curves back in place, it is time to reseal the raw steel. Remember, do not touch the steel with bare hands. That will contaminate it. Now is a good time to wipe the panel down with phosphoric acid to give it some protection.

Smoothing Metal

Don't trust your eyes. Trust your sense of touch because your hands can feel things your eyes can't see. You can also use a jeweler's torch to heat up very small areas. You will need to quench the metal even more quickly if you use this advanced technique.

But First, A (Geeky) Note about Steel

While it certainly looks like solid metal, it is actually a semisolid substrate made from a crystalline structure. When the steel is put through a form press to be stamped into panels, such as doors, hood, and body, the pressure realigns the steel's atomic structure so it will keep a memory of that shape and alignment of molecules.

If the steel is stretched or cracked with a dent or a ding, the molecular bond is broken. Dings and dents cause tension in the steel. The steel wants to go back to its original shape. So, if you can relieve that tension, the steel will automatically go back to its original shape.

Metalwork is literally about moving tension in the steel with your bare hands (and some handy tools). It's an old art form that very few craftspeople know how to do anymore, especially because most modern car bodies are made of plastic or composites instead of steel.

---

what's needed. Do you have a lot of parking-lot dings, hail damage, or an old wreck? Don't jump in and go for the deepest part of damage to beat it out; you'll just stretch the steel. Instead, follow the *first in, last out* pattern as you work. The deepest part of impact is generally the first point of contact, and that will be the last area you work on.

With rough hammer and dolly work, the goal is to get it close. You don't need to make it perfect yet. We just want to see what we're working with right now. Working with an assortment of dollies is best. Choose the one that best suits the panel.

After a few hours of work, your arms will be numb and your ears will be ringing. The panel is getting closer to perfection, so keep going. With a few more hours of beating on metal, the dolly shapes have changed. You're getting closer to bringing out the shrinking disk.

Now it's time to start shrinking the steel. You will recurve the curves and straighten out the straights. You will still have high and low spots, but don't worry about them. Using the shrinking disk will take care of the high spots you've been noticing as you work. Be patient and let the metal go back to where it wants to go.

Work until you're happy with it. If you go too far, you can stretch the steel. Just reverse that stretch by using a shrinking disk to get it back in shape.

Filler, Finally

After metalwork is finished, there may still be some areas that need help. Choose a two-stage filler (never a single-stage variety) to finish the panel surface and leave it level and smooth. This is about curving the straight parts and straightening the curvy parts as needed. Use fine sandpaper and feather out your work area to blend.

Use the right chemistry for your application. There are three types of filler:

Epoxy Resin: This has the best durability for high vibration, heat, and wear areas, such as doors, doorjambs, and the engine bay. Use small quantities.

Talc-Based Filler: This is the best for minor surfacing.

Spot Filler: It is super lightweight for pinholes and minor scratches.

Filling Bodywork

1 *Hey, what do you know? We have more dents and dings to play with. Our project panel was full of filler, which all came off in blast. This panel will take about four hours of beating to get it into shape.*

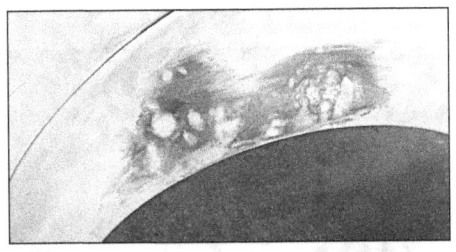

2 *Use 40- or 80-grit sandpaper on a block to define the area that you need to address. Rough it up to reveal the bare steel. Those are your high spots.*

Filling Bodywork *Continued*

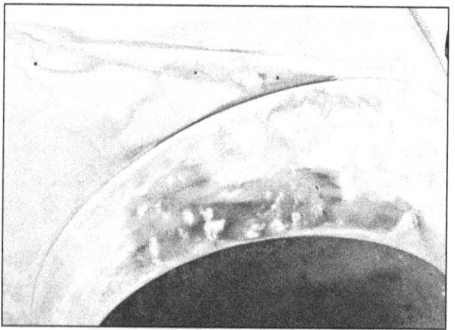

3 It's time to pick up the shrinking disk again. While this fender is close enough for a filler job, if you want it to be straight and shiny, it's not close enough yet. There's more work ahead.

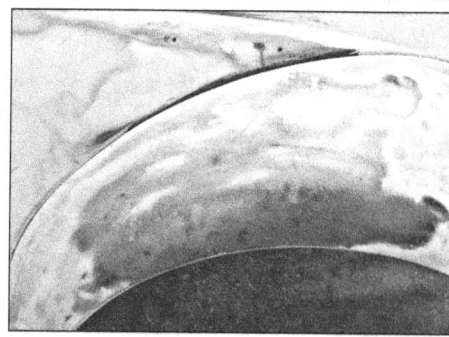

4 After you are mostly satisfied with the results of the shrinking disk and the shape of your curves, go over the repair area with 80-grit sandpaper. Then, it goes back into sealer.

5 Apply your first round of filler. Typically, we will use one called Kitty Hair on high-vibration areas. Apply multiple thin coats until you have the desired thickness.

6 Time to break out the long-blocks and some 40- or 80-grit sandpaper or your trusty dual-action sander. You will level, or cut, this to get it close to where you want it. Don't expect to get it done in one pass.

7 This is the next layer of filler that goes on your panel. Once again, apply multiple thin coats rather than slathering it on. Let it harden before you start cutting, otherwise you will foul your sandpaper up and get paste in it.

8 Using the longest, stiffest block you can comfortably work with, work in a crisscross pattern. This will help keep your planes in line. Remember, you are not working on a flat panel or a straight edge. Curves are good.

9 This is what you should end up with after all that body work and dust. Thankfully, you were wearing your dust mask!

Filling Bodywork *Continued*

10 At this point, make sure to remove all dust, debris, oil, grease, and contamination from the body, and clean your work area well. This 1968 Standard Beetle is ready to go to the next step.

11 Three good layers of high build later, it is time to let the body sit overnight. Then, we get to start sanding again.

12 Here is a good example of some smaller low spots missed during the rough filler process. These small divots and pinholes will be taken care of with two-part spot putty.

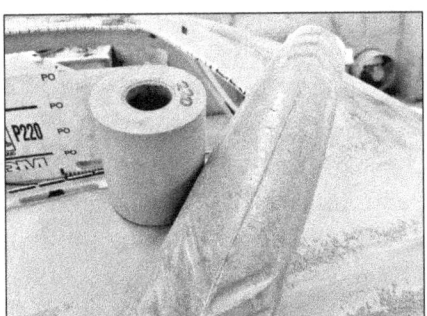

13 Continue cutting the panels until you are satisfied with their appearance, increasing the abrasive grit throughout the process. Midway through the cut, if you still have any low spots, use some spot putty. You should have enough high build down to make it all level and smooth. Don't be afraid to stop and reshoot more high build if you need it. It's easier to catch now than later.

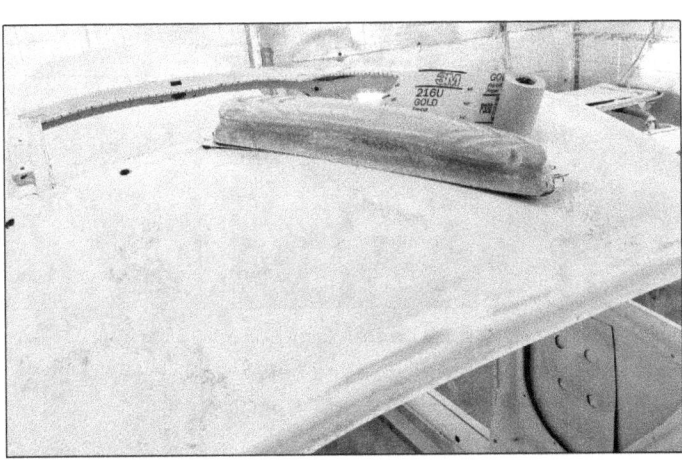

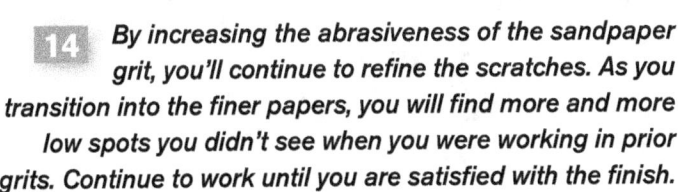

14 By increasing the abrasiveness of the sandpaper grit, you'll continue to refine the scratches. As you transition into the finer papers, you will find more and more low spots you didn't see when you were working in prior grits. Continue to work until you are satisfied with the finish.

You've now hammered and dollied the metal to within an inch of its life. After you've gone over it with a shrinking disk and gotten the metal as close to smooth as you possibly can, it's time to do filler.

Typically, we'll use Kitty Hair around high-vibration and high-wear areas, such as around doorjambs, door edges, and the rear valance. The reason for this is because Kitty Hair is an extremely dense and durable material. It is a resin epoxy, rather than a talc epoxy, which is not nearly as strong or durable.

For filler application, it is easier to use metal spreading spatulas than the plastic versions. The metal type will hold a true edge for a lot longer, which means they will not need to be replaced or refaced as often as the plastic kind. Spatulas with rough edges will lead to drags and voids in the filler.

The mixing board is also important. Some companies make disposable sheets you can use for mixing. A better option is a glass cutting board because it's reusable, cleanable, and scrapeable. Whatever you do, do not use cardboard. Cardboard contains oils and waxes that will transfer onto your bodywork and cause problems during the paint process.

Make sure you have enough hardener in the filler material. Follow the manufacturer's directions to get the right mix. If you over-catalyze, it will harden too quickly; if you under-catalyze, the filler may never harden.

As you mix, work with a downward motion, not stirring or whipping the material. That way you can avoid adding air into the filler, which will lead to voids or pinholes.

After you get a nice, consistent mix, there should be a slight color change in the filler. The color should be consistent. If it is not, continue to mix it until it is uniform.

When it's time to apply the filler, the best way is to use two metal spatulas: one a little larger than the area you are working, and the other about the same size as that area. Apply the filler in a very thin layer over the area. You can always come back to add more, but if you start with too much material, you may end up with an adhesion problem. After each pass with the spatula, be sure to knock the material off of the edges so you don't start getting excess filler coming off the spatula.

Use hand blocks or pneumatic tools to knock down any high spots in the filler. When working with rough filler, use 80 or 120 grit. When working with finer fillers, use 180 or 220 grit. When working with glaze putty, use 320, and finish it off with 400 grit. The lower the grit, the faster and more aggressive the cutting. The higher and finer the grit, the less it will cut and shape the filler. Once you're finished filling, you'll be ready for sealer.

Congratulations! You've gotten your car through one of the most time-consuming phases of restoration: rough and finish metal. While it will never be perfect (trust us, it's easy to drive yourself crazy trying to get it dead-nut straight), it is no doubt in much better condition than before you started.

Sealing all the work you just did is critical to protecting the fillers and steel. Always use a good two-part epoxy, which is available from local paint stores. Don't use cheap, inferior products; you don't want to waste the work you have just done or the cost of the paint you will soon apply.

When doing your final sealer coat, double-check to make sure you have sealed 100 percent of the body. This means the interior and the exterior.

It's time to inspect your work. You are either ready for color or you need to apply some more filler. At the shop, we do one more cut on the final sealer before sending cars into the paint booth.

CHAPTER 5

Prime, Paint, and Polish

The proof is in the paint job. The paint process is where the Beetle you pictured in your imagination finally comes to life. If you're aiming for a patina ride, this is another chapter you can skip. But if your heart is set on a smooth, shiny paint finish, this is a chapter you'll want to bookmark because you'll be here a while.

Even if you've never painted anything but a room or a watercolor in junior high art class, you can paint a car. No problem. This is a whole different kind of painting anyway. Great paint skills take time and practice to build. There's always room for improvement.

Along with this book, YouTube offers some excellent tutorials for your technique. You'll know you've crossed the line into restoration obsession when your playlist includes tutorials on paint, polish, and, for the truly hardcore, washing your microfiber towels.

In this phase of your restoration, you'll be priming your car, painting it (color and clear), and then polishing it.

Primer

The first step of paint is to spray the project with epoxy primer to seal in the fillers and protect the metal from hydroscopic reactions. Most talc-based fillers absorb ambient moisture, and the sealer will cover any bare metal that may have been exposed during filler work.

The goal here is to spray nice, even, thin coats to completely encapsulate the body. Generally, we apply three coats, but check your manufacturer's instructions. Enough material has been applied when no filler is visible underneath the primer. The filler will actually draw the primer in to form a tight chemical bond. Always keep a wet edge as you work to prevent adhesion problems.

This is the final step before going into color and clear. You will catch any pinholes and edges that may not be quite right. Look for small high spots you can feel but can't see.

Safety During Painting

There are a few safety items to use during this step. Keep a box of latex gloves (or rubber gloves if you're allergic to latex) on hand to protect the surface of the car as well as your hands. Safety glasses are important to protect your eyes from the airborne chemistry. Keep an eye-wash station handy in case you get something in your eye. Some of the chemicals can cause serious eye injuries.

You absolutely need a respirator so that you can breathe safely during your shoot. We recommend the PAPR system from 3M. It is spendy, but being able to breathe properly makes it a more-than-worthwhile investment. Always keep a fire extinguisher within reach. These chemicals are highly flammable. ■

Primer Supplies

- Dawn liquid dish soap
- High-buff primer
- New 5-gallon bucket
- Paint guns: at least three good guns or a kit with interchangeable tips, caps, and needles that will all work on the same paint gun
- Pneumatic dual-action (DA) or electric sander
- Sanding disks and sandpaper, including grits of 800, 1000, 1500, 2000 wet and dry, and finishing disks 3000 and 5000 grit
- Stiff hand blocks
- Two-part epoxy primer
- Warm water

Shooting Primer

Spray the car body and secondary panels with primer. Follow the epoxy primer with a high-buff or sandable primer. This is a thick primer that's used for leveling and surfacing.

Use a long-block to get your curves curvier and your straights straighter. In fact, use the longest footprint block possible for the panel being worked on. That'll help smooth the transitions. Some folks use pneumatic or electric DAs or sanding files (that's not what we do at the shop, but it's certainly acceptable for a home build). Add a seal coat to cover any primer or metal that was exposed during final prep. To do this, apply the sealer, let it cure, and then long-block one more time to catch anything missed. Don't forget to add more primer to any areas that were corrected.

That last step allows you to get anything you may have missed. This is the last look and feel opportunity you have before adding color and clear to the Beetle. The darker the paint color chosen, the more preparation work will show. The smoother the body, the closer you can get to a mirrorlike shine.

Paint

The protective coating and color of paint will make a Beetle beautiful and shiny while also protecting it from environmental corrosion. Paint gives the car character, and you can create a whole different feel or personality for your car with the paint you choose.

Always use the best-quality materials you can. It's better to spend once than to have to spend twice to correct a bad product choice the first time around. Don't be afraid to try painting. You might be self-taught, but so are most of the paint masters! In the end, shiny is just scratches you can't see.

If you don't want to take this part of the project on yourself, look for a restoration shop. We don't recommend going to a collision shop because their business model relies on speed rather than painstaking levels of care. Some hobbyists take their cars to a local trade school or community college and pay the automotive paint department a nominal fee to have the students practice their skills on their car. As always, you'll get what you pay for.

Safety During Painting

If available, shoot in an Occupational Safety and Health Administration (OSHA)-approved paint booth to increase the safety factor. By painting in a paint booth, you'll have the benefits of a controlled environment. The paint, hardeners, and reducer are all temperature- and humidity-sensitive. You'll also get better results because you'll have correct airflow during your shoot.

If you are painting in your garage, be sure the garage is well-ventilated. Also make sure that any paint fumes you exhaust out of the building are not going toward an electric fan. If there were to be a spark, you'd have an explosion. Your neighbors and family would not be amused.

Correct, clean airflow is a crucial factor for creating a flawless paint

Apply an even layer of epoxy primer to prepare for painting with color and clear. This primer provides a good seal to protect the surface and gives it the kind of tooth needed for good adhesion.

finish. With the correct airflow, dust and dirt cannot settle onto your very sticky new paint. Dust and dirt in your paint environment are the enemy. Work clean!

Be aware that the chemicals you're spraying are toxic. Even limited exposure to these chemicals can cause significant health concerns. If you can smell the fumes, get out of the area. Examine your setup and improve your ventilation before continuing.

Your paint distributor can help you figure out how much of each product you need. Every paint brand has different best practices. It is vital to follow manufacturer's recommendations to the letter.

Paint Parameters and Practice

There are three crucial parameters that go into every paint job. First, know how much fluid is going through the gun. Second, know how fast the paint is going through. And third, know how much fluid is being laid down. You'll need to achieve the right mix to avoid runs, sags, and dry spots. It is important to become familiar with the paint manufacturer's spec sheets. In particular, you want to know how much overlap you need to get a beautiful result. The recommended overlap rate ranges from 50 to 70 percent.

Unless you paint professionally, practice your technique before shooting your car. A bit of practice will give you a good feel for the equipment and the paints you're using. Once paint is shot, it's difficult to fix. If you mess it up to the point where you can't stand the sight of your paint job, you'll probably end up sanding it back to primer and repainting. The second go-round on a paint job is significantly less enjoyable than the first time around.

Painting Supplies

There are three options for painting: a single-stage enamel, where the color and shine is all in one layer (old-school technique); separate paint and clear coat (more common today); or a waterborne system (instead of VOCs, the solvent is water). The waterborne system is tricky to shoot and much more expensive, but it's your only option if you're in California.

Here's a list of the equipment and tools you will need for the paint phase:

- Air compressor
- Air dryers
- Air lines
- Clear
- Hardener
- Paint gun
- Reducer

Good shops use a variety of paint guns, tools, and quality paints. Clean, dry compressed air is a must. A three-stage air filtration system is shown.

One more reason to practice is that paint is expensive, especially if you choose red, black, or blue paint. Those colors have a higher pigment content; therefore, they are more expensive.

One of the best ways to get a feel for the shooting distance and angles of your paint gun is to practice with wooden paint sticks. Cut the sticks to 6- and 8-inch lengths. Tape one of the sticks to the end of your gun. Then, pretend to shoot. Pay attention to how far away you are from the surface and how far the paint pattern fans out. There's a correlation between the distance you are away from the surface and the fan pattern.

Take your time and chemically clean the body once more. Remove all contamination from dust, dirt, etc. You will be surprised how much contamination floats around in the air.

With a 6-inch fan, you should be approximately 6 inches away from the surface. Likewise, with an 8-inch fan, you should be approximately 8 inches away. You will have to adjust for paint viscosity and ambient temperature.

Then, graduate to painting with colored water. Fill the paint cup with a combination of water and food coloring and shoot at a piece of cardboard. There is no need to don your mask, respirator, or goggles this time, unless you want to go for the full effect.

Practice just the way you'll shoot. You should be able to see the material hit the surface. Move at an even pace. If it's blurry, you're shooting too fast, and you'll get dry spots. If the material is dribbling, you're shooting too slowly, and you'll get runs and sags.

Start Painting

You are now ready to start with the real paint. Wear proper protective gear while mixing paints. The chemicals can be hazardous to your health if you breathe them in without protection.

If mixing paint, paint manufacturers provide recommended mixing ratios. Follow the ratios and use a small digital scale to achieve exact mixes.

Proper setup of your spray gun is important. For example, a 6-inch fan will require a 6-inch distance from the painting surface. The first coat of color should be applied lightly with a 50-percent overlap pattern from one pass to the next. It will be semi-translucent, but don't worry about coverage at this point.

The paint manufacturer will specify approximate flash times (drying time between coats). Temperature and humidity may factor in to shorten or lengthen that time. On your second pass, apply the paint perpendicular to your first pass and use a 70-percent overlap this time. Let the paint flash again.

On the third and final coat of paint, shoot in the same direction as the first coat, going with a 70-percent overlap for good coverage. After allowing the final coat of paint to flash fully, in preparation for clear, run a tack rag to remove any dust or specks of foreign matter that may be present. Otherwise, the clear coat will make them glaringly obvious.

Painting Your Beetle

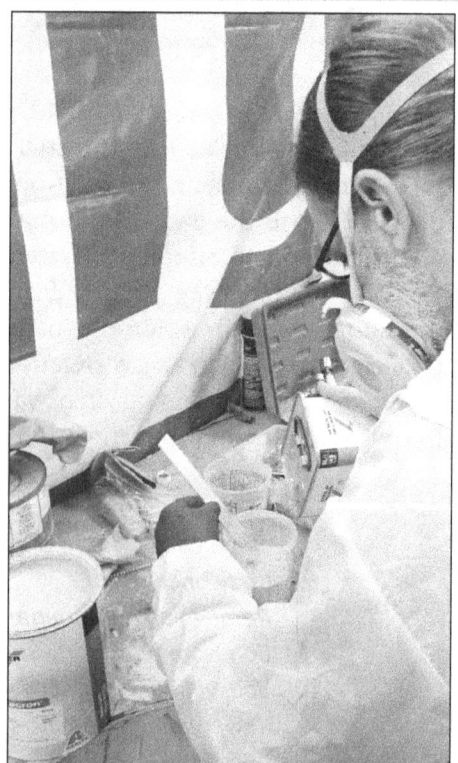

1 Clean and prep the car. After it's ready to shoot, mix the paint to the manufacturer's specifications.

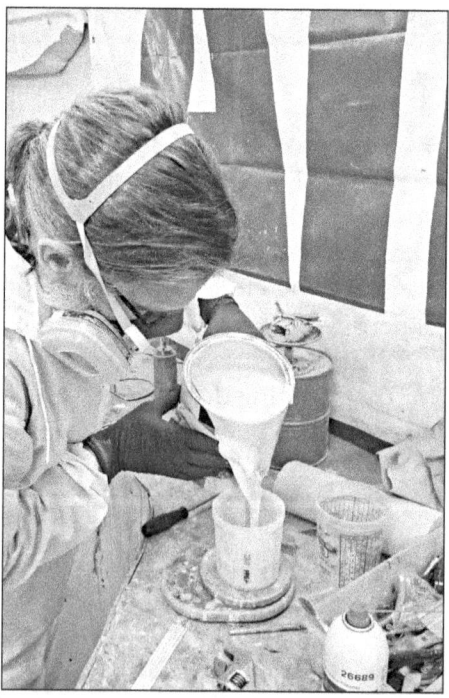

2 Pour the paint into the paint cup, taking care to not spill any of its content. Remember, paint is expensive, and a lousy pour could result in a costly mistake.

3 Set up your gun with a 6- to 8-inch spray pattern. Most paint manufacturers include specifications on the setting that will work best with their paint. Paint gun manufacturers also include guidelines. These specifications may contradict one another; in that case, you may need to experiment to find a balance between the two.

PRIME, PAINT, AND POLISH

Painting Your Beetle Continued

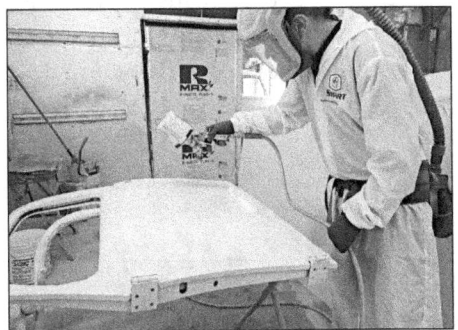

4 Lay down a base coat of color with a 50-percent overlay, always keeping a wet edge as you paint. Spray the entire car body; do the doors and secondary panels separately later.

5 When shooting color, there is no rush. The first pass should always be fairly light. Remember, you're going to do several coats. So, if you miss a spot, don't worry about it. You'll get it later.

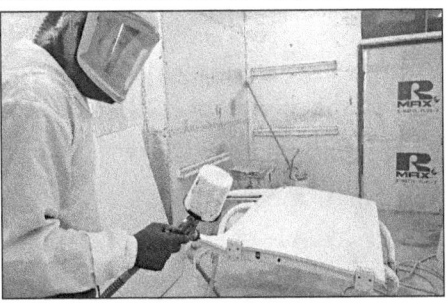

6 Let the paint flash according to the manufacturer's specifications. Paints are temperature sensitive. There are different reducers and hardeners to use in varying ambient temperatures. Check your paint manufacturer's specifications.

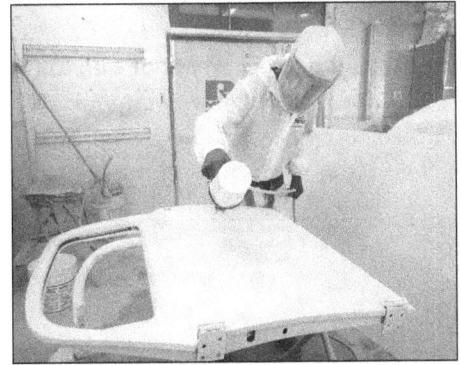

7 Spray with a 70- to 80-percent overlay, painting in the opposite direction of the first pass. If your first pass was going back and forth horizontally, this second pass goes up and down vertically. Keep a wet edge as you paint.

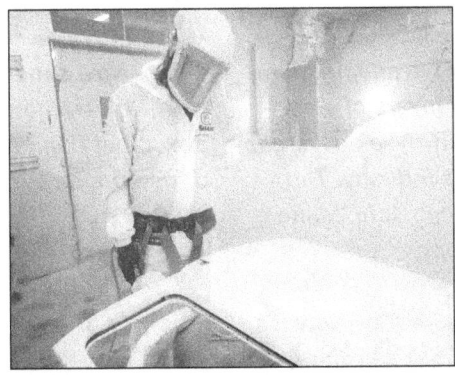

8 Allow the paint to flash again per your paint manufacturer's recommendations. If you don't wait long enough, the prior coat will outgas and cause a flaw called solvent pop.

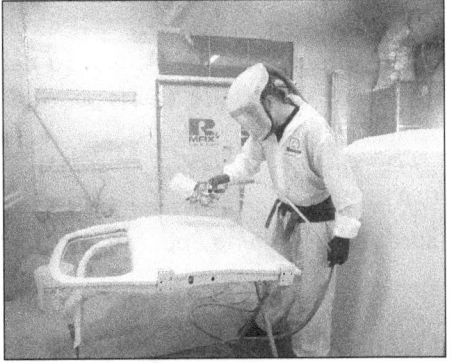

9 Apply one more coat of paint, painting in the same direction as the first coat. Two or three coats is usually enough, so repeat if needed. Always let the paint flash between coats.

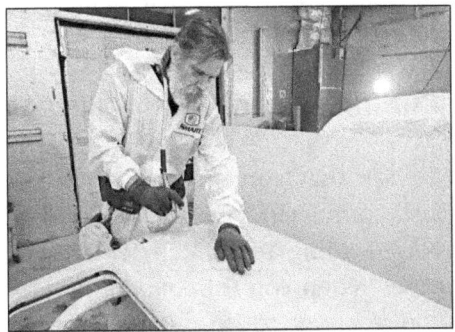

10 Wipe the surface with a tack cloth to remove any dust or debris before spraying with clear.

11 After the third pass in your color shoot, let the chemistry flash per the manufacturer's specifications. Then, inspect your work. Look for any runs, sags, drips, or weak spots in your paint. If you find any debris, scuff it out with 800-grit paper and repair with a light mist of paint.

HOW TO RESTORE YOUR VOLKSWAGEN BEETLE

Clear Coat

The next step is to apply the clear with a 50-percent overlap. The goal is a slight orange peel in the finish. It will almost look like a dry spray. This gives the next coat something to attach itself to.

With the second coat, spray with a 70-percent overlap. It will show a lot more gloss and depth, as well as more orange peel. This is normal. Repeat the process for a third and fourth time. With each new clear coat, shoot perpendicular of the direction of the previous coat.

Clearing Your Beetle

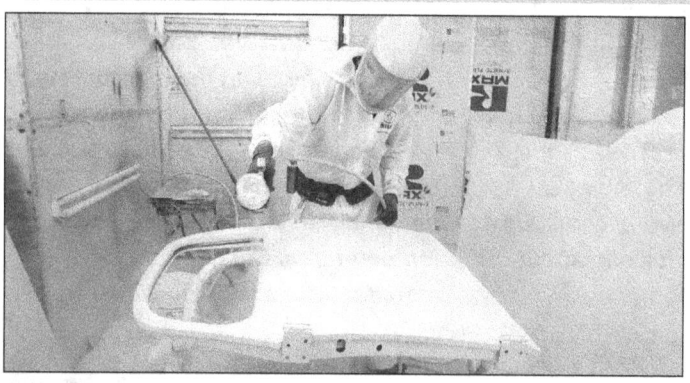

1 Apply a mist coat with a 50-percent overlap. This thickness will give the subsequent layers of clear something to adhere to. Let the clear flash. Tyvek coveralls are a must. They are fairly standard in the industry. They will help produce a cleaner job while staying safe. Make sure your breathing apparatus is OSHA approved.

2 Now shoot a 70-percent overlap wet coat with the clear. Slow the gun down to put more material down, but don't slow down so much that sags, runs, and drips appear. Let the clear flash again.

3 Now it's time to really lay the clear down. You'll paint perpendicular from the last coat with a 70-percent overlap pattern. At this point, the clear should be laying down like glass.

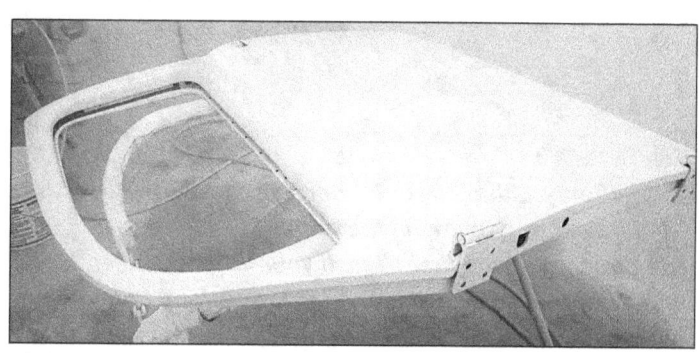

4 Let the final clear coat dry. Turn off the lights. Leave the ventilation on for three hours. Walk away. If you have access to a professional booth, bake according to the paint manufacturer's recommendations.

Once you've applied paint and clear on the main body, do the same with your secondary panels. Rather than painting and flipping those panels to get all the sides done, it's easier to suspend a pole from the ceiling of your work space and hang the panels from the pole. Some painters prefer to use a laundry rack rather than a pole. Either way, you'll be shooting panels from some rather strange angles. Don't forget to stay hydrated. You will sweat more than you think is possible.

If you're not baking the paint, let it air dry for 48 hours or so. If you don't let it dry that long, you'll wreck the finish by moving forward too fast. If you wait much longer, the paint will get so hard that it's hard to do the next steps.

Cutting, Buffing, and Polishing

See that gorgeous paint job you just completed? In the next phase, you're going to scratch it. On purpose. When you think about it, what you're about to do is work through a sequence of scratching the finish with progressively finer scratches, and that's what makes for a shiny finish.

PRIME, PAINT, AND POLISH

Sanding the Clear

1 We generally start with 1500 wet/dry paper. By leveling the surface and removing all orange peel, this prime cut will leave your paint job more level and remove imperfections from the clear coat. You want a flat, level surface.

2 Starting with 1000 or 1500 wet/dry paper (depending on the finish), soak the paper in warm water and liquid dish soap for 30 minutes before you start. Your first pass will be a crosshatch pattern.

3 Start leveling the clear coat. This means taking the high areas (orange peel) down to create a consistent, smooth surface. Be careful not to cut too far down. If you remove too much paint, you'll have scars, scrapes, and maybe even cut through the clear coat and into the color.

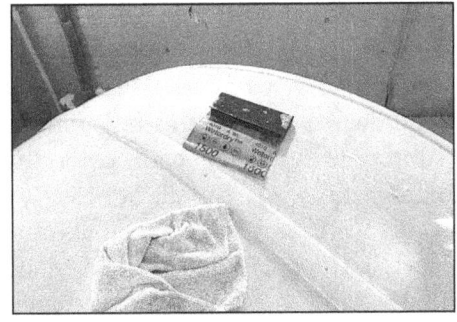

4 After your initial cut, clean the panel thoroughly with a 50-50 mix of isopropyl alcohol and water. Use brand-new microfiber towels and change your water often.

5 Move on to the next grit of sandpaper by 1,000 grit, follow the same crosshatch pattern. Continue the process you've started.

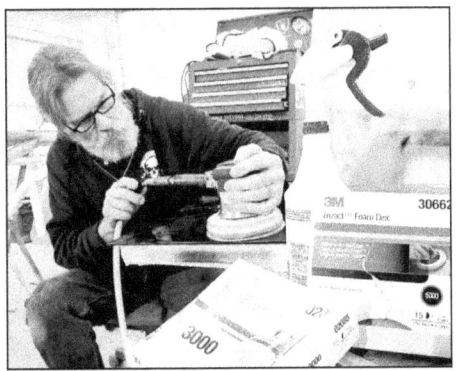

6 When the cut is complete, switch to a nonwoven abrasive pad and use an electrical or pneumatic DA wet sander. At the shop, we go from 3000 up to 5000, but decide for yourself how far to go before switching to polishing mode.

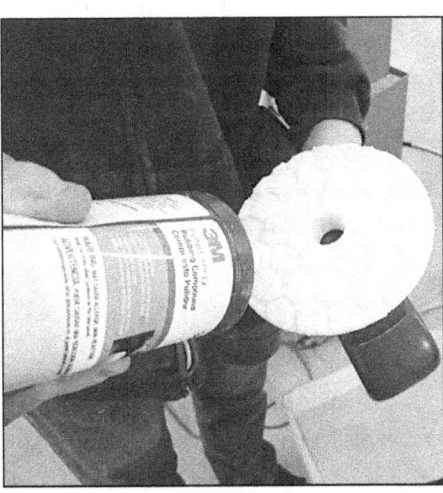

7 Priming your pad is important. With polish, a little goes a long way. If you use too much, you'll coat everything around you with polish.

HOW TO RESTORE YOUR VOLKSWAGEN BEETLE

CHAPTER 5

After the 48-hour drying time, assess how that clear coat looks on your car body and secondary panels. The better it looks, the higher the grit you'll choose for the next step.

Clear Coat Sanding

Choose your sandpaper between 800 and 1500 grit to remove surface imperfections and create a level surface. Use the stiffest rubber-backed block you can get. Sand a small section of the panel, work the next section of the panel, and continue working in small areas at a time. It will make the job easier.

Different panels require different light and angles to see the surface. We find that using an LED light at a 50-degree angle works best for our shop. The lighter the paint color, the harder it is to see the surface clearly.

Now that you've taken all the trash out of the paint and leveled it, it's time to refine your scratches. Repeat the leveling and cleaning process, increasing the grit each time up through 2500 grit. You want to make the smoothest, most consistent surface possible.

With each round, the finish gets shinier. To achieve the ultimate finish and to reduce your polish time, use woven abrasive disks. In this case, we are using 3M's Trizact non-woven disks with a foam interface pad. Finally, switch to chemical abrasives to finish this phase.

Polish It Up

Just when you thought your Beetle couldn't get any shinier, it's time to make it do just that. The more you refine the surface, the more it shines. Polishing removes progressively finer scratches. Next, you'll do a three-stage polish using an electric or pneumatic sander, polishing compound, and the correct foam pads for the compound you use.

At the shop, we use three sizes of polishers: 1, 3, and 6 inch, all of which are electric DA polishers. We are not fans of rotary buffers because they have a steeper learning curve for a hobbyist, which means damage can be done by burning the painted surface with too much heat. Spook's personal favorite is the Rupes brand of polishers and its line of polish pads. For the polish products themselves, the favorite around here is the Perfect-It line of polishes by 3M. For an inexpensive model, you might want to look at Griot's Garage polishers.

Apply four pea-sized dabs of polish directly onto the pad. If it's a brand-new, fresh pad, which is recommended, apply the polish to the pad and then daub it onto the body panel. Start on the lowest speed setting, work the polished area (about 2 x 2 feet); then, increase the speed until you reach about 38 rpm. Spook uses a six-pass process: one up, 50-percent overlap, and back down to form a box. Then, reverse the pattern. Repeat the process until you've polished the same area a total of six times.

Once polishing is finished, clean the panel with isopropyl alcohol and a little bit of water.

The pad will get dirty and clogged as you work. The best way to clean it is to turn the machine off and hit the pad with compressed air to remove the chunks. You can also take the pad off the machine, clean it, then reassemble the machine and turn it on. But make sure you put the head into a bucket so that you don't sling water all over the place.

On Level 1 of polish, use the most aggressive polishing pad from the set of three. The goal is to remove the scratches from the last round of hand cutting, when the 5000-grit DA pad was used. Keep moving up one level with a less-aggressive pad and polish. Work in small areas to remove microscratches. Clean the panel between each round of polish by using isopro-

Tools Needed for Polish

- 3 different pads
- 3 different polishes
- Clean water
- Dual-action sander (DA)
- Eye protection
- Gloves
- Isopropyl alcohol
- New microfiber towels
- Respirator (depending on the chemicals you're using; check the manufacturer's specifications)

Once you settle on an abrasives line you like working with, use the entire product line. They are designed to work together, and you'll get the best results possible.

PRIME, PAINT, AND POLISH

pyl alcohol and water to remove any contamination remaining from the previous process.

Level 2 continues to remove micro scratches with a decrease of the aggressiveness of the polish and pads. The next stage of polish will be finer. You don't want any previous paint residue scratching into the next level of shiny.

Move up to Level 3, repeating the whole process with the finest

Polish 'Til Your Arms Fall Off

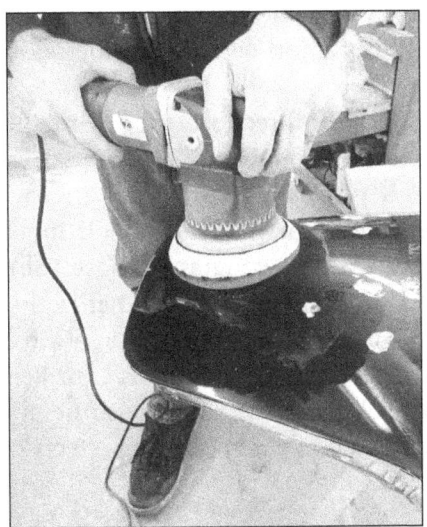

1 Use the most aggressive polish and matched pad to work in a 2x2-foot area where possible. Work in smaller squares to get faster results. At this point, don't worry about slight scratches or holograms. Polish until your material no longer cuts or disappears.

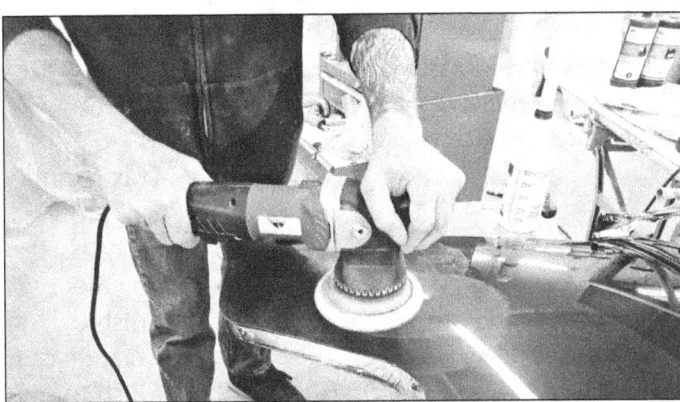

2 Work a 2x2-foot square area. Work up and down and then side to side, going over each area with a total of six sets of six passes.

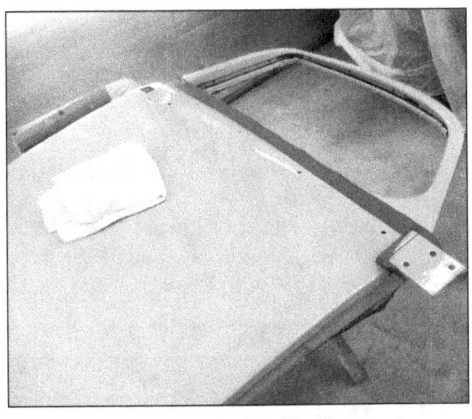

3 Clean the surface with a 50-50 mix of isopropyl alcohol and water. Use a brand-new cloth to remove the polish entirely.

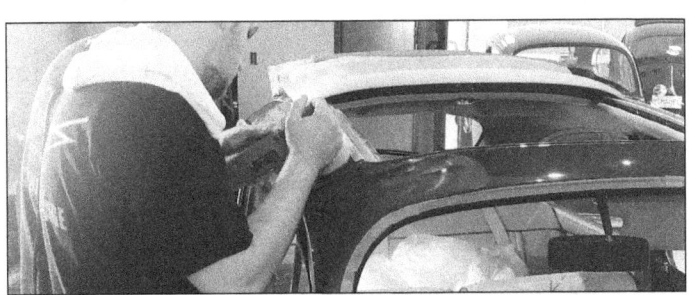

4 Change the machine and pad size as necessary. The smaller the heads, the faster the rotation, but the tighter the corners you can get into.

5 Then, move up to Level 2. Use your second-most-aggressive polishing pad and its corresponding polish. Follow the same pattern as the first phase of polish. Clean the whole surface again.

6 Now that the car is all polished and cleaned, it is as shiny as it will ever be. Be sure to take steps to protect that finish. Use wax, polymer, or ceramic; it's your choice. Only do so after the paint has fully cured, which takes 90 days minimum. Check the manufacturer's specifications.

CHAPTER 5

Always choose wax that is high quality. Our preference is to do a machine application process.

Painting Tips

Don't wear jewelry while polishing. This is for your own safety and to protect your car's finish.

If you have long hair, tie it back so you don't scalp yourself. It's hard to let your hair flow in the breeze if you've ripped it out with your DA. This goes double if you have a beard.

pad and polish you have. Clean the entire surface once more.

Take your work out into the sunlight when you've completed these steps. Be prepared to be impressed by what you've created.

Caring for Paint Finish

While you've probably been washing cars since you were a little kid, now it becomes serious business. Washing your Beetle correctly will protect its paint from dirt, debris, atmospheric contamination, and bird poop (surprisingly acidic). Normal driving damages paint unless you wash and polish it right.

IMPORTANT: Do not wash or wax your car for three to six months after paint and polish. It takes that long for the chemicals to outgas. Check the specifications from your paint manufacturer. Its recommendations will vary depending on whether you baked your finish or let it air dry.

Always work in a clean, well-lit area for detailing, cleaning, or waxing your car. Never work in direct sunlight.

Choose Your Protectant

There are three levels of protectant:

- Wax (from beeswax to Carnauba) will protect the finish for 2 to 3 months.
- Polymer sealant will protect the finish for 6 to 12 months.
- Ceramic coatings will protect the finish for 5 to 20 years.

Wax or polymer sealant can be done by anyone. Applying a ceramic coating is extremely difficult to do right and very easy to mess up. It's not a process for amateurs.

Washing the Car

Here's what to do:

1. Wet the car.
2. Use two clean buckets: one for washing and the other for rinsing.
3. Dip the mitt in the wash bucket, and then apply a couple of soapy coats on one panel at a time.
4. Before moving to the next panel, dip the mitt into the rinse bucket. Make sure you avoid any contamination so you don't scratch paint. You're rinsing the mitt, not the car. Then repeat on the next panel.
5. Once the entire car has been washed, rinse it with the hose.
6. Dry the whole car with a chamois or compressed air.
7. Wipe with a fresh microfiber towel. If using hard water, be extra careful to dry it well so no spots are left behind.

Apply Wax or Sealant

It's imperative to now coat the shiny new paint job with something that can protect it for years and years.

For wax, do not work in direct sunlight. Work small sections and spread wax on with the foam applicator that came with it. Let it dry and then buff it off with a new microfiber towel.

Sealant directions vary by manufacturer, so apply accordingly.

If you can see your face in your paint job—or read this book in its shiny finish—congratulations! Paint and polish applications are hard work, and you should be very proud of what you have done. Not only is your Beetle looking good, you've also helped to stave off the devastating effects of oxidation. Well done!

Tools Needed for Washing

- 2 clean buckets
- Compressed air
- Dawn liquid dish soap
- Hose
- New microfiber towels
- Warm water
- Washing mitt

If applying wax by hand, do so in small, circular motions. Take on a small section at a time rather than trying to cover it all at once.

CHAPTER 6

THE BEETLE PAN

Most modern cars have a unibody construction, meaning it's all one piece with everything bolted together. Some Volkswagens are the same, including the glorious bus. Early Porsches are also built with a unibody construction. While there are some advantages to the unibody style, there are also some disadvantages.

The Beetle is built on a pan, which is the backbone of the car. In essence, the pan is where the rubber meets the road. Most of the mechanical systems are attached to the substructure. A lot of the work for the engine, suspension, transmission, and brakes is actually done best with the body off of the pan. It's easier to see and to get to everything you need.

The transmission is part of your pan (or chassis) build phase. Installing a transmission is part of a restoration, so we will review the basics in this chapter. In the next chapter, we will go into much greater detail on building a transmission. The best plan is to read both chapters before beginning work on the pan. That way you'll know your options and you'll get the big picture before you get in up to your elbows in grease.

Tools Needed

- Assorted beams: 2-inch and 4-inch, either stock or narrowed
- Drop spindles, either stock or drop
- Large rubber mallet
- Metric socket set
- Open-ended metric wrenches
- Ratchet
- Sway bars
- Torque wrench
- Urethane bushings

Restoring a Pan

Before you begin, always use a jack and jack stand when working underneath a Beetle. Chock both sides of the wheels so the car can't roll away. Keep your work area clean so you don't trip, drop objects on the car, or have contamination issues from junk in the air.

During the disassembly phase of the restoration project, the Beetle's body was unmated from its chassis, or pan. If the pan was sent out for blast, no doubt you had a bit of a shock when it came back to you. The pan is closest to the road, and after splashing its way through puddles, being subject to rock and salt assaults in snowy areas, and possibly enduring decades of neglect, most pans are way too rusty to salvage. It's not uncommon for cars that come in

Metal might corrode, but rubber will rot and be less visible due to atmospheric conditions and age. It is hard to spot the worn components. If in doubt, replace them.

HOW TO RESTORE YOUR VOLKSWAGEN BEETLE

for restoration to be Fred Flintstone mobiles, featuring an unobstructed view of the roadway through gaping holes in the pan that were eaten away by rust. Even though nobody will ever see the pan once the Beetle is back on the road, it's well worth the time and effort of restoring it well.

Pan Types

The pan has evolved over the years. There are two basic versions out there, and there are some oddities out there too! The first version has a swing-axle rear end with a link-pin front end. It uses part of the outer axle tube as one of its attachment points to the rear spring plates. In the front, the link-pin beam is a little narrower from top to bottom than what is found in the second type.

The second is the independent rear suspension with a ball-joint front end. This type uses a trailing arm, which houses the bearings and bearing assembly (generally called an A-arm). It uses a double-CV live axle. This one's front is wider than the link pin, and it uses a ball-joint instead of link-pin suspension components.

The weird part comes in with the crossover years from 1966 to 1968. Some models in 1966 have a ball-joint front end and a swing-axle rear. Most 1967s have this configuration, and some 1968s do too. By 1969, Volkswagen completed the transition.

Pan Removal

The pan is the foundation of the car, so the structural integrity of the chassis is integral to the safety of the car. That means it's a one-piece unit that everything else hangs off of or is attached to; it's the automotive equivalent of a house's foundation.

Removing the Floor Pan

1 It's time to get started on your dirty, grungy old pan. A little elbow grease—okay, a lot—and compressed air will go a long way toward getting your pan clean.

2 Remove the body, transmission, axles, wheels, tires, and rear suspension if you haven't already. Bag and tag everything you take off so it's easy to reassemble.

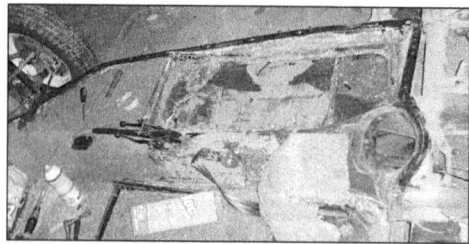

4 Remove the tar board (sound deadening material) on the front of the pan and discard it.

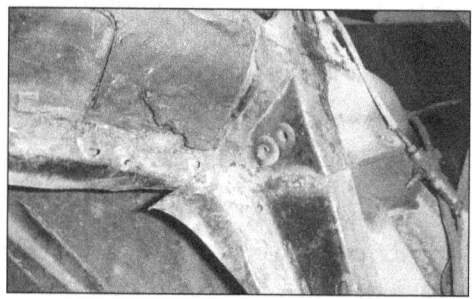

5 Remove the rubber grommets that are in the rear and front of the pan. The hard brake line goes through them.

3 A fully disassembled pan with the transaxle removed is shown here. The only things left to take off are the emergency brake handle and cable.

Removing the Floor Pan *Continued*

6 The master cylinder comes out next. It's attached with two bolts on the inside of the cabin (at the Napoleon's hat). You can try to save your brake lines or just cut them out of the way.

7 Unbolt the front wheels. Take the drum brakes off, then remove the spindles, tie-rods, steering box, and shock absorbers.

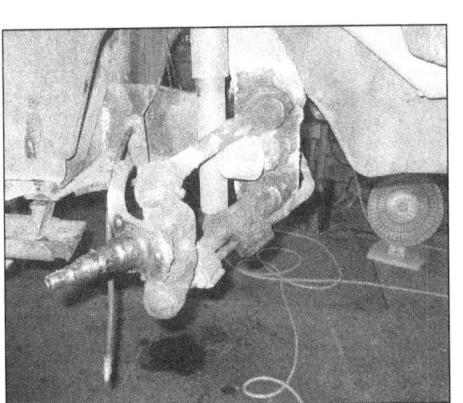

8 You don't need to remove the drums to remove the front suspension. It can be done as a complete unit. But we recommend doing so to reduce the weight of what you're lifting.

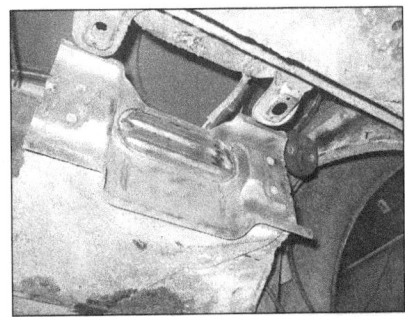

9 Here we've cleaned up the frame heads to show the access panel. It is now time to remove the shift rod (the oval piece in the center of the frame head).

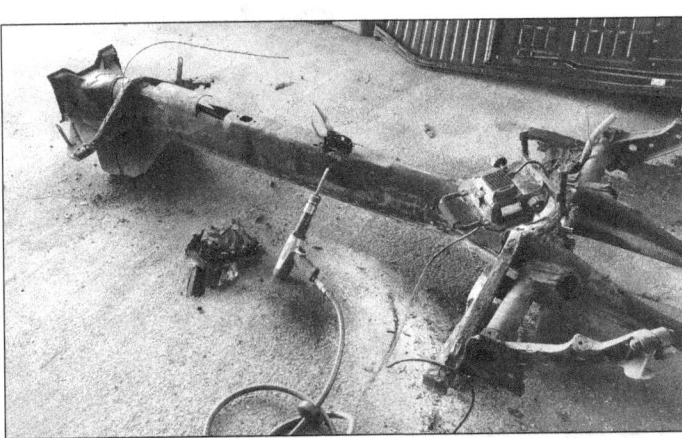

10 The pans are attached on a lip to the backbone and spot-welded in place with a bead weld on the Napoleon's hat. When removing the old pan material, be careful to remove only the pan layer.

11 Replacement pans need to be trimmed to fit in place. This requires putting them in, marking them, and then making adjustments with a grinder.

Removing the Floor Pan Continued

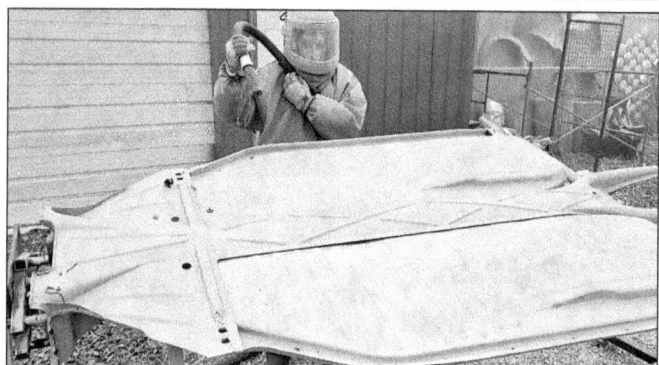

12 Sandblasting is usually the best option to prepare for the next phase. You can paint, apply rust-preventing coating, or powder-coat after this point.

13 After sandblasting, we are applying POR-15 to the pan and frame horns. This is done with a disposable chip brush while wearing protective gear.

14 At this point, you can reinstall your transmission, control cables, brakes, hard lines, and front and rear suspension. The more you can complete at this stage, the better.

15 It's starting to look like a pan again. The more bits, pieces, and components you put on, the closer you are to being done.

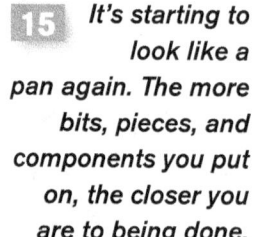

16 It's easiest to install the sound-deadening material at this point in your build. It will reduce rattling and road noise and provide some degree of thermal protection.

Sorting Parts

Use two plastic tubs as you sort through which parts you'll keep and which you'll replace. The contents of one tub goes to blast; the other tub's contents will be replaced. You can keep your project moving forward while the pan is out for blast by cleaning and painting any parts you plan to keep and reuse.

THE BEETLE PAN

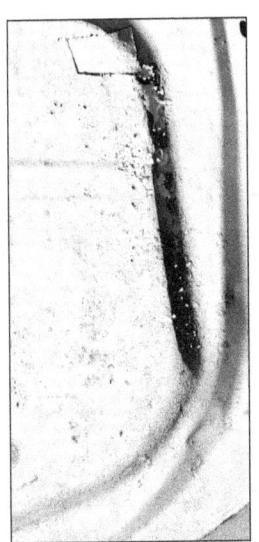

Sometimes you don't need to sandblast to find the holes. This is the result of many years of neglect and abuse. Since the pan is the structural backbone of your car, this is unsafe.

The body has been removed for ease of disassembly of the components shown. Everything needs to come off. If it can be removed, remove it. Assess the condition of all the parts of the pan. We sort the parts into two groups: keep and reuse or throw away and replace.

Remove all of the old carpet padding, tar boards, and anything else attached to the tunnel. Don't worry about the pans because you will be replacing them. Remove any cables, the emergency brake, clutch cable, throttle cable, and pedal assembly. Disassemble the front suspension, including the master cylinder and brake lines.

Now the fun part begins. Take everything off the pan: bolts, nuts, retaining washers and plates, pedal assemblies, and assorted bits of rubbish. Some parts will be needed later and some won't.

The drums don't need to be removed in order to remove the front suspension. It can be done as a complete unit. But we recommend doing so to reduce the weight that will be lifted. Pull the shift rod out from the tunnel. It comes out of the front.

After disassembly, inspect the floorpans. They are held onto the backbone with a series of spot welds going along the tunnel, the front Napoleon's hat, and the rear frame horn. If the floorplans need to be removed, cut them out and fit replacements. Send the pan to blast after the floorpans have been put in.

We recommend coating your floorpan with either a POR-15 treatment or having it powdercoated or painted. Then, reassemble the pan using new bushings, seals, and cables.

If you are adding sound-deadening material, which is always a good idea, now is the time to install it in your pan.

Pan Reassembly

Now that the pan has been replaced or repaired, cleaned, and

Floor Pan Reinstallation

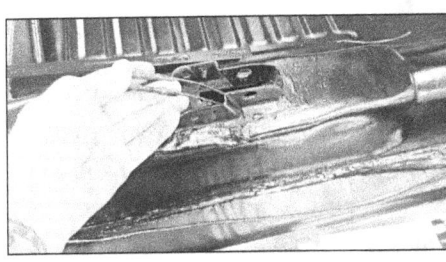

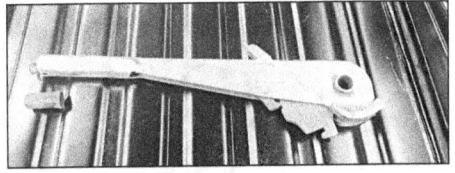

1. *There are two emergency brake cables: one for each side. They slide from the frame-horn side toward the front of the car and up through the hole where the emergency brake handle goes, resting in fixed tubes inside the chassis.*

2. *Next, hook up the emergency brake handle.*

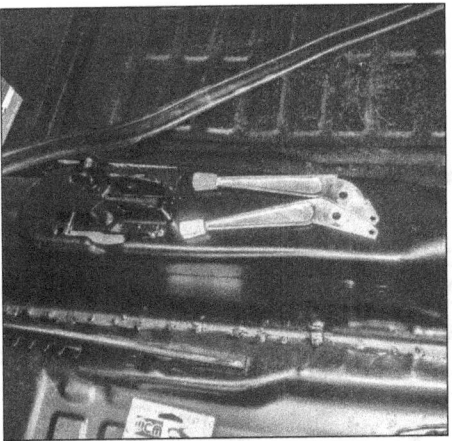

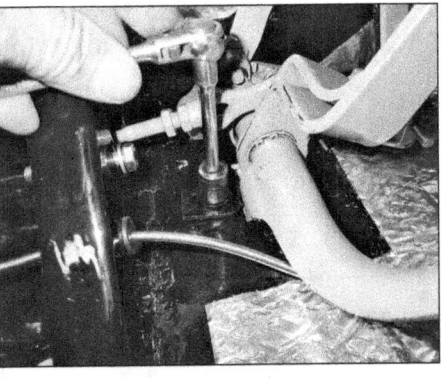

3. *Hook up the heater control knobs and levers.*

4. *Attach the clutch cable onto the interior of the clutch rod. Slide it into the tunnel. Set the brake pushrod into the master cylinder hole. After sliding it all together, bolt it down with two 15-mm M10 1.25 bolts. Torque them to spec.*

5. *Install the brake rod and spring first. The pedal stop is a small plate that prevents the clutch pedal from coming too far forward.*

Floor Pan Reinstallation *Continued*

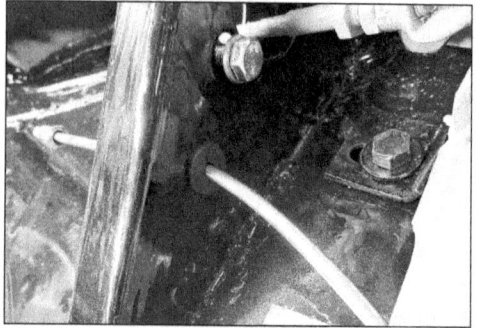

6 The brake line passes through the Napoleon's hat. Run the hard brake line through the Napoleon's hat first, then install the brake line grommets (one on each side). They have a split in them. A little liquid dish soap and a plastic push tool will be helpful for this job.

7 Install the brake master cylinder next. The brake light switches should already be screwed into it.

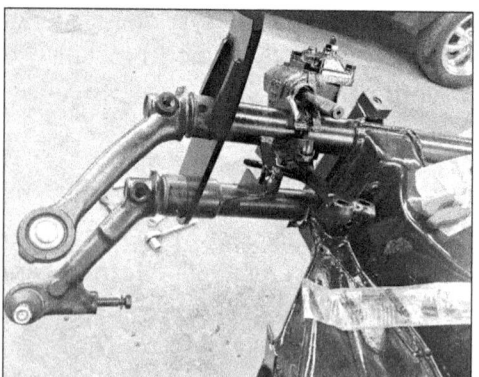

8 After the torsion rods are installed, install the torsion arms with the freshly pressed ball joints. Next, bolt up the steering box and Pitman arm.

9 Install the spindles and the backing plate. See chapter 8 on brakes for discussion and instruction about upgrading your brakes. Install the rotor (if you are going with disc brakes). Be sure to grease the wheel bearings and install the grease seals.

10 When installing brake drums, make sure to use the correct size retaining spring and pin. The replacement kits include three sizes in the same package. Use the right size for your model.

11 There are many aftermarket choices for performance brakes. One of the best is made by Wilwood. The faster you can go, the better you need to be able to stop.

painted, it's time to put it all back together. Place jack stands in the four corners for maximum stability. Pay attention to where bolts need to be fastened and keep those spots open and easy to access. Whip out the photos that were taken during disassembly. They are the best guides to follow for your specific vehicle. You'll be putting it together the same way it was before you took it apart.

Start with your cables. You will usually have the following cables: the throttle cable, clutch cable, air cables to the rear, air cables to the inside ducts, and the emergency brake cable. Refer to your disassembly notes and pictures and start positioning and reattaching the cables. Use grease on them to help extend their service life.

It is easiest to first lay out all of the components. Make sure you have everything before starting assembly. If you are missing any parts, do not continue without them.

Our project Bug has two heater-control levers alongside the emergency brake: one controls the flaps, and the other opens and closes the heater boxes. There are three cables that hook into the two rods.

The pedal assembly is next. It's easier to do it now than to save it for later. If put off, you'll end up lying under the dashboard once the car's body is back on. That's not very comfortable. This way, you'll be able to see what you're doing, and you get to skip that particular automotive yoga session.

The brake rod and spring come next. Then, install the pedal stop, which will be bolted to the floor. Next, run the main brake line (it goes from front to rear) along the driver-side tunnel. Make sure you use grommets on both front and rear when you go through the firewall.

Next comes the front suspension. Essentially the front suspension will be built hanging off the pan. Bolt the beam to the front bulkhead using the four bolts. Next, install the torsion bars and all four torsion arms (with the ball joint pressed in).

Assembly on the pan is about halfway complete. The front suspension has been attached, the master cylinder and hard lines have been installed, and so has the pedal assembly.

During the final assembly of your beam, the last step is to inspect every nut, bolt, and fastener to make sure nothing falls off when driving. Don't worry about attaching the upper shock mount at this point. If you are installing drum brakes, install the brake hardware. Then, install the drums. If going with disc brakes, install the brake calipers now. Finally, install the axle caps.

Wheels

The next question to answer is whether to change the bolt pattern for your restored Beetle or keep it stock. Until 1967, Beetles all had a 5x205 bolt pattern. Then, they went to 4x130. It's a matter of taste. Just google the different styles so you can determine which you prefer.

You'll find lots of aftermarket rims are available now too, which just adds one more feature you can customize. A popular choice now is to go with a Porsche pattern, which is 5x130.

In addition to the bolt pattern, you'll also need to choose the width of your rims. Stock width is 4 to 4.5 inches, but a popular aftermarket choice is to go with 5.5-inch rims or even larger. This choice gives you more meat on the road and a more menacing look overall. Don't forget, your front and back rims don't have to be the same size. It's not uncommon to see much wider rims on the back than the front.

Suspension

A Beetle's attitude comes from its altitude. From the friendly, almost puppy-like "let's go play!" enthusiasm of a high-rise Baja to the sinister "low and slow" look of a slammed Beetle that barely clears traffic lane markers embedded in the pavement, you've got a few options. There's also stock height, if you want to roll that way. It's all in the suspension.

Every decision you make regarding your suspension can impact other elements of your build, as well as how your Beetle handles on the road. The profile chosen for your Bug really boils down to personal preferences on its look and how you plan to drive it.

The Beetle's suspension is about more than just good looks though. It also controls steering, how the front

The decision to go stock or add performance upgrades will factor into many other decisions as you build your pan. The higher the horsepower, the stouter your suspension must be to handle the power.

and rear axles operate, and how well the car absorbs bumps in the road. A car's suspension determines how rough, smooth, tight, or loose its ride is.

Your pre-restoration suspension is likely to be worn out, which is a safety concern. It's tough to control a car if it's out of alignment or the suspension is shot. For both appearance and safety's sake, the work done to the suspension is an important part of the restoration.

Suspension Upgrade Options

Suspension is just one component impacted by the engine size. If using a souped-up engine that's packed with go-fast goodies, a strong suspension is needed to back it up. Upgrades will be needed for the brakes and suspension to handle the extra power.

Pay attention to the bushings. Choose stiffer bushings made of urethane rather than rubber to firm up how the car handles. These upgraded bushings will have a tighter feeling in how your Beetle steers. You'll also notice an overall improvement in responsiveness with this type of suspension.

Gas-filled shocks are a stronger option than oil-filled ones, and coil-overs are an even stronger option than gas- or oil-filled shocks.

We also recommend upgrading the sway bar to help keep the car under control through turns. This upgrade will give you tighter cornering and traction control. The standard is an approximately 3/8-inch sway bar. Upgrades are often 5/8, 3/4, or even 7/8 inch. Any of these will work, so take your pick, based on the desired stiffness and cornering response you want.

Finally, there are aftermarket kits for custom suspensions. While costly, they are very well engineered and will handle better than any other modern car out there.

Drop It Low

If you like the look of a Beetle that's been slammed to the ground, you'll need to do a suspension upgrade to lower the front end. There are a few different ways to get this look.

One option is to install drop spindles, which essentially relocate the actual axle upward by about 2.5 inches. This is predominantly a bolt-on solution, which means it's an easy way to lower the front.

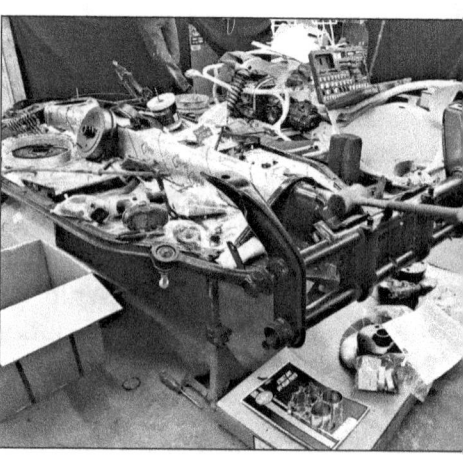

While you can piecemeal a suspension bushing kit together using parts from different manufacturers, it's better to find a kit that has everything in one box. Check with your favorite parts supplier.

Oversized sway bars with poly bushings are always a smart design choice to increase a car's handling ability. If using OEM rubber components, you will get a bit of a softer ride.

A truly stiff suspension can be supported by coil-overs. Gas struts are a nice in-between option for maintaining your car's stability and handling.

Upgrading the front sway bar or adding a rear sway bar is a fine way to be able to carve the curves. Just because it's larger doesn't make it better. Make sure to have a balanced setup. Drop spindles are always a good way to pick up 2.5 inches of suspension drop without changing the front-end geometry. The spindles are also readily available from your favorite parts supplier.

Another way to lower the front end is by changing the adjustable beams. That's a little more involved than just using a bolt-on upgrade. Adjustable beams make the center pivot of the beam moveable so that the desired ride height can be set and locked in. Adjustable beams are available in do-it-yourself kits or as new replacement parts.

The third option is to install narrowed beams for a super low look or if you want to put wider wheels and tires under your car. Most narrowed beams are available in an adjustable option as well. The most common formats include 2, 4, 6, or a whopping 8 inches. You can use any combination of narrowed beams and adjustable beams along with dropped spindles to achieve whichever style of *low* suits your fancy.

Negative Camber

Whether gawking online or drooling in-person at a Volkswagen show, you're likely to see Beetles with back wheels angled outward, sometimes at angles that seem impossible to drive. That's negative camber. (Neutral camber is the normal stance.) Most people either love the negative camber look or hate it.

There are a few downsides to negative camber. Some say it is bad for the transmission. It makes the Beetle a bit harder to control on the road, especially in bad weather conditions. The suspension is more likely to bottom out with this wheel configuration. Finally, the inside of the tires will wear out about twice as fast as neutral camber.

Still, negative camber fans say it's such a cool look that they just don't care about the downsides. In their eyes, it's the price you pay for being cool.

Slight negative camber is not a bad thing. It will help the car grip the road as well as lower the vehicle's center of gravity. Flipping over is not all it's cracked up to be. The ground clearance will suffer though.

Offset or notched plates are generally a good idea while lowering the rear of your car. This will help maintain proper geometry and keep the car driving under your control.

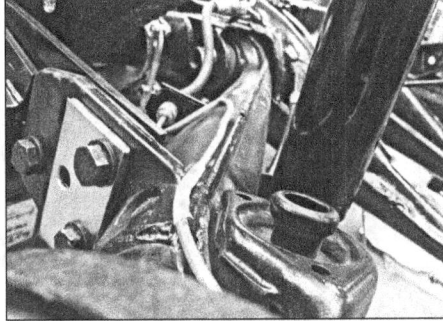

Another option is to go with an adjustable spring plate to fine-tune your Beetle's rear height and maintain level from left to right. These nifty little adjusters make it possible to fine-tune even further.

If offset spring plates are installed, the amount of force negative camber exerted on the axles can be decreased. This setup will straighten the tow-in on the front end. To reduce some of that tow-in, extend the spring plates back and upward.

Rear Suspension Installation

On 1968 and earlier Beetle models, the rear axle is part of the transaxle assembly with the axles attached to the differential. On 1969 and later models, Volkswagen went to an independent rear suspension (IRS) setup instead. With an IRS, each axle sort of floats independent of the other. When the transmission is out of a pre-1968 car, the rear suspension is pulled along with it. On an IRS car, only the transmission comes out, and the car will still roll. Due to Beetle differences from year to year, consult the official service manual for your model as you work.

Adding quality wheel bearing grease on the end of your splines will help prevent squeaking. It will also help protect against surface rust.

The spring plates are keyed onto a torsion rod. This will set your ride height. Changing where it sits in the keys will change the suspension height.

Set the outer rubber bushing. Most kits come with a little bit of grease for the housing to help prevent squeaking.

CHAPTER 6

The Lowrider Beetle (Sort Of)

In some circles, the measure of a car's cool factor is being able to make it practically dance in place. Up and down, all jaunty angles at the touch of a hydraulic-control button—that's the lowrider scene, and you'll find Beetles in it right along with big old muscle cars.

A rising trend in Beetle suspensions is to put it on airbags so that it can drop its stance to rest a fraction of an inch above the pavement with the touch of a button. Touch that button again, and the Beetle rises back up to a drivable height. It's all done with airbags, which let you ride on a cushion of air. Airbags can be configured to lift and lower the Bug front to back and/or side to side. ∎

Installing Your Rear Suspension

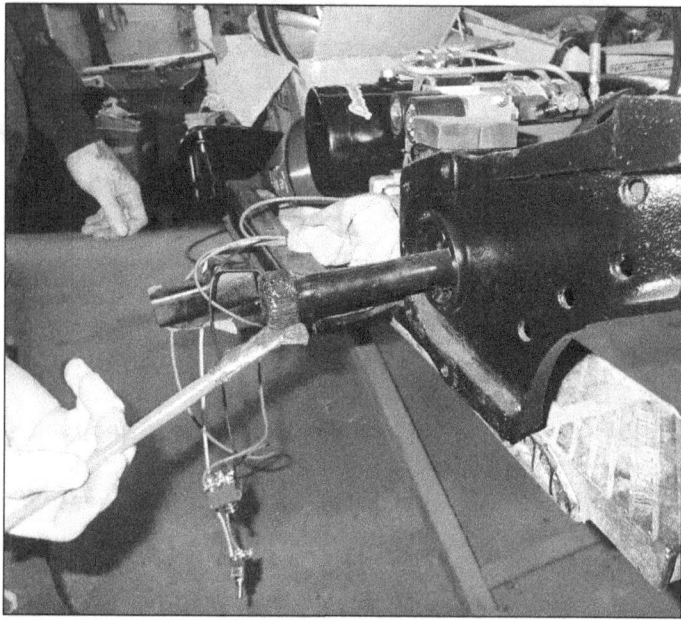

1 Install the rear torsion springs into their spline keyways. Use a little bit of assembly lube to do so.

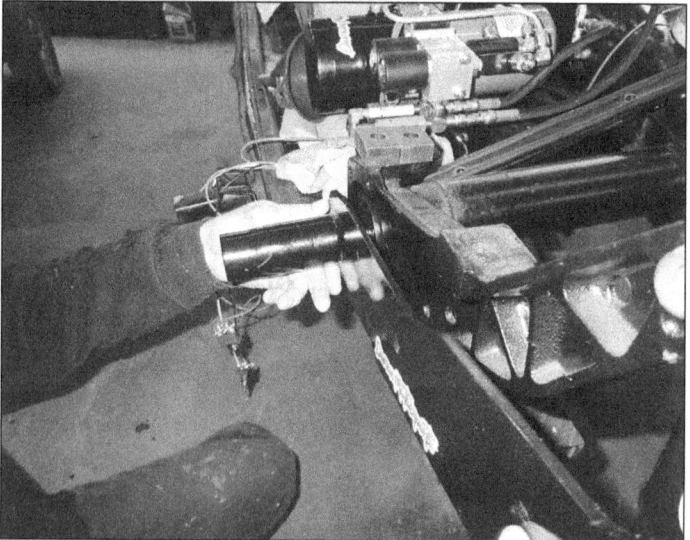

2 Install the spring plates on each side. Make sure to set the spring plates at the correct angle, otherwise the car will sit unevenly, too high, or too low. Don't forget the rubber bushing behind it.

3 Install the rubber bushing in front. Drive it home.

4 Bolt all of the transmission mounts to the transmission prior to installation. You can either use the original rubber style or urethane mounts.

HOW TO RESTORE YOUR VOLKSWAGEN BEETLE

Installing Your Rear Suspension Continued

5 *The spring plates, transmission, rear suspension, shock absorbers, clutch cable, heater cables, throttle cable, and hard and soft brake lines are shown. Next, you'll attach the axles and install the rear brakes.*

6 *This is what a complete rear suspension and brake lines looks like. It's almost ready for body and pan mating.*

Installing the rear transmission mounts to the mount bar before installing into the vehicle is easier than doing so in the reverse order. A little bit of Loctite on your transmission mount bolts will help keep everything in place.

Be sure to use a nose-cone seal to seal the transmission to the tunnel of the pan. Grab a buddy to help maneuver the transmission and axles into place. Or try it on your own with the help of a floor jack.

Once the two front, two rear, and six spring plate bolts are secure, the transmission installation and rear suspension are in. Next, bolt in the shock absorbers. Run the clutch cable through the Bowden tube. Attach the clutch cable to the transmission. Then, install the rear brakes. See chapter 8 for step-by-step brake instructions.

Beetles with an independent rear suspension setup have a few differences you'll need to know about. The transmission will go into the car in the same basic manner as detailed above. The major difference is that the axles will bolt into the transmission and trailing arm, respectively.

CHAPTER 7

TRANSMISSIONS

Transmissions have always had a certain mystique about them. Essentially, the transmission is a bunch of moving parts meshing together to allow a vehicle to move down the road. They are not engines. They are the mechanism that transfers the power the engine creates into motion.

It's not uncommon to overhear budding classic car restoration hobbyists say something similar to, "I build engines, so that transmission will not be a problem." To that we say, "Baloney!" Even mechanical maestros sometimes find themselves stupefied as they peer into the black box.

VW Transaxles

The engineers at Volkswagen had the foresight and thought needed to make a transaxle that would endure some of the harshest conditions and keep on working. Modifications over the years have improved reliability and function, allowing VWs to take you almost anywhere you want to go. Some of those transaxles are still on the road today and have never been rebuilt. Their track record proves that Volkswagen had a great idea right from the start.

1968 and Earlier

On the 1968 and earlier models, there was little an owner had to do other than make sure the axle boots were not cracked and leaking gear oil. Axle boots were easy to change, and the owner could complete this job at home rather than having to take it to a mechanic. The transaxle would function normally if the gear oil was monitored and kept at the appropriate level.

1969 and Older

The 1969 and later models are prone to having the constant velocity (CV) joint boot crack, which requires replacement. If not caught early enough, the CV grease is slung out of the joint, causing premature failure of the joint. Although it's not a hard repair to make, replacing the CV boot requires more time than the transaxle boot of old.

If problems arose, mechanics had to listen closely while driving the car. This subtlety is part of what earned the transmission its mysterious reputation. What someone might think is a mainshaft bearing could just as easily be a wheel bearing.

Repair versus Replace

Mysteries aside, you've got two good options when it comes to your Beetle's transmission. You can replace it or you can rebuild it.

When the transaxle is torn down, inspect all of the parts and the condition of the case. Assess its condition to get a better feel for whether you should repair or replace your transmission. Replacing worn parts with good used ones will work most of the time, but you are taking a greater chance that those *good* used parts won't fail.

We won't sugarcoat it: rebuilding a transmission is not a project you want to dive into on your own if you haven't done it before. Even seasoned Volkswagen restoration hobbyists usually prefer to hire this part of the restoration out. It's a complicated, time-consuming, high-stakes game once you crack open the black box.

If you decide to go with a pro for a rebuilt transmission, make absolutely certain that you choose a transmission shop experienced with classic Beetles. Find a shop that offers a solid warranty and that uses new parts in its rebuilds. While it sounds like common sense, not every shop does this.

Transmission Upgrade Options

Aside from the repair-versus-replace question, you also have a broad range of transmission upgrade options that can change its performance and durability. You can choose from a stronger differential, close-ratio gears, Rhino cases, and the list goes on.

One popular upgrade for a Type 1 Beetle transmission or transaxle is known as the pro-street. It is a super differential with welded third and fourth synchronizer hubs, hardened keys, and billet aluminum side plate.

For a Type 2 Beetle transmission on 1968 and later, there is an upgrade known as a freeway flier. For this, owners usually will change the ring and pinion to achieve freeway speeds.

Another choice for the performance-minded owner would be a new aluminum Rhino case with better gussets for strength. Your wallet may not like that option as much, but your get-up-and-go sure will.

Everyone has a different opinion on how to go about achieving the same result. The best transmission option for your Beetle is the one that suits your driving scenario at a price you can afford to build or install well.

Transmission Rebuilding

First, an important note. When we talk about building transmissions, there are so many little nuances with the different models that we cannot possibly cover every detail. The following information will deal in generalities and not so many specifics.

Once a transmission arrives for rebuilding, the unit is completely torn down to a bare case for inspection. The builder will look for worn teeth on the gears, metal pieces in the bottom of the case, and any other obvious things before the gear stacks are separated from the gear carrier.

The ring and pinion gearset is normally the first to be inspected. Once the side covers are removed, the differential is removed and the ring gear are inspected for any major flaws. Any wear or broken teeth means it is time to start looking for another set.

The input shaft will need to be removed. This is accomplished by

Tools Needed

- 36-mm flywheel socket
- Gear spreader
- Milling machine
- Output shaft seals
- Socket set
- Spline alignment tool
- Steel press
- Transmission jack
- Wrenches

Inspect to make sure the pinion drive teeth are smooth and not broken off. Any chips or abrasions on the teeth will make the pinion shaft unusable for further rebuilds.

Ring-gear teeth are inspected for any chipped or pitted teeth. Pits do not change the strength of the tooth, but they will cause it to eventually make noise. The noise causes many daily drivers to replace that ring gear. However, some off-road Bugs are not worried about noise and will use a pitted gear.

Transmission Safety

When working on the transmission in the car, make sure you always chock the wheels and use jack stands. Many people have been critically hurt or even killed because they did not follow simple safety protocols. If you are a first timer, do not attempt any rebuild unless you have a knowledgeable builder to guide you along the way. Proper tools and jigs are needed to correctly position the shift forks and other functions of the transmission.

The nose cone inspection is very important. We make sure that the top inside part of the inner nose cone is not gouged out. This will happen if the mainshaft bearing bore is not tight and allows the bearing to axially move, pounding the nose cone. Pictured here is a reusable nose cone.

This 1969 VW Beetle gear carrier shows that this mainshaft is held in the bearing with the later concave washer and circlip. No distinct corrosion is noted. Earlier models have two large nuts screwed onto the end of the shaft and locked on with large, bendable washers.

The propane torch is used to heat the transmission case and open the pinion bearing bore slightly. This allows extraction of the gear carrier without putting a lot of force on the extraction tool.

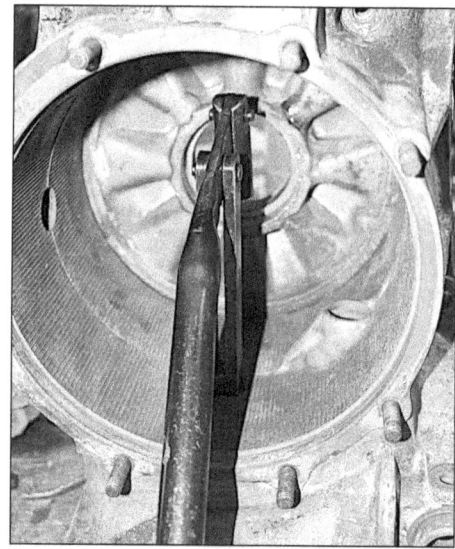

This tool allows the builder to put pressure on the pinion shaft and the rear of the differential housing to extract the gear carrier from the case. Once heat has been applied to the case, minimal force is usually needed to push the pinion shaft/gear carrier out of the case.

disengaging the circlip that holds the reverse-drive coupler in place. The coupler then can be slid off the mainshaft and up onto the input shaft. Next, the input shaft is unscrewed from the mainshaft and slid out of the case. At this point, the nose cone is removed and inspected for internal wear.

The wear point is where the mainshaft bearing contacts the back side. If the gear carrier has a worn mainshaft bearing bore, the bearing will have axial movement and will start to gouge the nose cone.

Now, you have two choices: mill 0.02 off the nose cone and use a thrust plate to stop any further movement or replace the nose cone with a new one. High-performance applications may warrant the use of the thrust plate to ensure no movement is seen in the mainshaft bearing. Once the nose cone is removed, the gear carrier can be extracted from the case. This gear carrier holds both the complete mainshaft and pinion shaft with all the gears and associated mechanisms.

If you have an earlier case that has a four-bolt pinion bearing, the four bolts holding pressure from the pinion retainer plate are removed. The nuts on the outside of the case are removed, and the gear carrier is ready for extraction.

Builders have a tool that allows them to exert pressure on the end of the pinion shaft while also exerting pressure on the backside of the differential housing. Once in place, the builder starts applying pressure to the tool arm and the gear carrier should start to slide out. Occasionally, a propane torch may have to be used to heat the underside area of the case where the pinion bearing sits so

TRANSMISSIONS

Here we show the extracted gear carrier on its side and the first-gear shift fork bolt removed from the brass shift fork.

The next step would be to pull the associated shift rail out of the gear carrier and remove the first-gear shift fork from the pinion gear stack. The third- and fourth-gear shift fork has yet to be removed.

The reverse-gear lever and pivot bar are removed with the pivot eye bolt still in the gear carrier (shown). Now, the reverse shift rail can be extracted from the gear carrier.

When all of the shift rails are removed, the gear carrier is placed on the gear carrier press jig and the mainshaft is pressed out. This will now allow the gear stacks to be disassembled.

the bore expands enough to allow the bearing to slide free with little friction.

Next, the real inspection begins. Normally, the reverse gear will fall out when the gear carrier is removed. Most of the time, the gear is worn beyond the point of reuse because the engagement teeth are folded over.

The first- and second-gear shift fork is removed first by loosening its respective bolt. Then, the shift rail for first and second gear is pulled through the shift fork, allowing the rail to be pulled out of the gear carrier. Next, the bolt for the third and fourth shift fork is removed, and its respective shift rail removed. The third- and fourth-gear shift fork will remain within the gear carrier and is removed once the mainshaft and pinion assemblies are pressed out of the gear carrier. The reverse gear mechanism will be removed by loosening its tension bolt and extracting the shift rail out of the carrier.

If the transmission is an early model with nuts holding the mainshaft and pinion shaft in the carrier, those are removed. If it is a late model, any and all associated circlips are removed from the shafts. The gear carrier is now ready to be placed in the hydraulic press and both shafts pushed out of the housing.

Once they are separated, the gear carrier will need to be disassembled by removing any detent plugs, springs, the two interlock pins, and any remaining reverse mechanism. These will be cleaned and used with the rebushed gear carrier upon assembly.

Inspection

Disassembly of the mainshaft and pinion shaft is when the builder gets to inspect the internal moving parts of the transmission. Mainshaft disassembly is straightforward because the fourth-gear thrust washer slides off along with fourth gear and its synchronizer ring.

The mainshaft is set into the hydraulic press, and the operating sleeve hub along with the third-gear and fourth-gear bearing races are pressed off the shaft. The hub assembly is taken apart and inspected for any cracks, broken teeth, or worn catch keys. Mainshaft inspection starts with looking at the root of second gear. If you see corrosion of the tooth root, it's time to start looking for a replacement shaft.

Something else to look for is wear where the mainshaft bearing fits on the end of the shaft. If the mainshaft was easily pressed out of the bearing or fell out of the bearing, it's time for a replacement shaft.

CHAPTER 7

First- and second-gear operating sleeves are usually replaced due to the reverse-gear engagement teeth being worn out by the reverse gear. Also, if the inner tooth is worn, this may affect the engagement with the associated synchronizer hub.

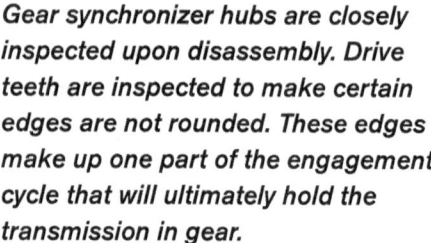

Gear synchronizer hubs are closely inspected upon disassembly. Drive teeth are inspected to make certain edges are not rounded. These edges make up one part of the engagement cycle that will ultimately hold the transmission in gear.

Third- and fourth-gear synchronizer hubs are to be closely inspected. If any of the topside edges of the engagement teeth are rounded, the hub will need to be pressed off the gear and replaced with good used or new ones. Those rounded edges are notorious for making the transmission pop out of gear.

Operating Sleeves

Operating sleeves play a vital role in positive shifting. The makeup of the engagement angle between the operating sleeve and synchronizer hub is really what keeps the transmission in gear. The VW factory's operating sleeves were only back cut on the fourth gear side and only on the drive side of the tooth. Over time, this would allow the operating sleeve to wear so the angle of engagement with the synchronizer hub would not properly hold it in gear. New operating sleeves have all four sides of third and fourth back cut to help alleviate this problem. Used sleeves may be reused if both coast sides of the tooth are back cut.

Early pinion shaft disassembly starts with pressing off the early keyed fourth gear since you have already removed the large nut before being pressed out of the gear carrier. Late pinion shafts need to be stood up in the hydraulic press and pressure applied to fourth gear so the bearing-race circlip can be removed. After the circlip is removed and pressure relieved on fourth gear, the gear and bearing race normally will start to rise off the shaft due to pressure from the spring between third and fourth gear.

Early transmissions will have a solid sleeve with a washer and shims to do the same thing as the late spring. Now, the third-gear circlip is removed, which allows for the rest of the pinion shaft to be disassembled. Third gear lifts off the shaft, then remove the first- and second-gear operating sleeve along with first gear and its clearance shim.

As before, the first- and second-gear operation sleeve is disassembled from its hub and inspected. Reverse gear operates off of this operating sleeve, so the engagement teeth for reverse are looked at very closely. First- and second-gear synchronizer hubs are made into the actual gear. The hubs and engagement teeth are closely inspected for any wear or roundness.

As on the third and fourth gear hub, if the teeth are bad, the gear needs to be replaced. To complete the disassembly of the pinion shaft, the first-gear bearing-race retainer nut is removed so that the shaft can be put into the hydraulic press and the pinion bearing pressed off.

The case itself then needs to be fully disassembled. Removal of the reverse driveshaft, inner-mainshaft bearing, and any remaining hardware is next. After this, the case and any side covers or nose cone are cleaned and blasted appropriately. All internal parts are then put into a parts washer. Some builders fill a plastic tub with parts solvent and let the parts soak for a while, and others just wash and dry them. Either way, the parts are dried and ready for any blasting and reassembly.

Don't Forget the Differential

Differentials are sometimes overlooked. Differential bearings will need to be replaced. Early differential bearings can be pulled right off the differential. However, late-model differentials will need part of the differential taken apart and the bearings knocked off with a flat punch. Bearings are then pressed on the differential housing and ready for installation. If late differential bearings are installed, the races should be kept with the associated bearing and installed in the side cover or case.

TRANSMISSIONS

Differentials will need to be checked for proper bearing fitment as well as bolt torque. In order for the differential bearing to be removed, eight bolts will be removed and the top plate separated from the housing. The plate will then be turned over and the bearing removed.

This view allows us to see if the ring gear is in good shape. The differential bearing was removed with gear pullers. If the bearing comes off the shaft with relative ease, that part of the housing will need to be replaced.

Reassembly

Reassembly of the transmission will take time and doesn't always go smoothly. Any time you are meshing new parts with used ones, fitment may cause problems. Whatever the case, the builder should take the time to make sure all the parts fit and will perform well.

Pinion Shaft Assembly

First, the pinion shaft is stood up to accept the pinion bearing. The pinion bearing comes in three parts and must be heated to slide over the shaft. Whether the bearing halves are heated with a hot plate or a propane torch, they need to loosely slide over the shaft during assembly.

Once all three bearing parts are on the shaft (the lower roller, bearing race, and upper roller), the first-gear bearing race is then heated and dropped onto the shaft. After cooling, the first-gear bearing and retainer nut are installed. The retainer nut is then torqued to the specified tightness and its collar is seated into the pinion shaft grooves. This locks the nut onto the pinion shaft.

Once the pinion bearing is on the shaft and torqued, the ring gear and pinion pattern can be tested. This pattern allows the builder to see how the pinion shaft and ring gear mate. It will also will tell the builder if the ring gear and pinion are worn out and should be replaced. The pinion shaft with the bearing and shims are inserted into the bare case.

Printing compound is applied to the ring gear next, and the differential is installed into the case with the appropriate side covers. The pinion shaft is then turned to allow the compound to mesh between the pinion and ring gear. This pattern will show any abnormalities between the two. If the pattern looks good, the differential and pinion shaft are removed from the case and assembly can begin. Otherwise, another ring and pinion must be acquired and printed.

Pinion Shaft Assembly

1 *Pinion shafts are built starting with a new pinion bearing. You can see that it is a three-piece part. Other parts are washed and laid out for proper assembly.*

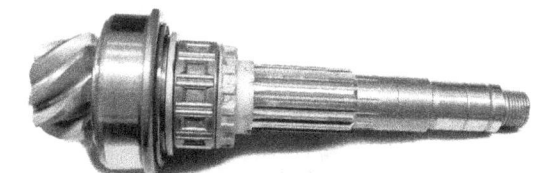

2 *The pinion bearing, first-gear bearing race, bearing, and retainer nut are installed, and the nut has been torqued to specifications. This assembly is now ready for its place in printing the ring gear and pinion.*

Pinion Shaft Assembly *Continued*

3 This view shows the coast side of the ring gear. When printing the ring gear, you are looking for where the ring gear and pinion shaft mesh. The above pattern is what you want to see on the coast side of the ring gear.

4 This view is of the drive side of the ring gear. The drive side will have more wear than the coast side. Again, you are looking for that centered tooth print at the meshing point.

5 The start of building up the pinion shaft begins with installing the four-bolt pinion bearing retainer (early models) and then installing first gear. This particular gear had oiling grooves cut into it some time ago from a previous builder.

6 After first gear is installed, we put the first-gear synchronizer on the gear then install the operating sleeve and hub assembly.

7 Next, install the second-gear synchronizer ring into the hub assembly.

8 Second gear is put into position by inserting the gear and its synchronizer hub into the synchronizer ring.

9 Then, install the third-gear bearing into the top of second gear.

TRANSMISSIONS

Pinion Shaft Assembly *Continued*

10 Third gear slides onto the pinion shaft and into second gear.

11 Third gear end play is now set, and the appropriate shim or circlip is put into place.

12 On this particular transmission, the tension spring is slid over the pinion shaft and rested on the third-gear circlip.

13 Fourth gear is now placed on the pinion shaft, and its drive splines are lined up. The gear will drop into place a little to give appropriate guidance when the gear is pressed on.

14 The front pinion bearing race is placed on the pinion shaft and readied for installation.

15 The completed pinion shaft is now placed into the press and pressure is applied to fourth gear. Once the gear is fully compressed against the compressed tension spring, the bearing race is pushed down on top of fourth gear and the circlip is placed in its groove.

HOW TO RESTORE YOUR VOLKSWAGEN BEETLE

First Gear

First gear always needs a certain amount of endplay to ensure it is not locking up during operation. Builders will put the first gear on along with a shim they think will give them the clearance needed. Next, the operating-sleeve hub will be slid on the shaft and pushed against the shim so the builder can take a feeler gauge and check for proper clearance.

When satisfied with the clearance, the hub is removed from the shaft and readied for assembly with the operating sleeve. If the transmission is an early one, the first gear is removed and the four-bolt pinion bearing retainer flange is slid on the shaft. Then first gear is again slid on the shaft, and assembly can begin.

Gear Assembly

When assembling the operating sleeve to the hub, the three slots in the hub must be aligned with the three indentions in the sleeve. This allows for the catch keys to fit properly and be held in place with the wire springs. New or re-machined operating sleeves are used to help ensure that popping out of gear does not happen.

Once the sleeve and hub are assembled, a new first-gear synchronizer is placed onto the gear. The first-gear endplay shim is installed, and the newly assembled sleeve and hub are dropped onto the shaft.

The builder must make sure the catch keys are fitted into the synchronizer slots, otherwise binding will occur. A new second-gear synchronizer is placed on top of the hub assembly and second gear is placed over that.

Second and Third Gear

Next, the second-gear bearing is installed along with third gear. If you have an early setup, a large washer is used, followed by shims, and then the solid spacer between third and fourth gear. On later setups, you will have an endplay circlip followed by a spring tension spacer between third and fourth gear.

Fourth Gear

Fourth gear is then installed followed by its bearing race. For early setups, the pinion shaft will stay this way until pressed into the gear carrier, then the large nut will be placed on the shaft. Later setups will have the assembled shaft placed back into the hydraulic press and pressure reapplied to fourth gear so the front pinion bearing race circlip can be applied.

Mainshaft Assembly

The mainshaft assembly will start with having the third gear, synchronizer, and bearing placed on the shaft. Assembly of the operating sleeve and hub are different from that of its counterpart on the pinion shaft. Again, new or re-machined sleeves should be used to help the transmission not pop out of gear.

Assembling the Mainshaft

1 Mainshaft assembly starts with the bare shaft cleaned and blasted.

2 The third-gear bearing is then lubricated and placed onto the shaft and on its respective race.

3 The third-gear synchronizer is now placed onto the third-gear synchronizer hub and placed onto the shaft and over its bearing.

Assembling the Mainshaft *Continued*

4 The third- and fourth-gear operating sleeve and hub are assembled and readied to be pressed onto the mainshaft.

5 Pressing the hub assembly on the mainshaft requires the builder to make sure the key and slot line up and the synchronizer ring does not interfere with the hub.

6 The fourth-gear bearing race is now heated and installed onto the mainshaft. Allow the bearing race to cool before installing the bearing.

7 The fourth-gear synchronizer is placed into the hub assembly along with the fourth-gear bearing placed on its respective race.

8 Fourth gear is placed over the bearing and slid into place.

9 The fourth-gear thrust washer is now put on top of fourth gear. This washer will keep tension between fourth gear and the mainshaft bearing.

The operating sleeve for third and fourth gear has catch-key indentions in every tooth. Builders must fit the hub as many times as it takes to get a smooth sliding action between the two parts. This smooth sliding action will show when the shift forks are being set.

Once the builder is pleased with this action, the catch keys and wire springs are assembled and the assembly is pressed onto the shaft. The mainshaft can either have a key or splines that the hub must slip over. Again, the catch keys in the hub must fit into the synchronizer slots to prevent any binding.

Fourth gear and its synchronizer can then be fitted to the shaft along with the bearing. The only thing left to install on the mainshaft will be the fourth-gear thrust washer for the shaft to be complete.

Gear Carrier

Having a re-bushed gear carrier is important. Let's start with the first and second gear along with the third- and fourth-gear shift rails. They routinely will have worn their respective bores in the gear carrier. Shifting movement of the steel rail in the softer magnesium carrier wears enough material in the bore to allow the rail to move and affect shifting of the fork. Also, many mainshaft bearing bores in the gear carriers are worn too much, allowing the bearing to slide.

The gear carrier will then need to have a sleeve machined in to allow a tight bearing bore. For these reasons, a re-bushed gear carrier is a must.

CHAPTER 7

Gear Carrier Reassembly

1 A gear carrier is shown with both first/second and third/fourth-gear shift rail bores re-bushed. This will allow the shift rails to move freely and not wear the material from the gear carrier.

2 This top view shows an assembled gear carrier with both mainshaft and pinion bearings as well as the three shift rails installed.

3 Pictured is the side view of a gear carrier with shift rails installed along with the reverse-gear mechanism.

4 Three separately completed parts of the transmission (gear carrier, mainshaft, and pinion shaft) are now ready to be mated. Make sure the third- and fourth-gear shift fork is installed into its operating sleeve before all three components are put into the press.

5 Shift rails are now inserted into their respective shift forks, and the reverse gear and its brass cradle are installed. The reverse-gear shift rail is now selected, and the reverse gear is slid onto the first- and second-gear operating sleeve. This aides with installing the completed gear carrier into the jig.

HOW TO RESTORE YOUR VOLKSWAGEN BEETLE

Reassembly of the gear carrier starts with inserting the detent springs and balls. Pressure must be applied to the balls to depress them enough for the shift rails to be inserted. Before the last shift rail is inserted (normally the first and second rail because it's in the middle), the interlocking pins are inserted and the rail slid in. The interlock pins make sure that you cannot shift on multiple rails at one time. That means no shifting into first gear and grabbing the third-gear rail.

The reverse-gear pivot eye bolt can be installed and put back in its original depth along with any parts installed on the reverse shift rail. A new mainshaft bearing can be installed as well as the new front pinion bearing. At this point, the gear carrier is assembled and can accept both the mainshaft and pinion shaft.

The assembled mainshaft and pinion shaft are stood up and the gears are meshed together. A new third and fourth steel shift fork is inserted into the operating sleeve on the mainshaft. The third and fourth shift rail will now have to be pushed out of the gear carrier until it's flush with the back side of the carrier. This allows the shafts to be pressed into the gear carrier with the third and fourth shift fork free from binding upon insertion.

The gear carrier is next taken to the hydraulic press, where it's pressed onto the mainshaft. Any nuts or circlips are applied to the mainshaft and pinion shaft. The third- and fourth-gear shift rail is then slid back down and through the shift fork. Insert the tension bolt and initially tighten.

The first- and second-gear shift rail is pulled out enough to insert the shift fork and then pushed back in so its tension bolt can be inserted and tightened. If appropriate, the reverse gear and brass cradle (or just the reverse gear) are installed on the pivot arm and engaged on the operating sleeve. This will hold the reverse gear in place while the carrier is installed in the shift jig.

Setting the Shift Forks

The last step before final assembly is to set the shift forks for smooth shifting. The completed gear carrier will have the pinion shim installed on the pinion bearing and the whole assembly installed into the shift jig. This jig allows the carrier to be mounted as it would be in the transmission case but with a lot of open room to adjust the forks.

When adjusting the shift forks, you are looking for the same amount of play when the transmission is engaged in first or second gear. The same goes for third and fourth. The reverse-gear mechanism is the last to be adjusted because it engages on the first- and second-gear operating sleeve.

With the completed gear carrier tightened into the jig, the task of adjusting the first/second- and third/fourth-gear shift forks can begin. The shift forks are slid along their rails to find the best median distance for proper shifting. Reverse gear is positioned once the first- and second-gear operating sleeve is centered.

So, once the first- and second-gear shift fork is set, it's time to set the reverse gear. While in the jig, both the mainshaft and pinion shaft should turn freely and separately. To complete the gear carrier, make sure all the bolts are tightened to the correct specification. Unbolt the gear carrier from the jig; it's now ready for assembly.

Final Assembly

Any internal case bearings will need to be installed along with the reverse driveshaft and input shaft seal. The case is ready to accept the completed gear carrier.

Gaskets and/or sealant is placed between the case and gear carrier. The gear carrier is slowly inserted into the case until the pinion bearing is stopped by the pinion bore of the case. A propane torch can be used to heat the case enough until the pinion bearing slides in.

Before going any further, make sure the reverse is on the reverse driveshaft and turns freely. This will save you from having to remove the gear carrier a second time to fix the problem. If you are going to paint the case after assembly, use any old nuts to tighten the gear carrier and other parts to the case. Most builders install new hardware after painting.

Now, the pinion bearing will need to be secured, whether it's with four bolts or the later pinion nut. Insert the input shaft through the new seal and install a new circlip past the groove. This allows the reverse-drive coupler to be slid up on the shaft, the input shaft to be screwed on the mainshaft, and the coupler to be slid down over the mainshaft. The coupler is now engaged with the reverse drive, and the circlip is installed in the groove.

Input Shaft Assembly

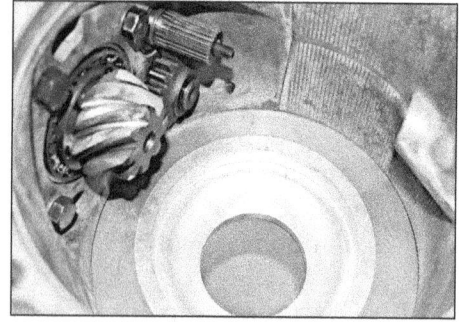

1 The input shaft is now slid through the new input shaft seal in the rear of the case. The new circlip and reverse-drive coupler are slid over the shaft.

2 The input shaft is ready to be slid up to the mainshaft and readied for installation. Align the input shaft internal threads with the mainshaft stud and start turning clockwise until the input shaft is snug against the mainshaft.

3 The input shaft is now turned counterclockwise to match up the splines of the two shafts. The reverse-drive coupler is ready for installation.

4 The reverse-drive coupler is slid from the input shaft down over the mainshaft; its outside drive teeth engage the drive teeth on the internal reverse driveshaft.

5 With the reverse-drive coupler in position, the retaining circlip can be slid in to hold the coupler in place.

Installing the Differential

Install the side cover (if applicable) on the opposite side of the ring gear (left side). Make sure to install the side cover O-ring, if applicable, and any sealant before installation. Tighten the nuts to allow the sealant to bond.

Lower the completed differential into the case, and rest the opposite differential bearing against the bearing race, making sure the ring gear teeth are properly engaging the pinion shaft. Next, install the other side cover as before, and the differential area will be complete.

The nose cone, if not new, will need a new seal bushing installed. When the bushing is pressed in the nose cone, it may cause enough shrinkage of the inner diameter that a reamer may be needed to open it back up for the hockey stick.

Apply any gasket and sealant to the nose cone and install it with the hockey stick. Now, let the sealant dry. If you want the case to look clean, take the time to pick the extra sealant off the case before painting it.

Before the differential is put into the case, the associated side plates must have the appropriate gasket or O-ring installed. Sealant is applied to help close any gaps or imperfections of the worn case.

TRANSMISSIONS

Use a good primer for the transmission case and then start painting. Apply several light coats of paint and let it dry for days to really set the paint up. After that, remove the fasteners one at a time and replace them with new ones.

Now you have a completed transmission.

There you have it. Clear as mud and twice as hard to do as it is to comprehend, right? While you might not want to tackle the transmission yourself, just knowing more about how it works and what goes into a rebuild will put you light years ahead of most VW enthusiasts. Because of the knowledge base, skill set, and special equipment needed to build transmissions, our advice is to entrust this part of a restoration to a professional. If you insist on doing it yourself, you'll want to amass a huge library of manuals and how-to books that cover this task in-depth for your specific Beetle model.

Final Assembly

Don't forget to install a new heavy-duty clutch cross shaft or have the OEM shaft welded so no arms break off in the future. Always install a new bronze impregnated shaft bushing and new spring to prevent any binding problems in the future.

Make sure to wipe the case with at least 91-percent isopropyl alcohol to get any remaining grease and other contamination off the case.

If you had a swing-axle transmission, you would install the axle and axle tubes to complete this. Otherwise, you would install the final drive seals and final drive flanges to complete the IRS transmission.

Tools Needed

- Blue Loctite adhesive
- Ground strap
- Wrench set
- Shifter coupling
- Transmission
- Transmission coupler seal
- Transmission mounts (front and rear)

Installing a Transmission

Whether you buy or build your transmission, you'll need to install it next. The good news is that this part of the project is much easier than rebuilding the transmission! Your transmission weighs 75 pounds or so. Wear steel-toe boots and safety gloves as you work.

Work on the front mount first.

Transmission Installation

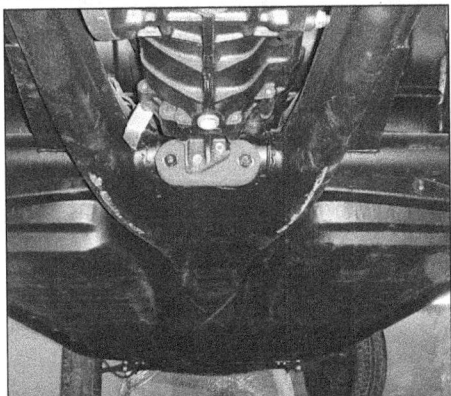

1 There are two types of nose cones associated with the VW Beetle. They take two different types of transmission mounts. Pictured here is the two-bolt style.

2 Ground strap installation is done by using a woven strap that attaches to the external case of the transmission. The strap is also attached to the frame horn of the car. This does nothing for the transmission, but it does help ground your engine.

3 The inner workings of the bellhousing are fairly simplistic. You have the output shaft from the transmission (the throw-out bearing will surround it), which is installed with two clips on the forks on either side of the output shaft.

Transmission Installation *Continued*

4 It is easiest to install the transmission when doing the pan build. While you can do it solo, it's a lot easier if you've got a buddy to help you wrestle it into place.

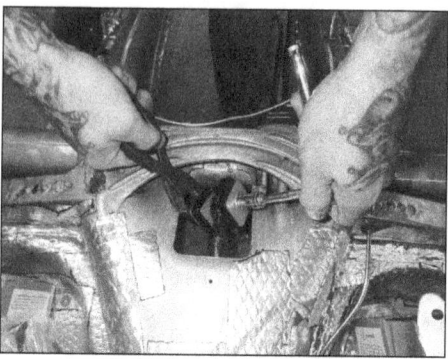

5 The shift-rod coupling isolates mechanical vibration coming through the shift rod up to the shifter. There are two isolators on either side that are attached to the shift rod with a bolt-and-pin configuration. It's held in place on the transmission with a retaining pin.

6 There are two rear transmission mounts. They are held onto the carrier by two nuts and bolts per mount and into the transmission case with two nuts going into captive studs in the mount.

It's easier to install the front mount to the transmission before installing it into your car. Install the front nose-cone seal to the body. The nose-cone seal is a small piece of rubber that will seal the pan to the transmission to keep water and debris out.

There will be two or three studs (depending on the year of your Beetle) from the mount into the transmission. Fasten them securely to the transmission.

Work on the rear transmission mounts next. Attach the rear transmission mount to the transmission cradle, bolting the studs through the cradle with four 13-mm bolts and wave washers. Once the cradle is assembled, loosely attach the mount to the bellhousing. Make the attachment with four 13-mm bolts and wave washers. Tighten the bolts once all of the attachments are made.

Now that the transmission is ready to install, slide it into place, centering the cradle with the two 35-mm frame horn bolts and wave washers. Torque them to manufacturer's specifications.

From inside the car, slide the shift-rod coupling over the transmission shift-selector rod. Tighten the set bolt. Wire the set bolt in an X pattern over the transmission coupler to secure the coupler to the transmission.

Take one end of the ground strap and attach it to the 15-mm front mount stud. Tighten it to specifications. Add blue Loctite adhesive to keep the bolts from vibrating loose.

CHAPTER 8

BRAKES

Nothing beats the feeling of cruising along in your brand-new, very old Beetle. Well, except being able to stop. That's a good feeling too.

While some vintage Beetle owners are tempted to leave their old brakes alone, replacing and upgrading them is truly a safety issue. Some say these iconic cars were built to be as close to disposable as you can get. While the brake system works well if properly maintained, without that maintenance, it will fail. Corrosion, brake fluid degradation, and mechanical failures team up to limit the working lifespan of the brake system. Weighing these factors and dangers, the reasoning behind springing for a brake upgrade becomes clear. Stopping is good.

There are a few choices when it comes to brake upgrades. When they rolled off the factory line, Beetles used drum brakes to stop. Since then, disc brakes have been developed, which have better stopping power. They're self-adjusting and fairly easy to maintain, which is why our recommendation is an upgrade to disc brakes.

The idea of an upgrade may leave purists cold. If that's you, you will probably want to leave the brakes stock and stick with the drums. If your purist inclinations allow for a little wiggle room, source a set of Karmann Ghia disc brakes as a direct swap and avoid aftermarket parts. However, the safest option is to buy brand-new disc brakes from a reputable VW parts manufacturer such as SCAT or EMPI, or even buy brakes from the more exotic Wilwood line.

Brake Replacement

Our 1968 Euro Beetle project car came in with four drum brakes. The front drums were a little larger than the rears (70 up front versus 30 in the back). We're going to walk through a drum brake replacement in the back and a disc brake conversion in the front.

Drum Brakes

Drum brakes were adequate for the speeds most vehicles reached back in the day. At today's speeds, drum brakes are not as safe as disc

Old, worn-out brake components aren't much fun. You need to be able to stop before you can go. Would you trust your life to these rusted out brakes? No way.

Performance disc brake upgrades are fairly affordable and come in complete kits. You can get various lug patterns to match your taste in wheels.

HOW TO RESTORE YOUR VOLKSWAGEN BEETLE

CHAPTER 8

This Wilwood brake package is one of the best on the market today. It has four pistons for stopping power, vented rotors for increased heat dissipation, and a three-piece component design for flexibility in wheel patterns. What more could you ask for?

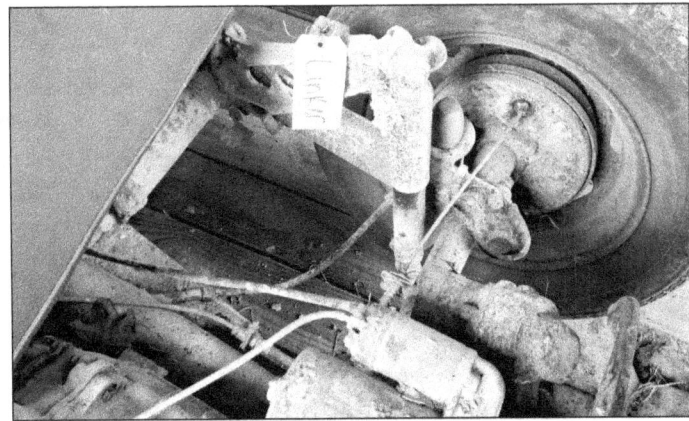

Three out of four brakes are probably old, icky, nasty, and nonfunctional. Upgrading the braking system is especially important if you want to take your Beetle out into traffic.

Tools Needed

- Impact wrench
- New brake kit
- New brake seals

You don't need a big toolbox to do your brakes. Gather a metric socket set, an impact wrench, your new brake kit and seals, and plenty of shop towels.

brakes. Drums have more moving parts and require more maintenance, which is another reason to do an upgrade.

Performing this upgrade won't change the appearance of your Beetle because the brake system is invisible behind the wheels. The only reason you might want to keep the stock setup would be if you plan to compete in concours-level shows, where you get points for having original, year-correct components.

Brake Fluid Safety

Brake fluid is highly corrosive and will eat anything it touches. Do not use old brake fluid that's been sitting around. Its hydroscopic nature means it will absorb moisture from the air and become contaminated. Once contaminated, your brake fluid can't contract and expand as needed, which means your brakes are not likely to work reliably.

A complete rear brake job should always include new brake cylinders, brake shoes, retaining pins, and springs. Always work clean to keep brakes from getting contaminated by dirt or grease.

BRAKES

Replacing Drum Brakes

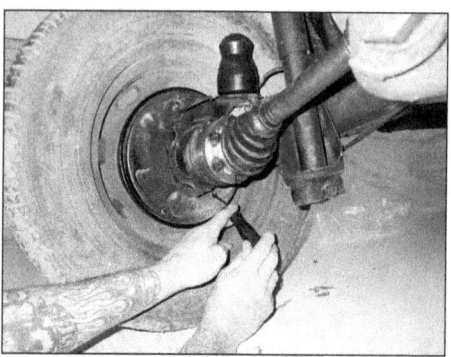

1 Reach around the back side of the first brake and remove the four rubber plugs in the bottom of the backing plate. You'll see star adjusters in two of them. Back the star adjusters off to relax the brake shoes so they're not in contact with the drum. Basically, you are un-adjusting your brakes.

2 Remove the wheels, which are held on with 17-mm lug bolts. An impact wrench is helpful for removal.

3 A 36-mm castle nut is fixed with a cotter pin. Remove the pin from the nut and axle using an impact wrench. Unbolt the castle nut and remove the brake drum.

4 The cotter pin is removed. Note the clean work surface. It's always smart to work clean. In fact, it might seem like you spend half your restoration project time just cleaning dirty parts. But before unbolting everything, cut the rubber brake hose from the back side.

5 While removing the entire assembly, pay attention to the emergency brake cable that is attached to it. After pulling off the backing plate, unhook the emergency brake from the mechanism. Then remove the entire brake assembly and put it all on the workbench.

6 With the backing plate removed, place the axle nut back on the axle so it isn't lost. Now would be a good time to inspect the suspension components while they are clearly visible.

HOW TO RESTORE YOUR VOLKSWAGEN BEETLE

CHAPTER 8

Replacing Drum Brakes Continued

7 Disassemble the brake shoes, keeping all springs, clips, and hardware. The new brake hardware kit includes these parts (springs, retaining clips, etc.), however, you never know when you will need parts. Clean and paint the backing plates and tension rods, and remove the star adjusters.

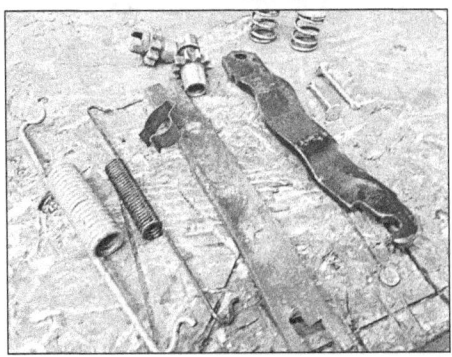

8 After disassembly of the brake drum, there will be a collection of miscellaneous rods, springs, levers, and retaining clips and pins. They all need to be cleaned and painted before they are reassembled.

9 Clean and polish the star adjusters. Apply a light coat of anti-seize on the part of the star adjuster that goes into the receiver, and reinsert them back in their retainers on the backing plate.

10 Insert the freshly cleaned star adjusters in the freshly painted backing plate. Install a new brake cylinder with an 8-mm bolt through the back. Set the new brake shoes loosely into their approximate location.

11 Reattaching the retaining pin is as simple as sliding the tensioner spring and retaining plate over, compressing the spring, and turning 180-degrees until it locks into place.

12 Attach an upper space slider and spring assembly to the upper part of the brake shoe. Attach your lower spring set and slider to the lower brake shoes. Then, set the brake shoes into their seated position.

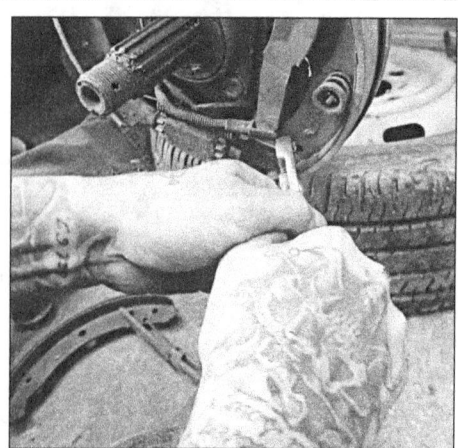

13 The lower tensioning spring is installed by sliding the front hook over the front brake shoe hole. Pliers are recommended to decompress the spring so it will hook into the back shoe.

14 This properly assembled rear brake drum assembly is bolted onto the car. Note that there are two different springs, and they are in the proper locations. The emergency brake will not function if they are reversed. Always use new hardware when you can.

15 Next, you're basically going to make a big sandwich. Two rubber rings will be like the bread with the larger ring closest to the axle, and a smaller one farthest out. First, take your new seal kit and mount the paper seal, then the backing plate, then a second paper seal, and then an oil seal. Reinstall the four bolts. Torque them to the manufacturer's specifications.

While a jack is fine for lifting a chassis up, wheel chocks and a jack stand are a requirement for working safely. They will help prevent the Beetle from falling on you while you work underneath. If you do not have access to an impact wrench and compressed air, you can loosen the lug bolts with a tire iron. If you go that route, your chassis needs to be on the ground with the emergency brake engaged.

For mid-1967 and onward, access to the star adjusters is done through the backing plate. Generally, there are two rubber plugs that help keep water out of the system. All four lugs are like this.

If you have a five-lug pattern, your adjusters will be on the wheel side. A wire brush will be helpful for cleaning off the castle nut before removing it. Sometimes the cotter pin is hidden under a thick layer of dirt. This nut cannot be removed with the cotter pin in place.

Remove the entire brake assembly from its connection point. Start with the rear, where four bolts surround the axle. Brake shoes wear unevenly side to side and back to front. This is caused by emergency brake wear.

Once the entire assembly is off the car and on the workbench, we can start to clean with a wire brush and paint parts to get them up to snuff. Freshly cleaned and painted parts are always easier to work with than dirty ones. Always apply a couple of light coats of paint instead of one heavy coat; adhesion will be better, it will last longer, and it will look nicer.

When doing brake service work, these spring-loaded retainers are the first component to be removed. A retaining pin goes through the backing plate, then through the brakes, helping keep the brakes in their correct locations. In order to ensure correct operation of your emergency brake's upper space slider, it must be slid between the two brake pads.

The tensioner spring must be attached to the brake shoes in the factory location. Take the backing plate and hold it as if you were going to bolt it up, but don't bolt it yet. Just let it sit on the axle stub for now. Then, thread the emergency brake cable back in through the backing plate and attach the retaining clip to the backing plate.

Now, it's all bolted back together and the new brake drum is ready to be installed. Hook up the hard brake line and the lever, and make sure to attach the retaining plate back onto the emergency brake cable.

Disc Brakes

It's a fairly simple procedure to install disc brakes on the front end of the Beetle. There are kits available that will bolt directly to the existing drum spindle. There are also kits that require you to change your spindle out, which is not much more complicated, but they are a bit more expensive.

Upgrading to Disc Brakes

1 Purchase a disc brake kit with spindles. The kit will include seals, bearings, calipers, pads, and new brake lines for the driver's side and the passenger's side. Follow the instructions that come with your kit.

2 Change the spindle to the disc brake spindle. Put the bearing races for both the inner bearing and outer bearing into the disc brake rotor.

3 Pack the bearings with wheel bearing grease, and then tap the inner seal in firmly. Grease the spindle with wheel bearing grease. Slide the rotor on with the bearings. Tighten the washer and a nut until the rotor is tight but still spins. Attach the grease cap next and tap it on.

4 Use the buddy system to bleed the brakes. This is easiest to do when the body is not on the pan. You can see and reach everything much more easily this way.

5 Put the caliper in place and bolt it on, making sure that the rotor is centered in the caliper. You can shim it inward or outward with the shims provided in the kit. Attach the brake line to the caliper and then into to the hard line. Then, bleed the brakes.

BRAKES

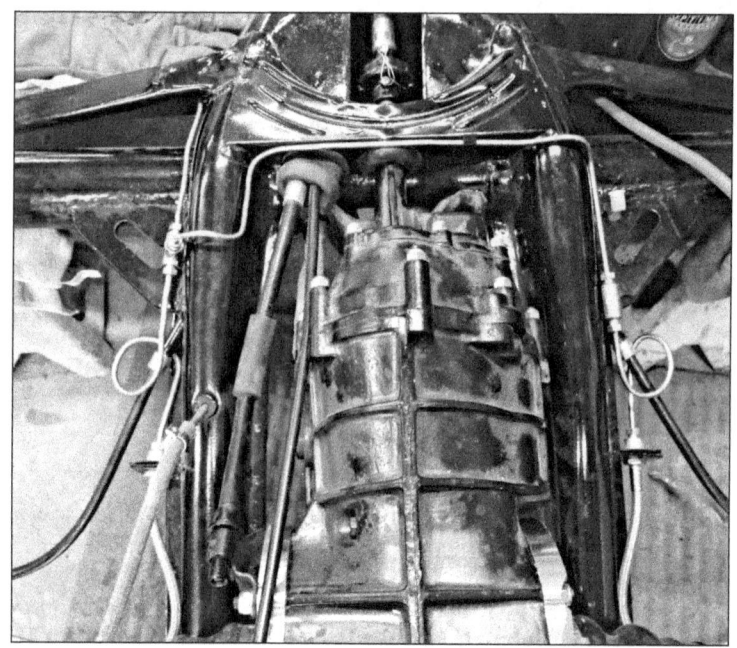

It's always a good idea to replace the hard brake lines. In a pan-off restoration, this is the easiest time to do it and make it look nice.

The pneumatic brake bleeder is a lifesaver. The tool makes changing fluid and removing all the air bubbles in the brake system a one-person job. The bleeders are available online.

There are five or six manufacturers of disc brake conversion kits. All are fairly easy to install, but it's a good idea to inventory the parts before starting installation.

With outer race bearings pressed into the hub, it is time to grease up the entire assembly and slide it into place. Make sure to pack the bearings full. After installing the wheel bearings' inner and outer seals and packing them full of grease, the retaining nut must be locked down. The last step before installing the wheel is locking the retaining bolt on the end of the spindle.

After assembling the disc brake kit, make sure there is clearance between the brake pads and the rotor. Shimming may be required to get the gap even on both sides. Shims come included with the kit.

Brake Lines

Even with brand-new upgraded disc brakes, keep a close eye on the brake lines. If there is cracking, damage, weeping, dew, or leaks, replace them. It's a matter of safety. Those original rubber brake lines will break down and cause unsafe driving conditions. Typically, brake lines only last three to seven years.

Bleeding Brake Lines

Fill your reservoir and then start with the rear right. Advance in sequence, moving closer to the reservoir. You can either use a pneumatic bleeder or you can go with the buddy system. Here's how both of those processes go:

Pneumatic Bleeder

1. Place the hose on the pneumatic bleeder.
2. Pressurize the canister.
3. Open the bleeder valve.
4. Let the air bubbles out.
5. Close the valve.
6. Repeat this sequence until you no longer have air bubbles escaping.

Buddy System

1. Have a helper pump the brakes three times then hold the brake to the floor.
2. While the helper has the pedal on the floor, crack open the brake bleeder and watch for air. There should be a steady flow of fluid with no spurts from air bubbles.
3. Repeat this sequence until all air is out of the system, clean brake fluid is flowing, and the brake pedal tightens up to a firm pedal feel.

Now that everything is installed, bolted up, and bled out, it's time to put the wheels back on. Double-check all of the connections, watching for leaks, drips, and kinked brake lines.

HOW TO RESTORE YOUR VOLKSWAGEN BEETLE

CHAPTER 9

BODY MATING

The A-Team's Colonel John "Hannibal" Smith may have been thinking about this next phase of your restoration project when he said, "I love it when a plan comes together." Except what will be coming together next is your Beetle's body with its pan. You'll be joining your painstakingly painted and polished body with your good-as-new (or new) pan that you coated in POR-15.

While taking the car apart was all fun and games in a demolition kind of way, putting it back together is another matter entirely. Now you have money in the game and probably a fair amount of minor scratches, burns, and bruises that show off your hard work. Where disassembly is a rather low-stakes task, and the worst thing that can happen is that you break something you're already debating about replacing, body mating is a much bigger deal.

Safety Reminder

Always wear steel-toe shoes in case you drop something on your foot such as a car body. You may still break a toe or two with a direct hit, but you'll fare much better than if you're wearing sneakers or flip-flops.

It is a good idea to wear safety glasses whenever you are working in your shop, even if there shouldn't be any sparks flying. Ample and clean space to work in is important so nobody ends up pinned against a wall or tripping over tools. Put away any tools you are not currently using.

Take your time, communicate clearly with your helpers, and listen closely to your spotter. This can be the difference between celebrating with pizza and beer afterward or rushing someone to the emergency room.

Body to Pan Reassembly

Modern cars are considered unibody, where the body and floor are one assembled component. The powertrain and subsystems bolt onto the unibody. In a Bug, you have most of those systems (suspension, transmission, emergency brake, fuel lines, and control cables) attached to the pan or chassis. The body is bolted on with a rubber seal between the pan and body. The reason for this setup is because the factories simply didn't have the capability to build unibody cars.

Cars today are essentially built as a single structural component. They have doors, a trunk lid, and a hood that can be removed, but that's about it. The suspension, engine, transmission, and all other components bolt directly to the subframe. The advent of the computer in automotive design and manufacturing led to a decrease in weight and an increase in structural rigidity.

The process of mating the body to the pan is not complicated. In a nutshell, line up the bolt holes on both components and lock them together with body pads and a seal. However, it's a process that takes time in order to avoid damaging the freshly painted body.

Eye protection is often an overlooked part of working safe. There is nothing worse than getting a burning shard of metal in your eyes, except maybe having to take the time for a trip to the doctor to remove it.

92   HOW TO RESTORE YOUR VOLKSWAGEN BEETLE

BODY MATING

Tools Needed	
• 13-mm socket, 1/2-inch drive is sufficient • 15-mm socket • 17-mm socket • Body pad kit (consists of six pieces, including rubber pads that the body will rest on top of when it's attached to the pan)	• Contact cement • Four sober buddies, plus pizza for afterward • Gold or silver permanent marker • Pan bolt kit • Pan gasket • Punch cutter • Rubber gloves

The pan bolt and retaining sets can be refurbished by blasting and painting. They can be color matched to the car, or a contrasting color can be used as an accent. Most people won't notice this tiny detail, but you will.

We consider this milestone to be the halfway point of a build. This is when we are starting to put stuff together again instead of taking it apart. Make sure to read through this section a few times before attempting the body mating. In the end, the actual mating will take less time than it will take you to read this set of instructions, but you want to be sure you do it right the first time.

Reattaching the Body to the Pan

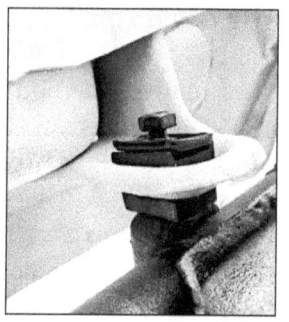

1 Place two of the medium-size pads from the pad kit on the front beam. The beam has two very small tubes on its shoulders. The pads go on the outer sides of the tubes.

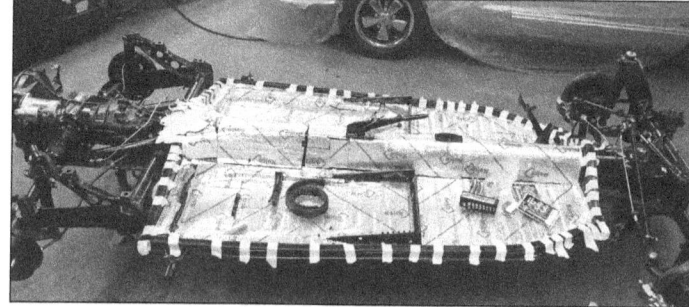

2 Double-check to make sure the pads are in place, the brake lines are installed, the throttle cables are ready, and the emergency brake cables and master cylinder are installed. Doing a pre-checklist now will save you some major headaches later.

3 While you can add sound-deadening material after the body is on the pan, we suggest getting everything done on your pan before the body goes on. The rear brake lines are another good example. While it is doable to install afterward, it is much easier to do it now.

4 There are two more points at the rear suspension that will also need medium pads. You will find them at what will become the rear wheelwell. The pads go on the rear suspension upper frame horn.

CHAPTER 9

Reattaching the Body to the Pan *Continued*

5 Depending on your model, you may also need to use a third set of pads. They go behind where the backseat will go on the lower side of the frame horn.

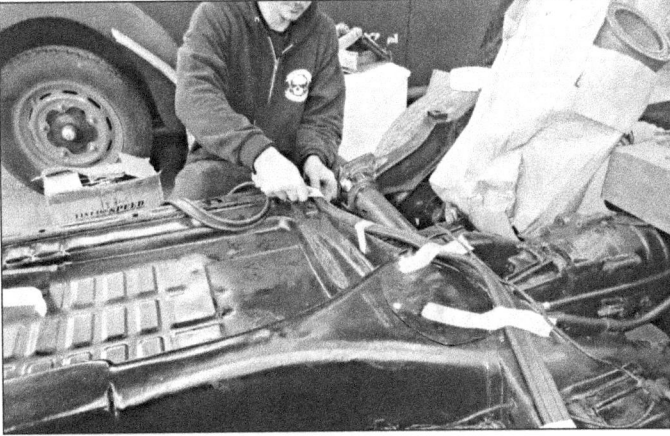

6 The pan gasket comes in a roll that must be cut to fit to the pan. Cut the front sections first. Glue them in place and tape them down until the glue sets.

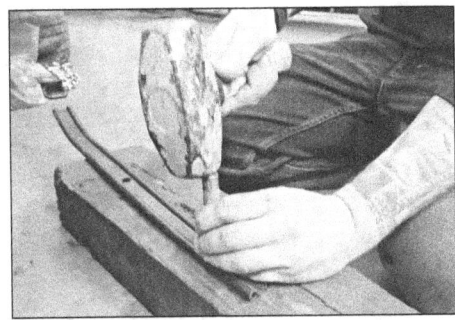

7 After mocking up the pan gasket and marking where the pan bolts attach to the body, prepunch the bolt holes. An inexpensive set of punch dowels is invaluable, but you can use a pair of scissors or a utility knife.

8 A light coat of adhesive will help keep the pan gasket in place. Tape it until the adhesive is cured. Remove the tape before setting the pan.

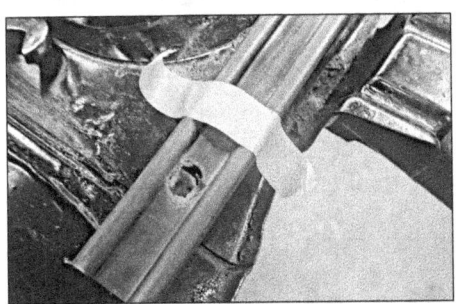

9 Cut the pan gasket to fit the top hat, then the rear, and then the sides.

10 After punching the holes, use an RTV or weatherstripping gasket adhesive to lock the pan gasket in place. Then, tape it until the glue sets.

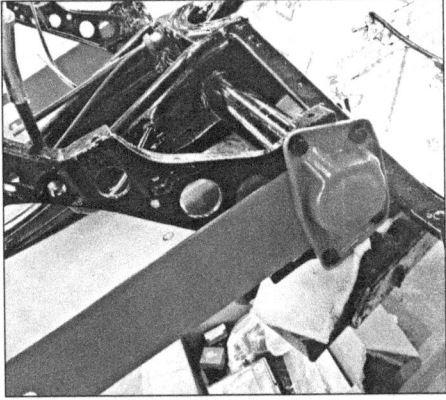

11 The pan gasket hole is punched and set. Don't forget the four rear body mounts. They are critical for keeping your Bug properly aligned.

HOW TO RESTORE YOUR VOLKSWAGEN BEETLE

BODY MATING

12 When resetting the body back onto the pan, the best arrangement is placing the body and pan side by side. This way, you won't have to carry it far, and there is less danger of dropping it.

13 Have a helper on each corner and a few sets of eyes to move the body. Remember to have everyone lift with their knees, not their backs. This is not a good time to throw out your back.

14 Set the body on the pan and make sure all of the bolt holes line up before fastening them. Once it is locked in, making adjustments is much more difficult.

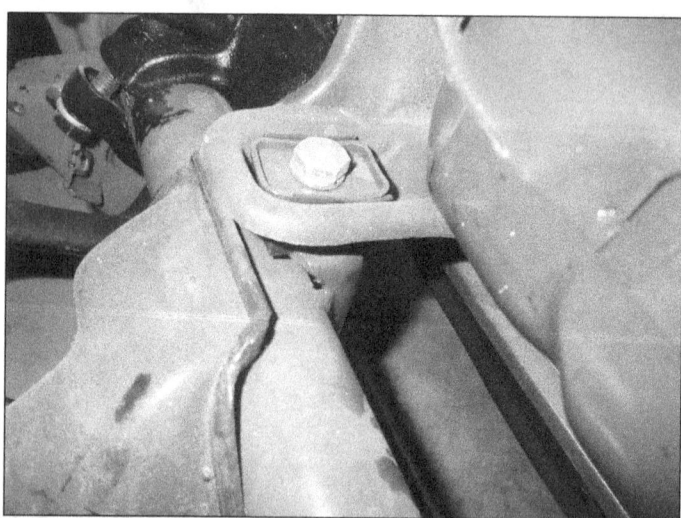

15 With the body set on the pan, there is another set of pads and retaining plates that need to be installed. One set is on the forward-most point at the beam (shown). The other set is behind where the rear tire sits.

16 There are four retaining plates and bolts that need to be attached under where the rear seats go. These are often overlooked on many home-built projects.

HOW TO RESTORE YOUR VOLKSWAGEN BEETLE

CHAPTER 9

Installing the Mica Tube

In the back of most late 1960s through late 1970s Beetles, there's a plastic or mica tube that must be installed in the body before it is mated to the pan. Make sure you do not skip this step. Otherwise, you will never get the tube in. It's the passthrough from the heat exchangers into the interior's heating system.

Buddy System

Grab some friends, and be sure they are the kind of friends who will take direction from you rather than joke around and potentially drop the Beetle on their feet. It may be helpful to make copies of these pages for them to read through before you start working. The smoothest body mating happens when everyone knows exactly what will happen and when.

Gloves On!

Everyone handling the body needs to put on rubber gloves. This is particularly critical if the Beetle body has been restored, painted, and polished. The oil in human skin can contaminate the finish. If you have decided to keep the natural patina, gloves are optional because there's not much harm that can be done to your finish.

There are upper and lower isolator pads to connect the front of the body to the beam. An upper plate and a bolt serve to maintain structural integrity on the front end of a Beetle. Double-check that the pads are in place, the brake lines are installed, the throttle cables are ready, the emergency brake cables are installed, and the master cylinder is installed.

Make sure the seal is attached to the pan securely and smoothly. The seal comes in a giant roll. The pan has 90-degree angles that you have to work around, so you will have to cut the seal to length rather than trying to bend it around the corners. It's helpful to lay the seals out in a dry run before you even think about using glue. Doing a mockup first is the equivalent of *measure twice, cut once* and will save you a major headache.

Use a gold or silver permanent marker to indicate where you'll cut for bolts to connect the body and chassis. Mark the holes, pull the seals off, and use a punch cutter to make the holes in the seals.

Start at the front of the pan at the front footwell. Cut the seal to length, leaving about 1/2 inch on both sides. You'll trim it later. Affix the seal with contact cement.

Then, move to the rear of the pan. Follow the same process of cutting it to length, leaving about 1/2 inch on both ends, and applying the seal. Next, do the same on the sides of the pan, starting with the driver's side and finishing with the passenger's side.

At this point, arrange the pan and body so they are side by side. This will make lifting, carrying, and maneuvering the body easier. Position one helper on each corner of the car body. The fifth person is the spotter, who needs a clear view of what's happening. The best position is on the far side of the pan.

Lift the body over the pan and slowly lower it into the correct position. The folks doing the heavy lifting will not be able to see exactly where they are putting the body, so the spotter must clearly communicate any adjustments needed before the lifters set the body down. There are four points to look at closely to make sure the alignment is correct. Check the two body mounts in the rear tire well, and then check the two body mounts on the front beam. Line these up straight and you'll be good shape.

Time to Bolt

Start bolting it all up. There should be 11 13-mm bolts along each side and 2 or 3 underneath the rear seat. There are 2 17-mm bolts on each side of the front of the car in the footwell area. Those bolts will go through a capture plate to help keep them secure.

There are two hard point attachments where the pads go in (they will be 13 to 14 mm). These hard point attachments go into the lower and upper frame horn on each side, for a total of four. Two of the hard point attachments are under the gas tank, attaching the body to the front suspension.

Before tightening the bolts all the way down, double-check that the body alignment is true and correct. Adjusting the alignment of body and pan is much easier when you don't have to do a bunch of unbolting and re-bolting.

CHAPTER 10

ENGINE

The restoration project began with taking the engine out. It's now time to make some decisions. The engine can be refurbished, meaning cleaning it, putting it back together, and calling it good. A brand-new engine can be built from scratch (the skills and machinery needed to do that take us way beyond the scope of this book). A brand-new engine can be purchased from a reputable builder, which is a good option if your checkbook isn't already cowering in the corner. A long-block will cost you a few thousand dollars plus shipping. A final option is to rebuild the engine, at least the top half of it.

The decision really comes down to what's worn out and what can be fixed. For example, an engine case can only be machined so much. If it's machined too far, the saddles will wear out where the bearings fit. When assessing whether to reuse or buy new components, keep in mind that it all boils down to the money spent and the quality of the parts. Parts that are built to last will cost money. Spend wisely.

The hardest part of engine building is the machine work. Unless you're an expert machinist, you'll need the services of a good machine shop that's experienced with VW engines. A good machine shop is likely to be booked solid for months, so plan ahead to get onto their schedule. Do not make a decision based on price. Get recommendations before signing on the dotted line. Patronize a shop that does shoddy work, and you'll have a lot of work to redo or pay someone else to do.

Whatever type of engine work you decide to do, it would be wise to pick up a factory manual as well as a book or two specifically about building air-cooled engines. Books, such

This is what you see when you split the case on a VW motor. Building from scratch is certainly not for the faint of heart. Even doing a rebuild is a challenging project.

Everything inside needs to be machined to work together but also be in the correct position to the other parts. One incorrect placement or out-of-tolerance gap will kill an engine.

CHAPTER 10

Bottom End versus Top End

Let's talk about your engine's bottom end and top end for a moment. These terms refer to a group of components and where they are located within the engine. The bottom end typically refers to the block, crank, cam, lifters, and distributor's drive gear. The top end includes everything outside of the engine block, including pistons, heads, rocker assemblies, carburetor, distributor, and the intake manifold or runners.

Engine Safety

While the engine is running, steer clear of belts. Watch for fuel spray, leaks, and distributor arcs. Be careful. Use the right tools when you work. It's easy to get hurt if you improvise and your tool slips.

Wear rubber gloves to help prevent oil, gas, and brake fluid from burning your skin.

Safety glasses are a must. It's also a good idea to wear a hat if you're working under your engine. This will help keep stuff from dripping on your head.

Be cautious with your engine stand. Some have only three wheels and can tip over. The best choice for stability is a heavy-duty four-wheel model.

---

as CarTech's *VW Air-Cooled Engines: How to Rebuild*, go into extreme detail for all types of Volkswagen. If you want to get into the nitty-gritty, this kind of book will be a lifesaver.

This book will take you through a top-end rebuild. It's more work and expense than just refurbishing but way less work and expense than building a brand-new engine. By doing a top-end rebuild, you'll know for sure that your engine is in good shape and you won't have to worry about leaks. As a bonus, you'll get to know more about your engine than most people ever will.

Engine Disassembly

Pull the engine out of storage and bolt it onto the engine stand so it's safe and easy to work on. Most VW engine stands require the pressure plate and clutch to be removed before you can mount the engine to the stand. Remove the 13-mm bolts holding the pressure plate to the flywheel. Remove the pressure plate, and the clutch plate will fall out. Now it can be mounted to the engine stand.

After many years of service, it is time to freshen up the engine. While the engine tins don't have to be cleaned and painted, it is recommended to at least get rid of the dirt and varmint nests.

After draining the oil, wrap the motor in plastic for removal. This will keep everything together, and it will keep the dirt and oil on the inside of the plastic.

Tools Needed

- 4 pieces of PVC pipe, about 1.5 inches long
- 3/8-inch torque wrench
- 8-mm wrench
- 10-mm socket
- 12-mm socket
- 13-mm socket
- 15-mm socket
- Crescent wrench
- Engine assembly lube
- Engine stand
- Feeler gauges
- Flat-head screwdriver
- New pistons and cylinders kit
- Ring compressor (you can rent from your friendly local auto parts store)
- Rubber mallet
- Snap ring pliers

Disassembling the Engine

1 Insert a screwdriver into the back side of the fan pulley. Remove the fan pulley bolt. Don't lose any shims that are behind the bolt or in the center of the pulley. The pulley will come out in two pieces.

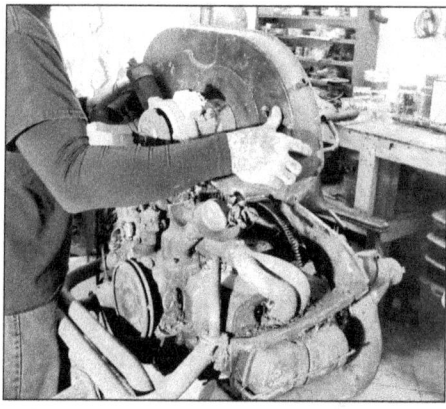

2 After removing your generator strap from the stand, loosen the two screws or nuts on either side of the fan housing. Lift up to remove the generator and fan housing as a unit.

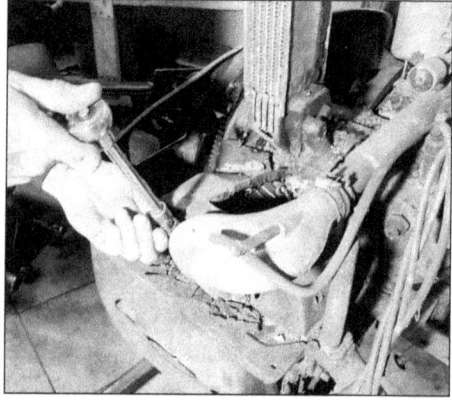

3 Loosen and remove the two nuts on either side of the intake manifold. Loosen the two intake boot sleeves. Then, lift the entire assembly out.

4 Remove the two 13-mm nuts and washers. Lift up on the fuel pump, removing it, the rod, and the base.

5 The distributor is held down by one 13-mm bolt. Remove it and the washer, then pull the distributor straight up. Try not to nick or damage the rubber O-ring on the distributor shaft.

6 There are four nuts and washers up front, two at each corner of the engine. They may be heat welded onto the exhaust studs. Some gentle persuasion may be necessary.

7 There are four nuts and washers also on the flywheel side of the engine. A rubber mallet may be needed to help remove them here as well. If you accidentally remove the stud from the case, it's not a big deal. Replacement studs are available from a Volkswagen parts house.

8 The engine tin is held on by a series of flat-head cheese screws to various parts of the block and heads. Start with the sled tins, then move on to the cylinder tins.

Disassembling the Engine *Continued*

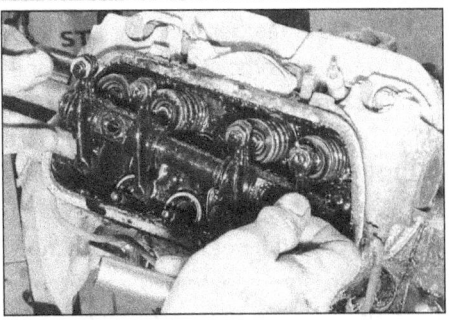

9 Unscrew the large bolt in the center first. Let the oil drain out into an appropriate container. Always dispose of your oil in an environmentally friendly manner. Most local auto parts stores will accept used motor oil.

10 The valve cover for a VW engine is held on with a wire bale. Insert a screwdriver from the top and pry it downward to pop the bale. Pull back the cover, making sure to remove the cork gasket with it.

11 Loosen the nuts and washers evenly, side to side. The valve cover bales are under strong valve-spring tension. If you do this evenly, it will not get hung up on the studs as it releases.

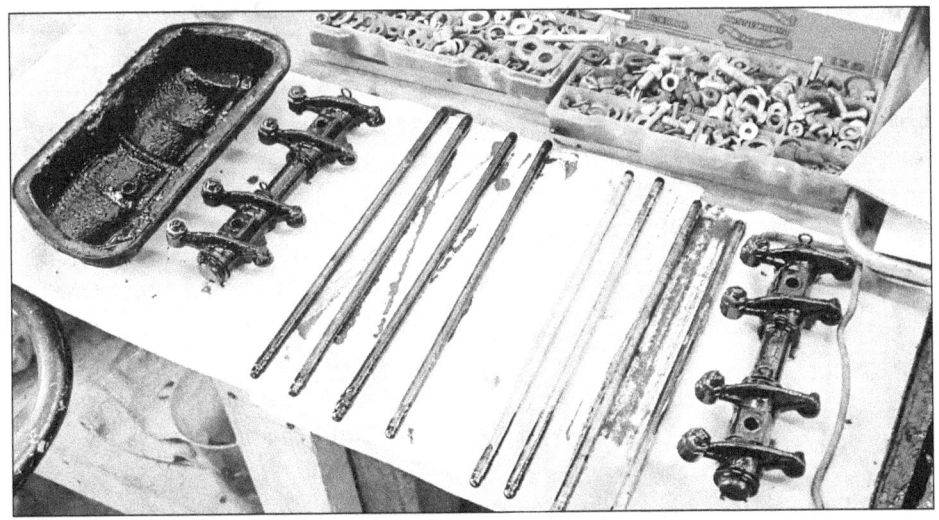

12 When disassembling an engine, it's a good idea to lay out the disassembled pieces and parts in the order and position in which they came out. That will help you keep track of your parts and also remember how it all went together.

13 There are eight head nuts and washers: four inside and four outside. Just loosen them. It's possible that the head studs might unscrew out of the case. If so, go ahead and remove it.

14 Grasp the head with one hand on each exhaust port. Pull the head toward you, away from the engine. It may require some persuasion to come lose if there is carbon buildup in the chamber causing it to stick. If so, tap with a rubber mallet to dislodge it.

ENGINE

Engine Disassembly Checklist

- ❏ Remove the generator or alternator from the engine. This can be done two ways: by removing the generator itself from the cooling shroud or, preferably, by removing the generator or alternator with the shroud as a subassembly.
- ❏ Remove the carburetor and intake manifold and fuel pump.
- ❏ Set the engine at top dead center (TDC) and remove the distributor.
- ❏ Remove the exhaust, if not already done.
- ❏ Remove the heat exchangers from the head. There's one on each side.
- ❏ Use a screwdriver to remove the engine tin.
- ❏ Drain the oil, if not already done.
- ❏ Pop the valve covers and remove the valve cover bales from one side, then repeat the process on the other side.
- ❏ Remove the rocker assemblies; they're held on with two 13-mm bolts and washers on each side.
- ❏ Remove the pushrods. Try to keep them in order as you disassemble. They are interchangeable but work best if kept in their original configuration.
- ❏ Remove the head nuts and washers. There are four inside the head and four outside.
- ❏ Remove the heads. Sometimes they get stuck. A gentle smack with a rubber mallet will help loosen them for removal. Insert lint-free towels in the lifter bore holes to keep the lifters from falling out.

Head Inspection

Now is a good time to inspect of all the parts that have been removed. You'll need to decide whether the heads can be reused or if they need to be replaced. Consult with a machine shop as you decide. At the very least, it's a good idea to replace the valve seats and exhaust valves.

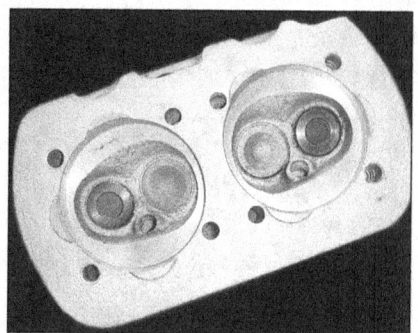

After removing the heads, inspect the combustion chamber. A little bit of soot and oil is normal. Look specifically for any cracks between the valves or spark plugs. If any are found, the heads are junk.

Piston Removal

Remove the pistons and cylinders next. The cylinders will slide out of the case. The pistons have a set of retaining clips that hold them in the wrist pin. The wrist pin attaches the connecting rod to the piston. Remove the clips and slide the wrist pin out. Then, the piston will come off.

Next comes the pistons and cylinders. We removed the oil coupler to replace the seals. Since you have gone this far, you should replace these seals at this time.

A machine shop will have the heads bead blasted if you ask for this service. The only drawback to this process is that it can be difficult to make sure that all the blast media is removed completely from the parts.

Now that the generator or alternator shroud and front pulley are off, it is time to remove the rest of the tin. Keep track of what comes off and the order in which it comes off.

HOW TO RESTORE YOUR VOLKSWAGEN BEETLE

CHAPTER 10

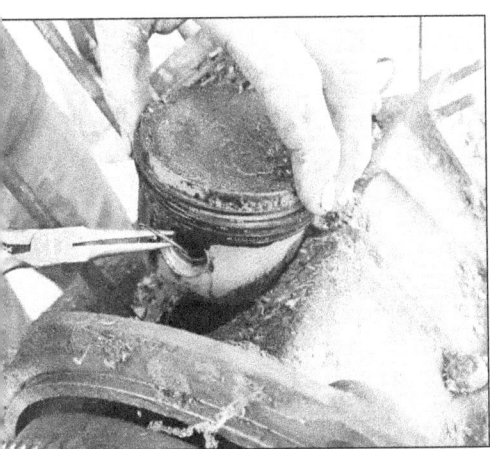

Use a pair of needle-nose pliers to remove the circlip from both sides of the piston. Using a wooden dowel and a rubber mallet, hit the wrist pin to release it from the connecting rod.

Here you see a reworked piston and cylinder. It has had a light cleanup, re-ring of the piston, and a re-honing of the cylinder. It's now ready to use.

With the pump pulley, tins, pistons, and cylinders removed, give the case a good cleaning. Use a wire brush, mineral spirits, and lots of rags to clean the outside of the case. Try not to get any debris inside the case. Be prepared to clean it for a while.

Buy a new piston and cylinder set. Rework or buy new heads if needed.

Engine Rebuilding

If rebuilding the engine, it's wise to make sure all components are within factory spec. A list of dimensions and tolerances can be found in any factory service manual. Much of this information can also be found on TheSamba.com in the technical section.

Of course, the engine tin could probably use some love. It can be sent out to blast or sandpaper can be used to clean it up. Once clean and prepped, spray it with a couple light coats of black paint.

After the engine tin is clean and shiny, put it all back together the same way you took it apart. Try to work in a clean environment, and make sure all your components that go into the inside of the engine are crystal clean with nothing but a light assembly lube on them.

Reassembling the Engine

1 Give the new pistons a good once-over. Make sure there are no nicks, burrs, or chips. Inspect the rings and the wrist pin for those flaws as well.

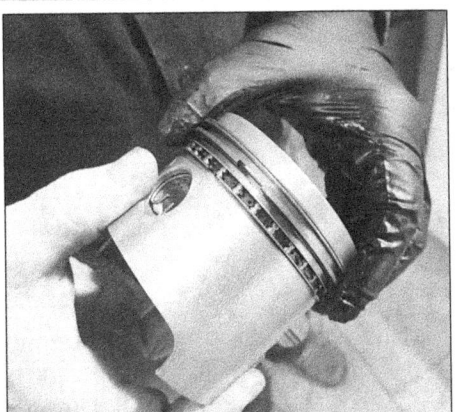

2 Make sure the ring gaps are not lined up. They should be 33-degrees offset from one another. Also, use a nice light engine assembly lube or oil to ease your installation process.

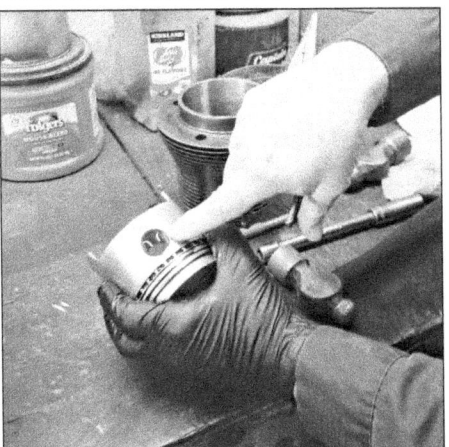

3 Install the inside-facing circlips first. Otherwise, there won't be room to insert the wrist pin later on. Use needle-nose pliers here. Make sure the circlips are in their receiving channels.

ENGINE

Reassembling the Engine *Continued*

4 Use a piston ring compressor. If you don't have one, borrow one for free from your friendly local auto parts store.

5 Hold the ring set in with the ring compressor. Slide the piston into the cylinder from the top. This might require some tapping from the wooden handle of your rubber mallet. Tap until it's all the way in.

6 Slide the piston down to the bottom of the cylinder. Do not slide it past where the rings are or else it won't go back in because the rings are compressed. Slide the wrist pin partway into the piston.

7 Lower the piston onto the connecting rod to the point where it lines up with the wrist pin. All parts should be well-lubed with a light oil to prevent damage during assembly and start-up.

8 Use a wooden dowel to tap the wrist pin home to the point where it makes contact with the circlip installed earlier.

9 Install the exterior circlip using a pair of needle-nose pliers to fasten the wrist pin in place. Try not to lose the circlip (everything is greasy and compressed).

10 Tilting the engine 90 degrees will make the setting of the pistons and cylinders much easier. With the ring compressor attached, slide the piston into the cylinder. Remove the ring compressor and slide the engine assembly onto the block. Insert the wrist pin, connecting the rods to the pistons.

11 Slide the new cylinder and piston combination home. We generally apply a small bead of liquid gasket to help seal the case. Do not use silicone.

CHAPTER 10

Reassembling the Engine *Continued*

12 After installing two of the pistons and cylinders, put retainers on them so you can flip the engine without them falling off. We use PVC pipe cut to length, washers, and a hand-tightened nut to keep it all in place.

13 After cleaning and inspecting the distributor and putting in new points and a new condenser, put a light dab of grease on the seal on the distributor shaft. That will prevent you from nicking it or tearing it as it is installed.

14 Rotate the engine counterclockwise to bring up the connecting rods for number-one and -two. Then, install the next set of pistons and cylinders.

15 Repeat this same process on the one and two side as you did on the three and four side.

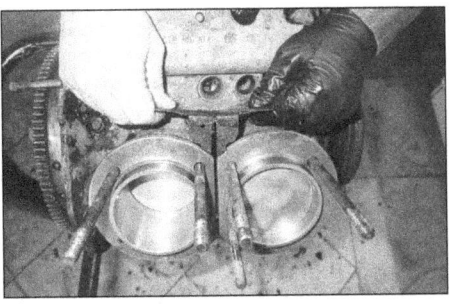

16 This small piece of engine tin may seem insignificant, but it is vital to install it at this point in the process. It's a small snap-in piece that attaches to the inner lower engine studs. It helps deflect air around the cylinder to keep it at a uniform temperature.

17 Slide the head down on the eight studs to where it is resting on the top of the cylinders. Be careful not to get caught up on the head stud threads or come down at an angle.

18 Here we've removed the head to show why it's important to set the head down loosely. There is barely enough room to install the pushrod tubes.

19 The pushrod tubes are in place with new seals. The accordion sections will compress down as the head gets tightened, providing an oil-tight seal.

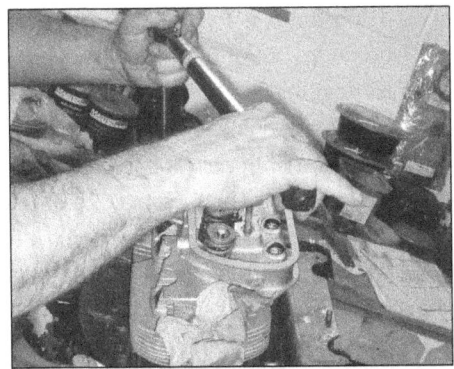

20 Tighten the case and head bolts using a two-stage tightening sequence (see diagrams 1 and 2 in the Engine Reassembly Checklist). Torque the first pass to 7 ft-lbs and the second pass to 15 ft-lbs.

Engine Reassembly Checklist

- ❏ Inspect the new pistons. Make sure they don't have any nicks, burrs, corrosion, or rough edges. Clean them with warm water and Dawn liquid dish soap, blow dry, and coat them with a light oil.
- ❏ Clock the rings. There's a set of three rings (fire-control and oil rings) that keep oil out of the combustion chamber and keep the explosion inside the combustion chamber. There are gaps in those rings that will close up under the engine's heat to provide a good sealed surface. Spread those gaps out evenly. They should not line up.
- ❏ Install one wrist-pin clip.
- ❏ Use a ring compressor to compress the rings.
- ❏ Slide the piston into the cylinder from the bottom. Don't go all the way in, but get the rings up into the cylinder.
- ❏ Slide the entire assembly down onto the connecting rod. Line the cylinder up with the visible studs. Slide until the connecting rod fits up to where the wrist pin is.
- ❏ Slide the wrist pin in.
- ❏ Insert the other wrist-pin clip.
- ❏ Slide the entire assembly in until the cylinder is seated with the case.
- ❏ Hold the piston and cylinder set on the engine case temporarily. Our shop usually uses a combination of small pieces of PVC pipe, a washer, and a nut to do this.
- ❏ Install the distributor. Use a little bit of grease to help the rubber seal stay intact as you slide the distributor in. If you proceed without installing the distributor, the distributor drive gear may pop out of the case and cause damage.
- ❏ Rotate the engine backward to bring the number-1 cylinder up to TDC by turning the pulley counterclockwise 180 degrees. The goal is to get the connecting rod to come up out of the case.
- ❏ Repeat this installation process until all four cylinders are temporarily installed.
- ❏ Pressure fit the air deflector on the bottom of the cylinders. It is a small tin plate that needs to be installed, otherwise your engine will not run for long.
- ❏ Install the heads next. With one side up, tip the engine up at a 30-degree angle on the stand. Remove the high side's temporary PVC retainers. Slide the head on partway.
- ❏ Install new pushrod tubes and pushrod seals.
- ❏ Slide the head down onto those four pieces, making sure the pushrod tubes are aligned correctly.
- ❏ Hand-tighten the washer and head nuts. Repeat the same process on the other side of the engine.

Inspection

After all four cylinders are installed, completely rotate the engine twice by hand. Look for snags, interruptions, rough spots, or anything else that doesn't feel right. It's a lot easier to fix now than later.

- ❏ Torque the cylinder heads next. Follow the pattern in diagram 1, torquing to 7 ft-lbs first.

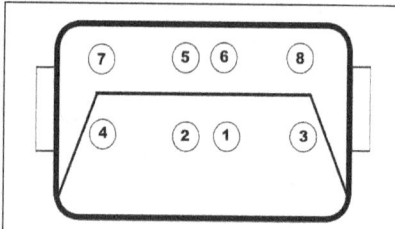

Diagram 1. When torquing heads, follow a two-stage, nonlinear process. This is how the engineers at Volkswagen designed the parts to be installed so that they will seat correctly. This diagram shows the torquing sequence for the first stage.

- ❏ Repeat, torquing to 15 ft-lbs, following the pattern in diagram 2.

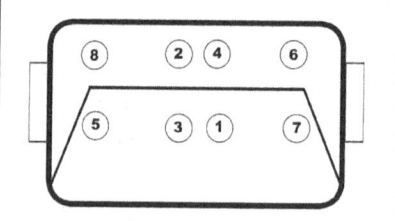

Diagram 2. This is the second stage for torquing heads. The pattern has changed, so follow it closely. Also, the first stage torqued to 7 ft-lbs, but this second time requires torquing to 15 ft-lbs.

- ❏ Pushrod tube length needs to be 7.53 to 7.56 inches in order to get enough compression seal from the cylinder heads. They have ribbed ends, which can be pulled to make the tubes longer if needed. Slide the pushrod tubes into their original location and orientation.

There are eight pushrod tubes in an air-cooled VW engine. Before installing them, pull the accordion sections so they are expanded evenly by approximately 1/4 inch. The left three here have been expanded. The far right one has not.

CHAPTER 10

Engine Reassembly Checklist CONTINUED

- ❏ Install the rocker arm assemblies. Don't forget the small rubber seal underneath them. Once the rocker assemblies are on, torque them to 18 ft-lbs with the rocker assembly backed all the way out. Repeat on the other side and rotate twice between sides. You should be back at TDC. If not, rotate it to TDC.
- ❏ Perform a preliminary adjustment of the valves.

After the head is installed and torqued to specifications, there should be two small rubber seals that go underneath the rocker assembly in the seal kit. Install the pushrods into the pushrod tubes at this point.

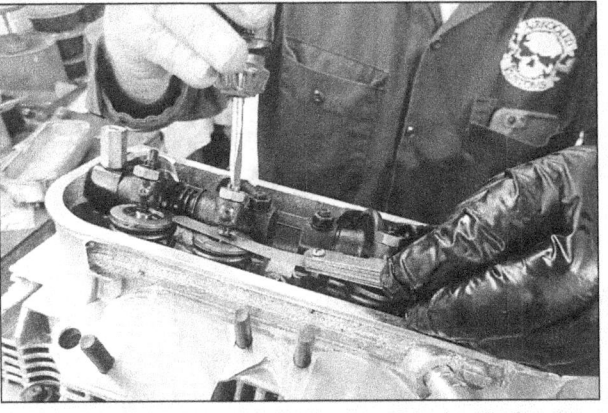

Before installing the rocker assembly, back the rocker adjustments all the way out. Set the rocker in place, add the wave washer, and tighten down the two 13-mm nuts to spec.

There's a specific order to follow in reassembling the top end. By following that order, there is less chance to misassemble or damage the top end of your engine. The goals here are to assemble it once, not have it blow up, and get it to function correctly the first time.

Valve Adjustment

To perform a valve adjustment, gather feeler gauges, a 13-mm wrench, and a flat-head screwdriver. Rotate the engine to TDC. Cylinder number-1 should be out; if not, put it there.

Slide the 0.006 feeler gauge between the valve spring and the tip of the rocker. If the space is more or less than 0.006, adjust the jam nut and screw inward or outward to get to 0.006. Tighten the jam nut without moving the adjuster. Recheck for 0.006 after you tighten everything down.

After checking the intake and exhaust on the number-1 cylinder, rotate the pulley 180-degrees counterclockwise to bring the number-2 cylinder to TDC. Measure, adjust, and recheck the number-2 cylinder.

Repeat this process with all four cylinders, rotating the engine back-

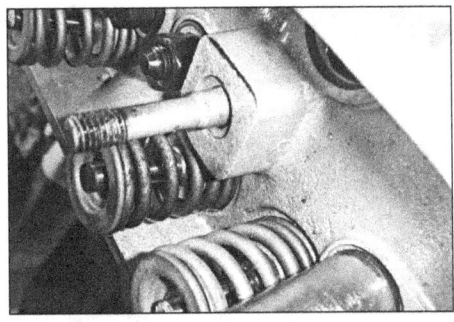

This little groove is supposed to have an O-ring in it. It is commonly missing or deteriorated. There is one per rocker stud. These will help keep the oil in the engine where it belongs.

ward 180 degrees to bring the cylinder you're working on up to TCD. The adjustment order is 1, 2, 3, 4.

If you are running a stock setup, install the valve cover bales next. Install the new valve cover gasket and then the valve cover and clip it into place.

Adjusting the Valves

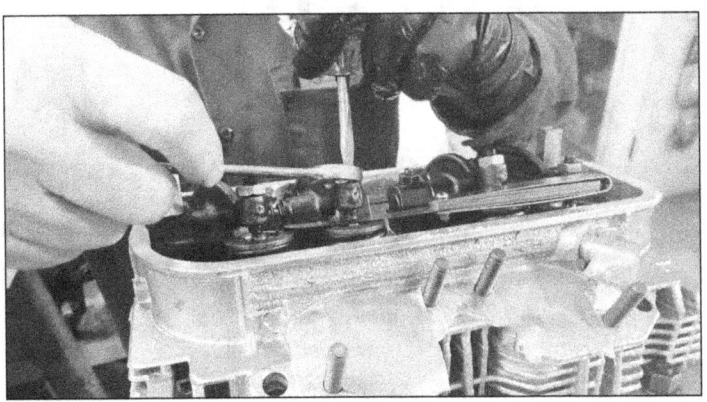

1 Starting at TDC of cylinder-1, adjust your valve lash to 0.006 with a feeler gauge. Tighten down the locking nut to keep the adjustment in place.

HOW TO RESTORE YOUR VOLKSWAGEN BEETLE

ENGINE

Adjusting the Valves *Continued*

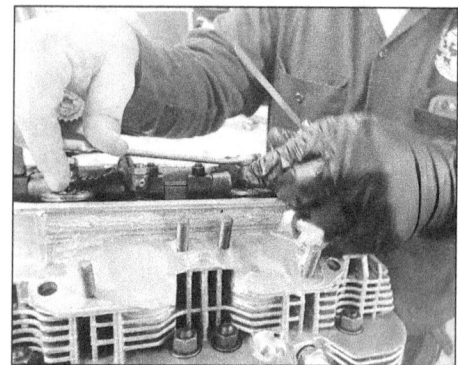

2 Rotate the engine counterclockwise 180 degrees to bring cylinder number-2 to TDC. Repeat the same valve adjustment.

3 Move to the other side of the engine. Rotate counterclockwise to bring cylinder number-3 to TDC. Repeat the same adjustment process.

4 Rotate by 180 degrees again to bring cylinder number-4 to TDC. Repeat the same valve adjustment process once more.

5 Put a light coat of grease on both sides of the valve cover gaskets. Place the gasket on the valve cover in its channel.

6 Slide the valve cover onto the head, taking care not to nick or pinch the cork gasket. The grease should help keep it in place. If it falls off, try again.

7 While VW factory valve covers are installed with the wire bale, the one shown here is a performance part. There are two 10-mm bolts holding it in place.

8 Now it is starting to look like an engine again. We use an old aluminum pulley to help locate where the new fuel pump will be installed.

HOW TO RESTORE YOUR VOLKSWAGEN BEETLE

Balance and Compression

Whether building, buying, or refurbishing the top end, balance is essential. How is the engine balanced properly? By measuring, measuring, and measuring. First, measure the area of the combustion chamber in the head. All four combustion chambers need to be the same size.

Then, measure the head height (where the piston comes up inside the cylinder and how much is left after the piston is all the way to the top of the cylinder). Use that measurement plus the cubic centimeters to adjust the compression ratio. Stock VW engines usually ran somewhere between the high 60s and the low 70s. For example, 7.3:1 is a good Volkswagen compression. Adjustments are made with shims between the top of the cylinder and the head.

Compression increases heat, and heat kills the engine. You want enough power to get down the road, but not so much that it generates more heat than is required. The compression ratio needs to be set at a happy medium so the engine doesn't overheat.

Engine Parts Worth Keeping

The parts that can be safely and efficiently refurbished and reused are the flywheel, pushrods with rockers, heads, and front pulleys. That's pretty much it. Keep all of the assemblies together so you don't lose anything as you work.

Every year, the shop hosts annual show where the guys build what they call a zombie engine. Basically, they clean a Volkswagen engine and put it back together with whatever used parts are around. It will probably run for a few minutes. Then, it's likely to throw a rod, send parts flying, and grind to a halt. An engine blow makes for good entertainment at a show, but if the goal is to actually use your Beetle, you'll have to do better than reused parts.

Pressed-In Plugs Don't Last Forever

The VW factory typically used pressed-in plugs to keep the engine's oil where it belongs. After 40 years of contracting, expanding, vibrating, and doing everything that a VW engine does, the plugs will loosen up. When we clean an engine case, we remove those plugs to clean all the oil galleries and make sure there's no gunk in there. To seal them back up, we recommend tapping them, putting threads inside, and then putting a plug in that's not going to leak. This way, if you ever need to get back in there to work on something, you can take the plug out and have access. If you weld those holes closed and then discover you made a mistake, it's really hard to fix.

Air Cleaners

Always use air cleaners, and always make sure they fit. If driv-

While this air cleaner might not be sexy, it works better than any fiber air filter out there. It works by directing the intake air to an oil bath (trapping any particles) and then changing direction to go in to the fuel charge. If you have a performance twin-carburetor engine, this is not an option without some custom fabrication work.

A Clean Engine Case

We clean all of our cases in a heat and chemical bath so that they come out looking just about brand new. If you clean the outside and the inside, you'll have a case so clean that it's nearly as good as new.

When the case returns from the machine shop, squirt all the parts down with WD-40. The last thing in the world you want is to have some kind of flash rust happening on the steel parts that were just cleaned and balanced. Aim to make them clean, then put them together as clean as you can.

With the engine all cleaned up, it will perform better. How, you ask? It is simple; dirt daubers, mud, and old grease will not dissipate heat as well as a clean case. Not only is the heat transfer more efficient but it's also a thing of beauty.

ing a stock older Beetle, it probably came with an oil bath air filter. Those are the best air filters to use. They're not pretty, but they work. If not using an oil bath air filter, then make sure whatever air filter you use fits correctly and is installed tightly enough. You don't want all the crud coming off the road to wind up going down your carburetor and into your brand-new pistons and jugs, and scoring everything up.

Stock Parts versus Aftermarket Parts

You'll want to use stock parts if you can get them. Many aftermarket parts are poorly manufactured. If you don't inspect correctly and make sure that your parts are balanced, your engine will wear itself out and die long before its time.

For example, there are little pins that sit in the main bearings and hold the bearings in the case. A standard engine pin will be less than 8 mm. Aftermarket pins are usually longer than 8 mm. If they're too long, then they cause a cramp on the bearing. That causes a hotspot, which causes wear, which is what you don't want to have.

To make sure the pins are the right length, get an 8-mm wrench and put the pins inside the open end of the wrench. If they fit, then they're the right length and will work just fine. If they won't fit, they are aftermarket parts that will need adjustments.

Depending on how many times an engine has been rebuilt, the holes that hold those pins can wear and become deeper than they should be. Adding some solder in the bottom of the hole will fix this. When it cools, measure everything again to make sure the pin at the right height.

After setting the fan belt tension by stacking shims inside the pulley space, rotate the engine via the belt. If not able to turn it, reduce the number of shims behind the upper pulley. The deflection on the belt should be no more than 1/2 inch at the center of the belt.

If at First You Don't Succeed . . .

Here's a very helpful tip: Your engine components only go together one way. If you're having difficulty, it might be tempting to think, *Maybe if I use a little bit of force it will go. I'll hit it with a hammer or get a bigger wrench.* That's almost always the wrong move. If it doesn't go together right the first time, take it apart, inspect it, and reassemble again. Usually, you'll find something simple that you didn't put together correctly the first time. When you catch it and correct it, you'll find it slips together easily.

Give Yourself a Clue

Review the photos you took during the disassembly process. Taking photos during disassembly is a marvelous idea because sometimes it is difficult to remember what a part looked like.

If there are two sets of a component, use one as a model. Simply put one set where you can see it and work on the other set, using the first set for reference. Then, use the newly refurbished set as a guide while you work on the remaining set. This way, you always have a working example to follow.

Test Throughout the Assembly Process

Working on an engine can be a matter of trial and error. If it is put together without testing along the way and it doesn't run right, how will you know what step of the process went awry? By testing every time a component is added, that guessing game is eliminated.

To test the engine, take a wrench and turn it over two complete revolutions after each component is installed. Make sure everything is turning easily. If it's not turning easily, take off the component that was added last. It is easy to identify what went wrong if testing like this is done throughout the process.

Why make two complete revolutions? That's because a four-stroke engine needs to make two complete revolutions in order for it to go through intake, compression, power, and exhaust stokes.

Keep Your Engine on the Stand

It's much easier to work on an engine while it's sitting on the engine stand. Working on an engine while lying in the dirt on your back under your car with no room is not nearly as much fun.

It is much easier to test and tune an engine while it is on the stand. The engine will behave a little differently in the car than on the stand. Don't rush this stage. Get everything ironed out now.

Gasket Guidance

Metal gaskets are preferable over paper gaskets. Paper gaskets are easier to fit, but if there is a problem, such as a stack fire or backfire, that paper gasket can blow right out of where it's supposed to be. Then, you have to take everything apart and put in another gasket. Metal gaskets take a little bit longer to put together, but once they're together correctly, you don't have that failure to worry about if a gasket gets blown out.

Engine Break-In

Got a brand-new engine? Follow this cam break-in process: Top the oil off and run the engine for 20 to 30 minutes at 1,500 to 2,000 rpm. Let everything get used to working with all the parts.

If it's only a top-end rebuild, run it for 20 minutes and then let the engine cool all the way. Once cool, check the valves and readjust as needed. Sometimes they'll change a little bit. Make sure that everything that was torqued down is still tight. Be certain to check the torque in the rocker arms and make sure everything is as it was before break-in.

Make sure your valve covers don't leak. During that 20-minute break-in, be sure to peek under the engine every couple of minutes and look at the valve covers. Valve covers usually leak right after adjusting the valves and putting it all back together again if the grease didn't hold the gasket exactly where it needed to be. That's easy to fix if you catch it in time. Any time the valve covers are removed, let the engine run for 10 to 20 minutes after they are put back on, then check and make sure those valve covers are not leaking.

Change your oil after you break in your brand-new engine.

Nuts and Bolts Check

Any time regular maintenance is done, go back and touch every single fastener. Make each is as tight as it's supposed to be or as loose as it's supposed to be; you want to make sure it's there and it's done right.

Oil Is Not Optional

One of the most important things you can do is pick the right type of oil to run in your project car. The oil that is produced for modern engines does not have the same stuff that it needs for the air-cooled engines. We use and recommend Lucas Oil that has additional zinc. You might also want to use Lucas break-in additive.

Change the oil every 3,000 miles and adjust the valves every time the oil is changed and you'll be fine. Beetles did not come with hydraulic lifters, which is not to say that your Beetle engine doesn't have hydraulic lifters in it because you can put just about anything anywhere. But as a rule, you are going to want to check the valve clearances every 3,000 miles and adjust as needed.

Keep the air filters clean and keep the oil topped off. It's a good idea to check the oil before starting the Volkswagen every day. If you don't start that Volkswagen every day, don't expect it to start after three weeks of sitting. Volkswagens don't run well if you don't run them. If not driven, it's best to start your Beetle, let it warm up, then shut it off until the next day. Just be sure to check the oil before starting the engine.

Whatever you do, don't run your Beetle low on oil. They are called air-cooled engines, but they're really oil cooled. If there isn't enough lubrication in the engine, then there isn't enough cooling going on. Anytime heat increases, wear increases; and when wear increases, so does the potential for failure.

Keeping the engine clean has its advantages. It is easier to see any leaks or if something is not quite right. Oil is a very important part of the system. Not only does it provide lubrication, it is also part of the cooling system, and there are only 2.5 quarts in your engine.

After the engine is off the engine stand, change the oil, adjust the valves, and install the refreshed powerplant.

Fan Belt

The fan belt is a critical part. It's smart to carry an extra fan belt under the backseat because sooner or later it is going to pop. When it does, all the air cooling and electrical will be lost. The battery will keep the headlights running for a little while, but when the battery goes dead, everything is dead.

Check the fan belt every day when checking the oil. To correctly adjust a fan belt, put the car neutral with the parking brake engaged, slide a crescent wrench on the nut that holds the pulley on the front of the alternator or generator that the fan belt goes around, and try to turn that alternator or generator pulley with the crescent wrench. Tension from the fan belt should turn the engine over if the engine is in neutral. If the car is in gear, the engine will not turn over.

If turning that alternator pulley does not turn the engine over, the fan belt needs to be tightened. It will probably require a couple of shims between the front and the back part of that pulley behind the nuts. Add shims if the belt is too tight; take shims away if the belt is too loose. When back together, turn it over by turning the nut on the alternator or the generator.

Fuel Line Safety

The German-style cloth braided fuel lines are not ethanol safe. Replace them with rubber-lined lines. Do not put the fuel filter in the engine compartment. Relocate it to behind the firewall by the heater boxes. We run one line up in front coming out of the gas tank and a second line in front of the engine compartment.

Keep Notes

A good little trick is to keep a notebook in the glove box. Every time the valves are adjusted, get that book out and write down the setting. Check to see what the setting was at the previous adjustment. If the number-2 exhaust was kind of tight last time, and this time the number-2 exhaust is kind of tight, then start saving some money because that number-2 exhaust stem is starting to stretch, and pretty soon it's going to fail. Repair it before it fails because after it fails, it shoots the valve through the top of the piston, fills the bottom of the engine with all kinds of little metal gunk, and you pretty much have to start all over again. ■

CHAPTER 11

THE ELECTRICAL SYSTEM

Oh, wiring woes. Most shops make the new guy learn how to do wiring and electrical gremlin chasing. Maybe it's because electricity is invisible, maybe it's the nearly impossible-to-decipher wiring diagrams, or maybe it's because it is nothing like the wiring in a house or other construction. Whatever the reasoning, this is almost everyone's least favorite part of the project.

Still, without electricity, a Beetle is nothing more than a very pretty hunk of vintage steel on wheels. There's good news and bad news here. The good news is that all you really need to install new wiring in a Beetle is the ability to read a wiring diagram. The not-so-good news is that these diagrams are challenging to read.

Wiring Harnesses

If wiring is such a pain in the neck, why mess with an upgrade? That's a logical question. It's a safety issue. Wiring degrades rather quickly over time. If a Beetle has been sitting outside, the sun's UV rays have been hard at work disintegrating the wiring. Rodents think wiring is about the tastiest snack there is. Matters get even more complicated if someone tried to fix the electrical system at any point. How wise would it be to trust your life to wiring that is decades old? How much wiser would it be to spend a few hundred dollars or so to get a brand-new wiring harness?

You could decide to build your wiring harness from scratch. Or you can buy a harness already built and coded to your Beetle's year and install it. It's no contest, especially when color-matched wiring harnesses are available from vendors. The only hitch with that option is that the

Care for some spaghetti? It looks like a mess, and it is a mess. Don't worry; we'll walk you through and get your electrical system squared away.

After 30-plus years and many thousands of heat cycles, the insulation on this wiring is probably worn out. Insulation gets brittle and can cause shorts or live jumps (arcs).

THE ELECTRICAL SYSTEM

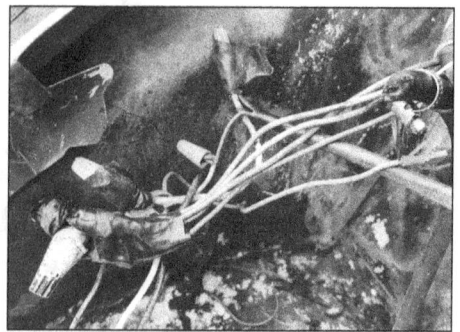

While this is not our idea of a fix, it was for someone. It might work, but it is not a safe electrical setup.

Many options exist for getting a new wiring harness. You can make your own, if you wish, and customize it to your needs. Or you can buy one that will work with your model.

Note the size differences between 6-volt and 12-volt flywheels and pressure plates. Depending on which one you have, you'll choose the starter appropriate for your project. This is important.

Electrical Tip

No doubt you've disconnected the battery already, but just in case you haven't, disconnect the battery. Identify wires that go to your fuse box. If wired wrong, it can burn the harness up or cause components to fail.

Wear eye protection. Things can fly when cutting, splicing, and soldering. And wire fragments hurt.

Soldering is hot. Set it somewhere safe and pay attention. Don't let wires fall over the soldering wire; they'll melt.

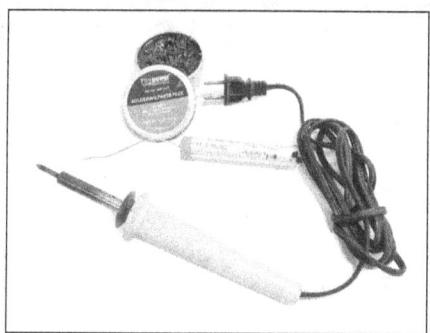

The soldering iron may become your new best friend. Be sure to get the correct flux for cleaning the connections before soldering.

Electrical continuity requires clean contact surfaces. Take your time. Clean up your fuse box, relays, and connector points.

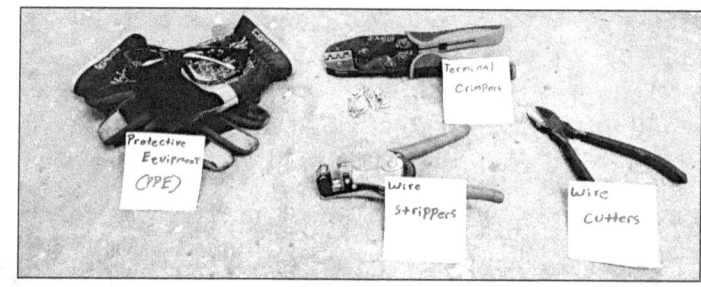

Here is a basic toolkit for running electrical. Each tool has its own uses, and you will need them all throughout your project.

color codes of the wires won't match the wiring diagram in the official service manual. That's because shops that build the custom harnesses typically don't have access to the enormous selection of wire spools that VW factories had. So while you won't get a wire-for-wire color match to the diagrams, you will get a basic schematic guide so you know what goes where.

Voltage

One detail to pay attention to as you buy a wiring harness is voltage. The options are 6-volt and 12-volt. They are not interchangeable. Consult an official Beetle service manual before ordering. With 6-volt wiring,

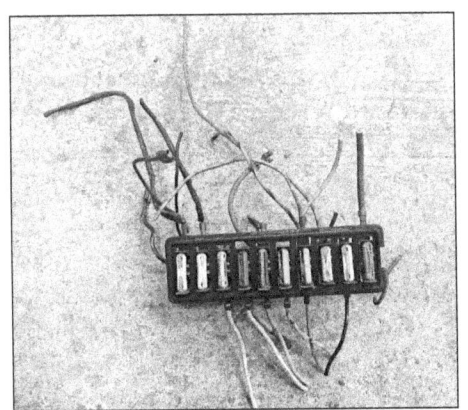

If reusing an old fuse block, it's a good idea to cut the wires with a few inches remaining. That will make identifying what goes where much easier. Take those photos!

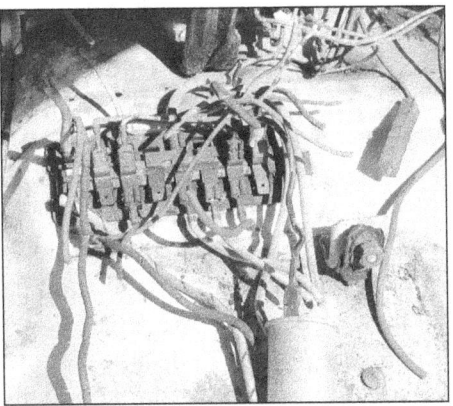

Take photos of an old harness before removing it. Cut it all out with wire cutters, leaving a couple of inches of wiring intact so you can see what went where.

Brand-new wiring harnesses are readily available, fairly easy to install, and will help a car's electrical system function like it did when it came from the factory. They're also rather inexpensive.

the wires are smaller and more brittle. The 12-volt wiring has a higher rating and allows more amps to go through it. If your Beetle is still running a 6-volt system, now would be a good time to upgrade to 12-volts.

Upgrading to 12-volts means upgrading the starter, flywheel, light bulbs, and gauges. Running 12 volts through a 6-volt gauge will fry it and may even start the Bug on fire. So if you do a 12-volt upgrade, upgrade all of your electrical components at the same time.

Wiring Harness Replacement

The wiring harness is the central nervous system for a car. It controls the lights, wipers, ignition, radio, turn signals, and anything else that can be turned on and off. Wiring harnesses are essentially individual wires loomed together as a bundle from their entry point to their exit point.

In the 1968 Beetle, the wiring harness ran along the driver's side from the trunk to the footwell, down the side of the doorsill to the back of the pan, then exited the pan into the engine bay. For later-year models, the harness may run up the package tray underneath the backseat and exit out the rear firewall. In earlier models, the harness started on the driver's side of the underdash, skirted the driver's side of the car, and ended in the engine bay.

The 50-year old wiring harnesses can be a nightmare. Age, neglect, and amateur rewiring is not only unsafe, it's also unsightly. It can cause glitches in the electrical system and increase the risk of a fire.

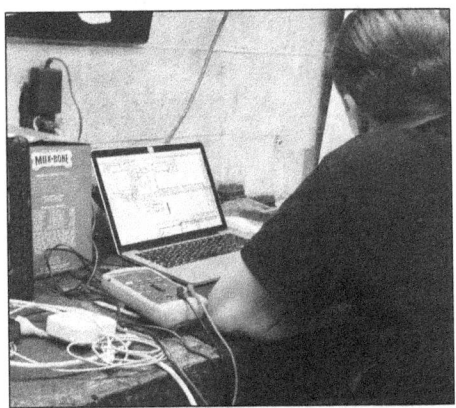

Don't be afraid of wiring. There are lots of resources online, including many hobbyist websites. You can find someone who's done what you're doing right now who can answer questions.

There are two harnesses for a Beetle: one for the rear and one for the front. The front controls the headlights, low- and high-beams, parking lights, turn signals, and horn. The rear controls everything else that runs on electricity.

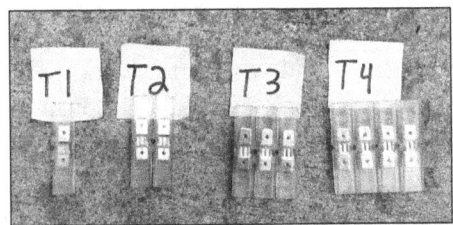

These are the four different T-connectors we use. They create junctions and jumpers within the system, and they are protected from the elements by their outside plastic coating.

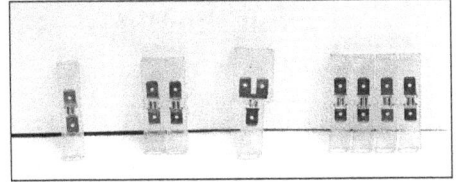

Save as many of the T-splices as possible. These are the plastic junction boxes with wires going in. T1 = 1 wire, T2 = 2 wires, and so on. These notations are also in the wiring diagram. The T-splices are quick disconnects featuring male and female ends.

THE ELECTRICAL SYSTEM

Period-correct replacement pieces are available. If you are looking for original equipment to restore, check with local VW shops or a VW graveyard.

Starting with the front may be the easiest way to go. Just read the diagram, then make the connections. Be glad you're not working on a Volkswagen bus, which is far more complicated.

If you get stuck, do some quick research online. There may be a video tutorial of someone installing or repairing the exact wiring task. Sometimes watching someone do it is a lot easier than trying to figure it out on your own.

Troubleshooting

When troubleshooting an electrical problem, 9 times out of 10 the issue is a loose or broken connection. The best way to chase electrical gremlins is by using a multimeter to check for continuity. For example, if a headlight is out, check the headlight itself first. If the headlight's bulb is not bad, unplug it and check to see whether there's an electrical signal from the plug. If there is no power at the plug, go back to the fuse panel to see whether there is power from the fuse that activates that particular circuit. Again, most problems originate from loose grounds.

The best way to go about troubleshooting is to be systematic and take notes as you track down what is causing the problem. Then start checking connections. Look for broken, damaged, or corroded wires. A good starting point is the headlight switch. The main power system starts there and branches out. Adjust the rheostat on the headlight switch. If it starts to smoke, make sure it's hooked up properly. There are documented cases where someone hooked the headlights to the rheostat where the dash lights should be. No wonder it didn't work.

During a gremlin hunt, just hope to never encounter the Magic Blue Genie (and yes, this is starting to sound like a game of Dungeons and Dragons). In the automotive world, this is a phenomenon you never want to see. After the Magic Blue Genie escapes, you will see a blue puff of smoke and your electronics won't work. It's a sure sign you shorted something out.

Weird Wiring Woes

Depending on the Beetle's year and service history, you may encounter some very strange wiring choices. In early models, the wiring for the brake light ran through the turn-signal switch. The ignition switch may be pulling double duty to run other components.

Also, depending on the year, the Beetle's fan switch may feature a basic three-pin system or a cannon plug system that runs other components. There were many more circuits built into later models, and they often piggyback from one component to the next, almost like daisy-chaining in a house. You may even encounter a situation where your right turn-signal control actually operates the left turn signal. That's a simple case of crossed wires.

Fuel-Injection System

Late model Bugs (1971 especially) came with crude fuel-injection systems called a D-Jet. Basically, they were junk. The system was temperamental and inefficient; if any connections were the slightest bit off, the car would run poorly. When it worked, it worked well. More often

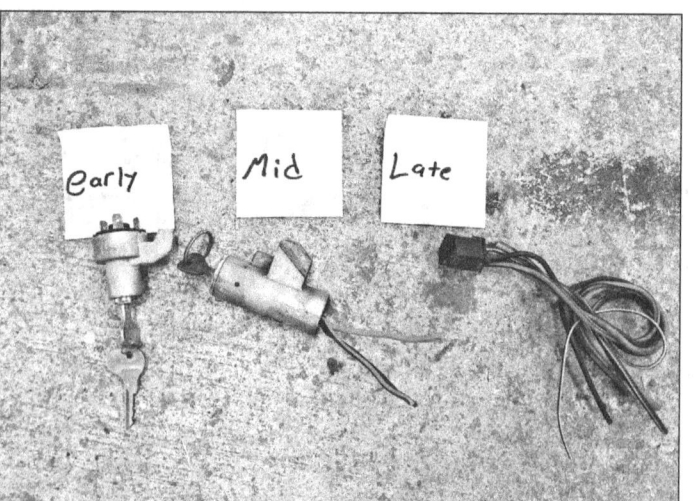

While all three of these ignition switches are the same part, they are very different and not interchangeable. Be careful to order correctly for your car's year.

HOW TO RESTORE YOUR VOLKSWAGEN BEETLE

Some Wiring Tips

There are a few things that can make wiring a little easier. They are:

Color wiring diagram: A colored wiring diagram will be a lot easier to work from than a black-and-white diagram. The black-and-whites include legends, providing a code for each wire. But with a colored diagram, you won't have to consult the legend constantly to figure out which of the black, white, or gray wires is supposed to be yellow.

Service manual: Be sure to get an official VW Beetle service manual. They can be found online. It's not a pleasurable read by any means, but there's no substitute in those times when you get truly stuck.

Simplified wiring: The simplicity of the Beetle's electrical system can be a stumbling block for hobbyists. If you've worked on a modern car's wiring, this one will seem primitive. It's easy to overcomplicate matters. Just keep that in mind.

Fuse block: Every Beetle came with a fuse block under the dashboard. To convert the fuse block to a spade fuse block, make sure to follow the wiring diagram closely and mimic the bridges as directed. Bridges are shown on the fuse-block diagram.

This VW factory fuse block might be old, but it will still function well if the contacts are cleaned. Looks like we need to clean these up now.

Document everything: We've mentioned it before, but it's impossible to take too many photos during disassembly. It is even more important with the wiring. It will be impossible to remember what goes where. Label everything, take photos, and you will be fine.

Opposite page: Here's a good example of a period, color-coded factory wiring diagram. This is much easier to use than the black-and-white version.

than not, it didn't work well at all. If you happen to have a fuel-injected Beetle that runs well, you can leave it as is; just upgrade your wiring harness and be on your way.

D-Jet was so bad that most owners tore it out at the first opportunity and switched back to a carburetor system instead. A carburetor system uses a basic wiring system. To illustrate, a fuel-injection system is represented with four pages of wiring diagrams. A carburetor system's wiring diagram fits on one page. Diagnosing issues with this simpler system is also much easier.

Converting from a fuel-injection system back to a carburetor system, will take a Beetle's electrical system from highly complex and rather unreliable to simple and more dependable. If replacing the wiring harness, you might as well make this improvement too.

The easiest way to know whether a Beetle has a fuel-injection system is to take a look. Does it have carburetors or throttle bodies? If it has throttle bodies, it's a fuel-injected system.

Even brand-new carburetors right out of the box need to be inspected and tuned to your car and atmospheric elevation. Look online or get a manual for your specific carburetor.

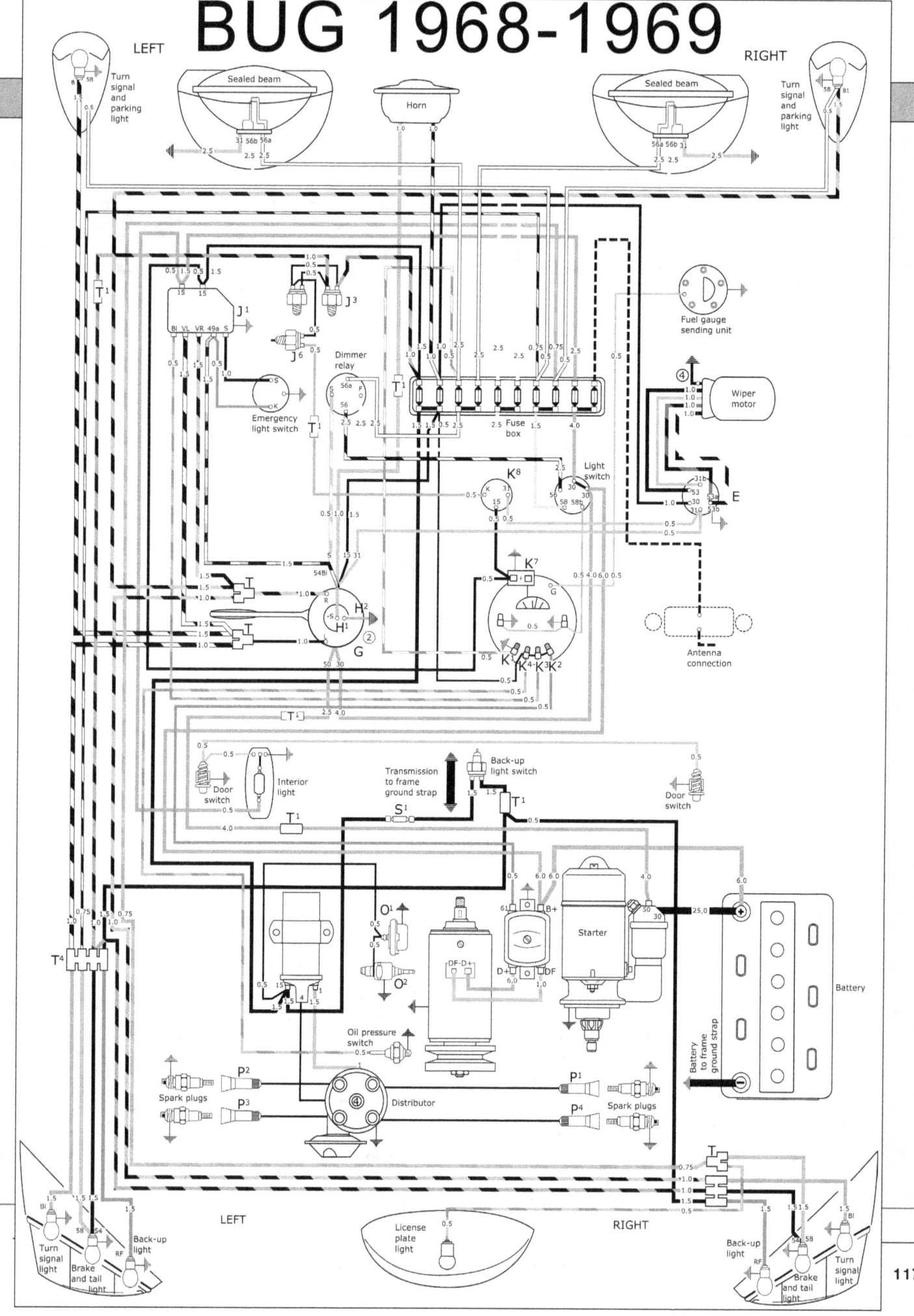

CHAPTER 12

Your Beetle's Interior

Other people see a vehicle's exterior the most, but what you'll see most is its interior. We've seen Bugs with new exteriors and old interiors. There's nothing wrong with driving around in your work in progress. But a complete restoration is a complete restoration: inside, outside, top, and bottom; it's all included.

As with the body and mechanical systems, there are some options when it comes to the interior. From the upholstery to the door cards, headliner, and handles, there is the option to make one from scratch, buy a custom option, or purchase from a VW parts house.

Make It

Those who are extremely experienced with upholstery and have access to a heavy-duty industrial sewing machine might want to do this part of the project themselves. Sewing a Beetle's interior is nowhere near as simple as patching a pair of pants or reattaching a button. The materials are expensive, unforgiving, difficult to sew, and can easily destroy a noncommercial sewing machine. Especially if installing a leather interior.

It's crucial to make sure you're up for the task. Leather hides are expensive, and there are no do-overs. Sew in the wrong spot, and you will have to look at those holes forever. Leather does not heal itself like fabric does. That said, if you have the equipment and experience necessary for crafting an interior, there's no better way to get a supremely customized result than doing it yourself. CarTech's book, *Automotive Upholstery & Interior Restoration* is a must-have to guide you through this task.

Buy and Bolt In

If sewing an interior is out of the question, as it is for most people, the other option is buying new upholstery and components. There are options here too. One option is to hire an automotive upholstery expert to create a completely custom interior. Another option is to purchase interior components that are ready to bolt in right out of the box. You can even buy bone-stock components from a VW parts house or interiors manufacturer.

Spend some time shopping around before you decide. If possible, see and touch the interior components before making your purchase. This is a great reason to go to a trade show if you can get in; you'll have the chance to touch and get an up-close eyeful before you buy.

Installing Sound Deadener

This material keeps down the road noise in the car and insulates the cabin. A package of sound-deadening material can be purchased through a

There are quite a few sound thermal insulations that are available at online retailers. We like using Noico or Rattle Trap. Just cut, peel, and stick it to the interior metal.

YOUR BEETLE'S INTERIOR

Tools Needed

- 1-inch and 2-inch binder clips (a case of each)
- Brand-new razor blades
- Contact cement or several cans of headliner glue
- Good fabric scissors (not utility scissors)
- Hair dryer (this is much safer and easier to use than a heat gun)
- Hog rings and hog-ring pliers (don't skimp out and buy a cheap set)
- Noico sound deadener (there are other kinds out there, but this is what we use at the shop)
- Roller tool
- Utility scissors

Safety

For this part of the restoration project, one of the most important safety measures is to make sure to work in a well-ventilated area. Contact cement will be used frequently, and it's not especially good to breathe its fumes.

Safety glasses are your friend too. You'll be working in odd positions, and you'd be surprised how many ways your eyes can get hurt if you don't protect them. Safety gloves will keep contact cement off of your hands. Finally, these are flammable components and chemicals, so keep open flames far, far away from your workspace.

VW parts house or local auto parts store. It's sticky on the back and shiny on the front. It will need to be cut to shape and then stuck onto the inside of the car's panels and body.

Choose a panel to work on first. Cut a piece of sound-deadening material to roughly the same size and shape as the panel. Peel off the backing. Stick the material to the panel with the shiny side facing out. Use a roller tool to smooth it into place. Using the surface as a cutting guide, trim the edges to make the material fit the panel.

Save Your Scraps

Keep your scraps as you go; you can use them on other projects as it won't be seen. Think of this part of your project like you're laying tile. Cut each section to fit as you go or to fill spots you may have missed.

Installing Sound Deadener

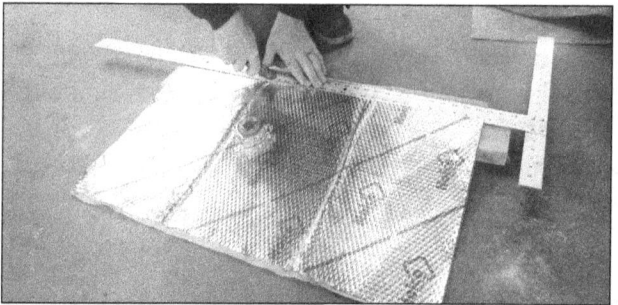

1 Use a fresh razor blade with a piece of wood behind it and a straightedge to make clean cuts as you trim the sound-deadening material to fit. You will go through a lot of razor blades in this step; they dull quickly.

2 The initial fit is a press fit with the backing removed. Guide your piece of sound-deadening material in place before tacking it down. Then, use your roller.

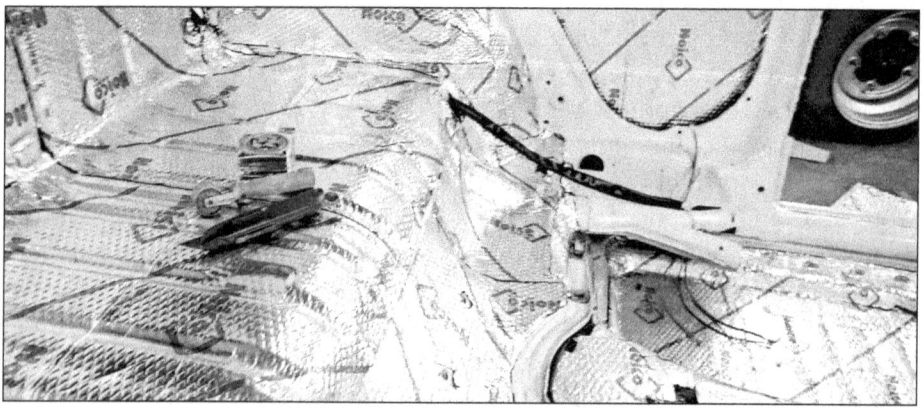

3 Try to cover any surfaces that will be covered by carpet, padding, or the headliner with sound-deadening material. This will help prevent noise and heat from infiltrating your cabin.

CHAPTER 12

Installing Headliner Padding

This step will give the headliner a smooth finish overall and especially on the edges. Most people use felt material here, and many use scraps leftover from assembling their seats. Headliner material can be purchased from online vendors, a VW parts house, or a local auto parts store. Note: If the windows have been installed already, they will need to be taken out for headliner padding installation.

It is very important to work in a well-ventilated area because of fumes from the contact cement.

Jute insulation is a nice product to work with. It will also provide a quieter ride and make the interior more comfortable.

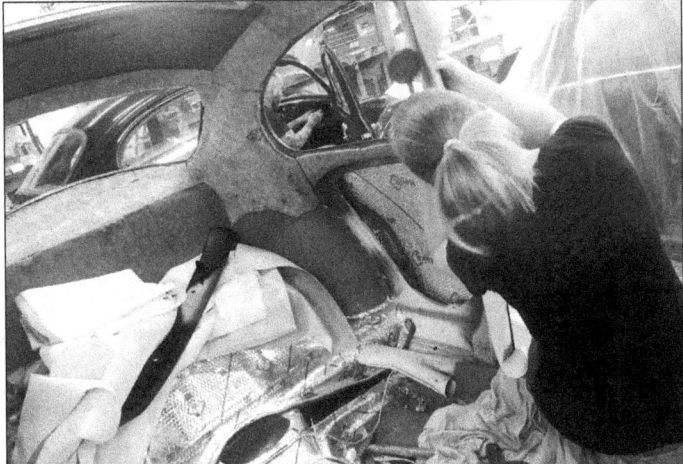

We like to increase the amount of padding that goes under the interior. As you can see, both B- and C-pillars have been covered, as well as under the carpet.

Tools Needed

- Contact cement
- Mason jar
- Paintbrush
- Sharp scissors

Hole Tips

Cut around the sun visor, rearview mirror, seat belts, and courtesy handle so those holes can be located later. Once the holes are cut, install the screws for those parts so that they can be found through the material. Feeling the holes without the screws is surprisingly difficult. Use a razor to cut a tiny hole in the headliner padding at the screw's location.

Pour a little bit of the contact cement into a mason jar and dip a paintbrush into the jar. This helps prevent cross-contamination and keeps your contact cement from drying out prematurely. ■

If using a whole piece of felt, it may be worthwhile to ask a buddy to help. One person will hold the felt in place. The other will cut it to fit the shape of your roof's interior. Then, glue it into place. If using scraps of felt, this job can probably be done on your own. Apply one piece at a time, patching it together like a jigsaw puzzle.

Installing Headliner

A headliner kit can be purchased from a Volkswagen parts house. Some Beetle owners decide to make their own headliners. It's not a horribly advanced sewing project to take on, but it's definitely a challenging one.

Most common headliner choices include velour and perforated vinyl. Velour is easier to work with, but perforated vinyl is more of a stock look.

If a headliner kit is purchased, it will come in a box and be mostly cut to shape already. However, it will likely be extremely creased. It will be easiest to work with if some of those creases are eliminated first. Ideally, this can be done by unfolding the headliner and lying it flat for a couple of days before working with it. That requires a lot of space, so if you can't lay it flat, at least drape it as gently as possible so the creases can fall out before starting installation.

There are six pieces on a headliner: two for the rear side windows, two for the B-pillars, the main headliner, and a piece that goes under the rear window. The bows that keep it in shape when it's installed should also be included in the box. Insert them into their casings, which vary in length.

Tools Needed	
• 1-inch and 2-inch binder clips (a case of each)	• Hair dryer or steamer
• Contact cement	• Headliner
• Disposable paintbrushes	• Mason jar
• Fabric scissors	• Putty knife
	• Sharp new razor blades

Installing the Headliner

1 The B-pillar is the first piece to install. Start at the top. There are metal tabs that run down the pillar to set into the groove. Once satisfied with the placement, close the tabs with a rubber mallet.

2 We have found that binder clips work well for headliner insulation. Purchase one box of small-size clips and one box of medium.

3 Stretch out the headliner and secure it to the window opening. Do not worry too much about the wrinkles at this point. The goal is to get the headliner in place, square to the car.

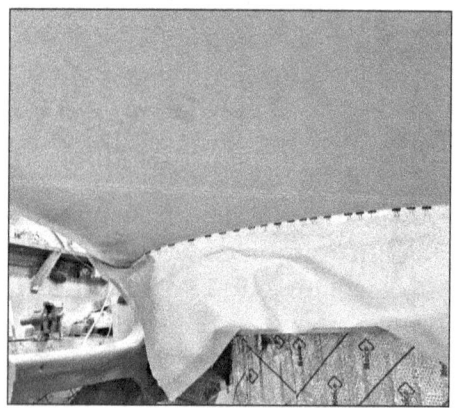

4 With some care and perseverance, keep stretching the material. Always work from the center out. Heat, pull, and clip. Repeat.

5 Once the headliner is looking like you want it, it is time to do some trimming. Just be careful not to cut too close.

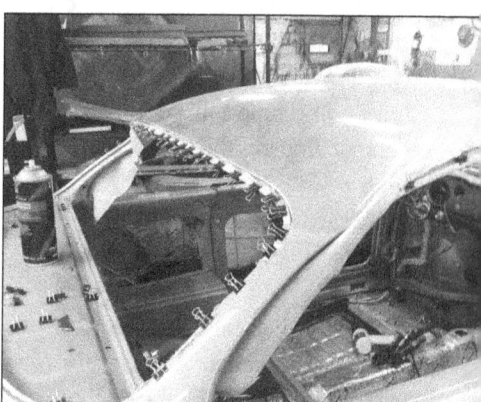

6 Starting in the rear window, trim only what is needed before gluing. Do not worry about the excess until everything is glued up.

CHAPTER 12

Installing the Headliner Continued

7 Start gluing once the headliner is in place and stretched out. Work in small sections, from the center out. We usually work back to front and then side to side.

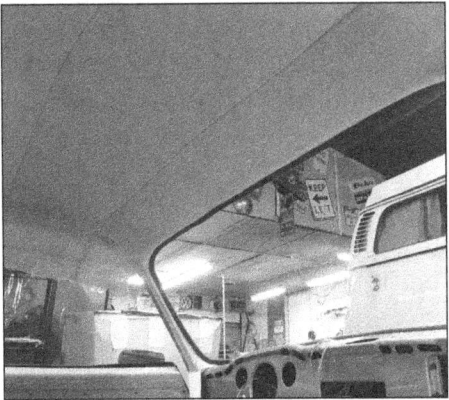

8 Let the glue set for 12 hours, until it's completely dry, then remove the clips. We will usually use an old piece of windlace to keep everything in place until the windows get set.

9 If any glue is on the headliner, now would be a good time to clean it up. Use a citrus-based cleaner because it won't stain the new headliner.

Plan your work first. We've found it's easiest to start with the B-pillars, then install the headliner by the rear window, then the main piece, and finally under the rear window. On the main piece, start at the back and work toward the front. Hold the headliner pieces in place with the clips.

Start in the middle and stretch the material out to the sides (rather than starting from one side and moving all the way across. As needed, pause to use a hair dryer to heat up the fabric. This will help get the remaining wrinkles out. As you stretch the material and hold it with the clips, trim away any excess fabric with scissors.

Repeat this stretching and clipping process twice more to make sure the headliner is smooth. Once all the wrinkles are smoothed out, start gluing. Peel back one small section at a time. Apply contact cement to both the headliner and the car surface, then put in place. Wait until the contact cement is dry enough to be tacky. Once the contact cement is tacky, apply the clips again to hold it in place as it dries completely.

Leave the installed headliner to dry overnight. Trim any excess material from the edges after the contact cement is completely dry the next day.

Emergency Brake Boot

Where the emergency brake sticks up into the driver's area, you'll want to install a little rubber boot. It doesn't really do anything other than sit there looking good, but it's a finishing touch you'll appreciate. They can be purchased through a Volkswagen parts supply house.

Installing Carpet

There's more carpet inside a Beetle than might be noticed at first

Installation of the emergency brake boot is simple. Lift up the emergency brake, slide the boot over the handle, then draw down around the mechanism. You'll want to adjust your emergency brake before installing the boot. This will make the adjustment process easier.

YOUR BEETLE'S INTERIOR

glance. Other than covering the entire floor, there's also carpet on the backside of the backseat and under the rear window. Purchase carpet as a kit from a VW parts supply house.

The key to installation without tears is working in the correct order. There are many types of carpet out there with varying quality levels. While the less-expensive carpets may look factory-correct, they are generally lighter weight and made from inferior materials. They don't fit quite right. Get a quality kit, even though it means spending a bit more. Quality carpet will last 15 to 20 years with normal use, while inexpensive carpet will only last 3 to 5 years because it will wear out much faster.

Tools Needed

- Chalk
- Contact cement
- Fabric scissors
- Mason jar
- Small paintbrush

New Carpet Installation

1 *When unboxing a carpet kit, lay the pieces out flat on the floor first. Be sure all pieces are included and also help ease the creases that happen during shipping.*

2 *Press and stretch the carpet by hand during the glue-down process. This will help remove wrinkles when covering curved surfaces.*

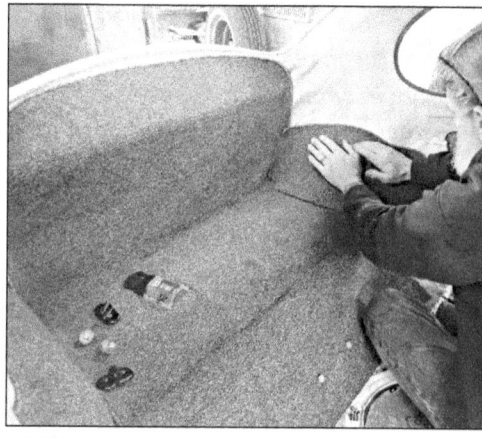

3 *The wheelwell carpet can be particularly tricky to install. Start at the center and work toward the outside in all directions.*

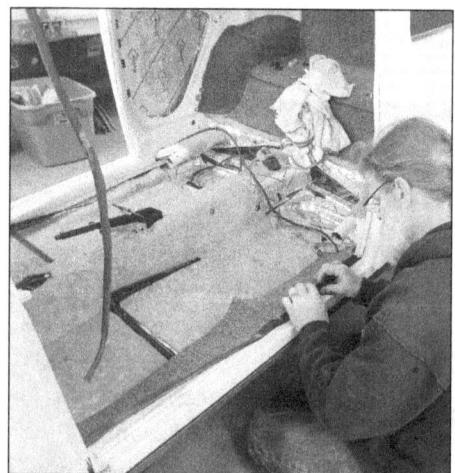

4 *In the 1968 and earlier models, there is a small retaining strip at the doorsill. The carpet edge tucks underneath it and gets smacked down with a rubber hammer.*

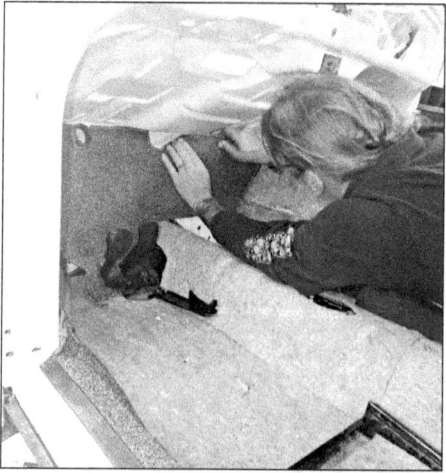

5 *When installing carpet on the front kick panel, start at the top right, then move to the driver's side. Finally, work your way down, smoothing the carpet as you go.*

6 *This piece of carpet is particularly challenging to work with because of the underlying shape. It's prone to wrinkles. To avoid them, set the top edge and B-pillar edge simultaneously and work toward the front of the car.*

New Carpet Installation *Continued*

7 Don't forget to cut small slits in the carpet for the seat belt attachment points. During the dry fit, install the bolts so they are easy to feel and cut those slits. Then, remove the bolts before gluing the carpet down.

8 In the carpet kit, there is a piece that goes onto the backseat. It's held in place with adhesive and an upper and lower retaining rail, attached with Phillips-head machine screws.

9 When installing the upper retaining rail on the backseat, line the existing screw holes up in the rail and the frame to make installation easier. The screws are stainless steel, so polish them before installing.

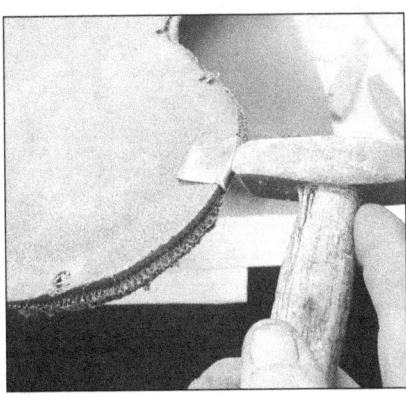

10 There are two aluminum strike plates on either side of the backseat carpet panel. Simply tap them in place and glue them down.

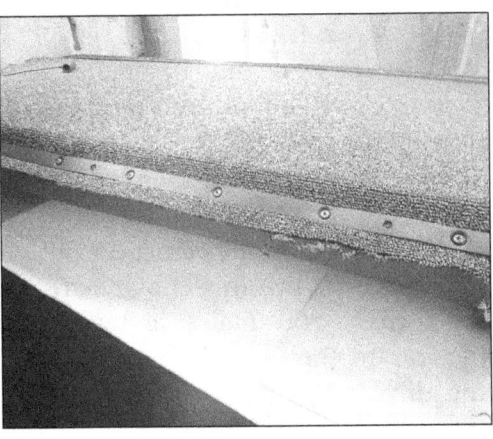

11 The lower retaining rail is attached the same way as the upper rail with the same stainless-steel screws. Line up the holes and you'll do it just right.

12 After the carpet goes in, there's still a lot of assembly that needs to happen inside the car. It's a good idea to use plastic carpet protectant. It can be found at a home improvement store.

Do a quick inventory to make sure everything is there and determine where each part will go. Then, determine the order of installation. Some pieces overlap, so it's important to install them in the right order, and the order can vary from one kit to another.

Install the piece of carpet that goes between the cargo area and the backseat. Then, install carpet in the wheelwells in the back. Next, install the carpet on the heater channels or doorsills, and then move over to the

YOUR BEETLE'S INTERIOR

firewall or kick panel up front where feet are placed.

The inner fenderwells come next. Working forward, start with the rear carpet that goes underneath the front seats and up over the hump. Cut holes for the heater controls, emergency brake, and seat belt mounts. Then, install carpet on the hump.

Work on the back of the backseat next. Make sure the lock for the rear upper seat is in the forward position, spring-tensioned to match.

After gluing and laying down the rear carpet on the backseat to the backer board, screw in the lower retaining plates. Attach the strike plates with a hammer and a set of Vise-Grips. The retaining plate has a total of eight Phillips-head machine screws that will hold the lower section of carpet to the bottom of the seat.

Finally, install the carpet on the floor itself. Do this in sections, starting at the back of the car and working toward the front, moving from the driver's side to the passenger's side.

Door Cards, Armrests, Door Handles, and Window Cranks

The door card pieces cover the door mechanism. They are typically made of cardboard or fiberboard. They can be purchased from an automotive interior supplier, or they can be made in a home shop.

The armrests, door handles, and window cranks are needed to operate the doors and windows. They can be found at a Volkswagen parts house.

Use cardboard to make a pattern of the door card. To do this, hold the cardboard up to the door card and use a pencil to poke holes in the cardboard. This way, you know where to

Carpet Tips

Work in sections, especially for bigger pieces. The carpet can get unwieldy otherwise. This is a wrestling match you need to win if you want your carpet to be installed correctly.

The carpet is likely to have cutting guides on the reverse side. If the carpet's rear side does not have cutting guides, you can use chalk. Simply rub the chalk on the car's interior where it will make sense to cut edges. Lay the carpet down, pile side up. The chalk will transfer to the back of the carpet. When lifted, the cutting guide that is accurate for your car will be chalked to the backing. ■

To keep the carpets clean as you work, use carpet-protecting film. It is available at most home supply stores.

If the old panels are salvageable, try to save them for patterns. Make a hard template out of a hard-plastic sheet. If there is only one panel, use it as a template for the others.

position the door clips. This is much better than trying to eyeball it while installing the door cards, handles, and cranks.

Once you have made new cards, install a thin sheet of foam, and glue and staple the material to the backside of the panel.

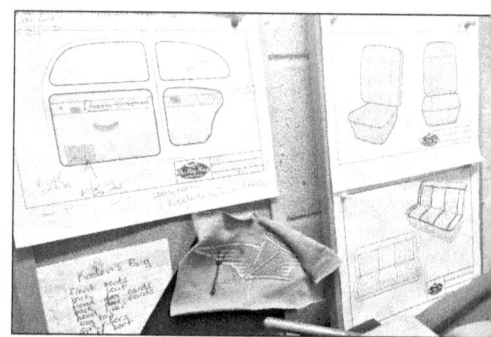

If you are planning to do a custom interior, it will help in the long run to sketch out what you want your car to look like. The sketch will serve as a guide as you go.

CHAPTER 12

Tools for Door Cards

- Armrests
- Buffer or escutcheon for door handles and cranks
- Cardboard to make door card patterns
- Clips
- Door cards (front and back)
- Door handles
- Door panel clips and grommets
- Masking tape
- Moisture barrier (helps prevent moisture from coming inside the vehicle, and it prevents mold and mildew growth)
- Needle-nose pliers
- Razor blade
- Rubber hammer
- Window cranks

Door Card Installation

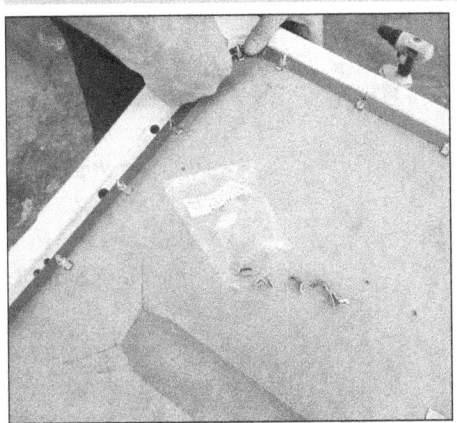

1 Purchase new clips from a local Volkswagen parts store. We prefer to use the original clips because they tend to give us fewer problems during installation.

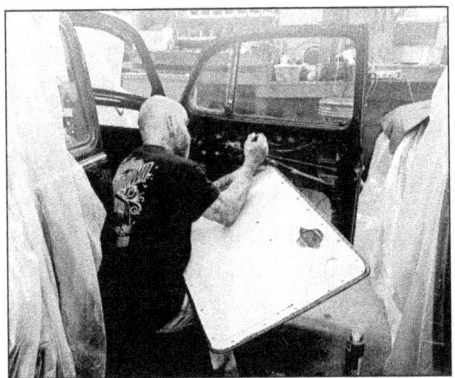

2 Using a pair of needle-nose pliers and a small flat-tipped screwdriver will make the installation of the door card clips a lot easier. Note: The window crank hole is not cut out yet. Do not cut a big hole. Once the panel is in place, make a small X cut at the correct location for the winder stem.

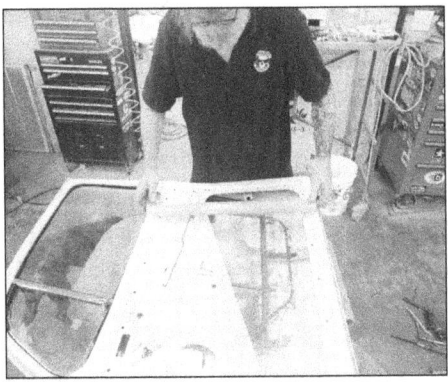

3 It is no longer needed to glue a piece of plastic in place for a vapor barrier similar to what they did back at the Volkswagen factory. Instead, purchase a roll of temporary carpet protector from a local home improvement store. One side is sticky, so it works great as a vapor barrier.

4 Use a brand-new razor blade to trim the vapor barrier to just inside the recess that the door card fits into. Make sure to leave a minimum of 5 mm outside the attachment point.

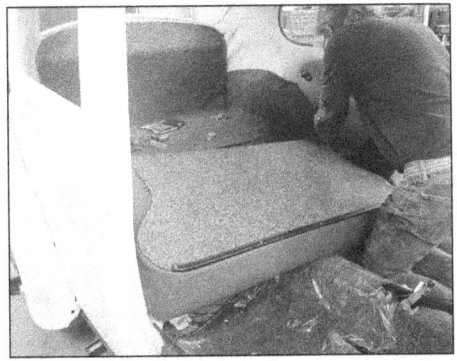

5 The lever catch is on the driver's side. It is spring-loaded and should work easily. When raised, it should click into place; when the catch is released, the seat should move easily without binding.

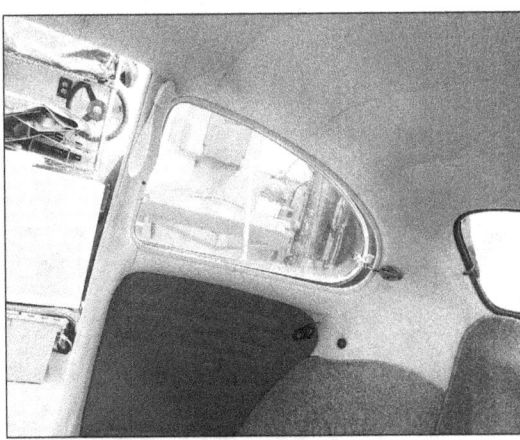

6 In this picture, the client specified pop-out windows. A matching-color windlace is installed on the pinch weld to give it a nice, clean fit and finish.

YOUR BEETLE'S INTERIOR

Protect Your Paint

Take the time to mask off the edges. This will help protect the paint from scratches as you work. ■

Mask off the edges to protect the paint. Most likely at this stage the Beetle has fresh paint and you wouldn't want to accidentally scrape a clip across top of the door.

Apply the clips to the door card using the needle-nose pliers. Guide the clips into the holes. Some builders prefer to start at the bottom of the door and then go up both sides and across the top. Others prefer to start from the top, so the door card will stay in place, making it easier to move around the sides because the door card isn't trying to fold over on itself. Adhere the moisture barrier to the edges of the door.

The window cranks should have been cleaned up and any rust residue removed. Now, it's time to put them back on the door. For stock window cranks, there's a screw in the center of the base. For aftermarket cranks, the fastening mechanism varies. Do the same for the back. Make a pattern, install the clips, then install the door card.

Lastly, install the backseat lever catch. The headliner, carpet, and door cards are now installed.

Interior Items

Now we'll turn our attention to the shifter, seat belts, courtesy handles, rear kick panels, visor, and rearview mirror. We'll be installing everything on the inside of the Beetle that is needed to bring the project nearly to completion. Some are necessary for getting the car mobile, and some are more about comfort. Volkswagens have a rather basic interior in contrast to modern cars.

Shifter

A shifter can be restored and reinstalled, or you can purchase a stock or aftermarket shifter from a VW parts house. Some Beetle owners get really creative with their shifter choices; we've seen everything from golf clubs to shotguns modified to work as a shifter.

A shifter boot will also be installed. The shifter and boot usually come as one unit. The range of choices is wide.

Tools Needed

- 13-mm wrench
- Flat-head screwdriver
- Shifter
- Shifter boot

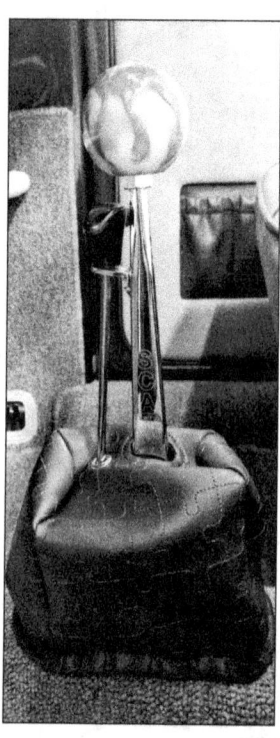

If running an aftermarket shifter, such as this SCAT short throw, it needs to have a boot to keep the interior looking sharp and the shifter mechanism working well for a long time by keeping dirt out of it.

Installing the Shifter

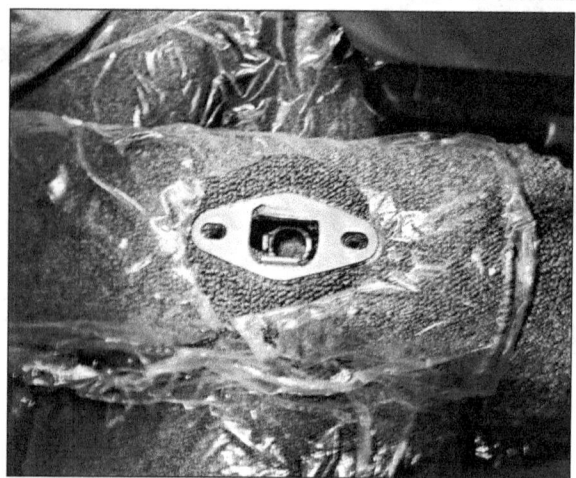

1 A stock Volkswagen shifter has a reverse lockout plate that must be installed with the machined edge up and toward the passenger's side. If this is mixed up, the car won't go in reverse.

2 Here is a semi-exploded view of a stock shifter configuration. Note all surfaces are cleaned, painted, and regreased.

Installing the Shifter Continued

3 When installing the shifter, the retaining spring needs to fit big-side down and little-side up. This is crucial in being able to engage reverse.

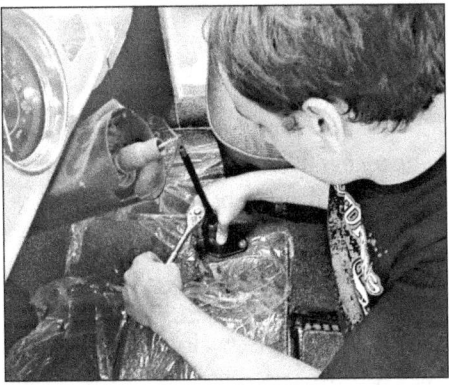

4 Try to engage the shifter in first gear when doing the primary installation. This will help with adjustments later.

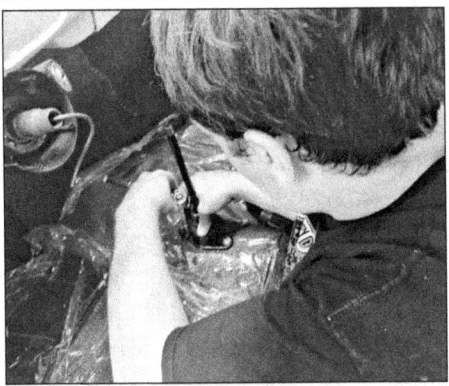

5 After doing an initial installation, some adjustments will be needed to engage all gears. This is done by loosening the two 13-mm retaining bolts, making adjustments, tightening down, and testing it again. Adjust until all gears can be engaged smoothly.

Make sure your car is in neutral, and chock the wheels or set the emergency brake.

Install the shifter base plate assembly. Ensure that the sloped side is on the passenger's side of the vehicle. The top of the slope should go toward the front with the lower part sloping toward the rear. Make sure the shifter spring is on the shifter. Grease the ball that goes into the shift rod so it won't bind. The shift should be smooth and easy. Install the shifter ball into the shift rod coupler and then hand tighten the shifter.

Put the vehicle into reverse and lock it down. Test drive it to make sure it's shifting properly. Adjust the shifter to your liking by adjusting the shifter baseplate to the left.

Seat Belts

Would you trust webbing that's half a century old to save your life? Of course not! No matter how dedicated you may be to the idea of building a restoration that puts a tear in the eye of any purist, don't reuse old seat belts. Get new ones, and what you might lose in authenticity, you will most definitely gain should you have an unfortunate lesson in physics at some point.

Purchase new seat belts from a Volkswagen parts house. Do not try to make them yourself.

Inventory all of the new parts. There is a left side and a right side. Lay them out on each side of the car.

Install the retractor base first. It will be easier with the seats out. Install the bolts in good and tight; you don't want them to come loose. Use red or blue Loctite to ensure they do not come loose. Refer to your Volkswagen's maintenance manual for proper torque specifications.

Courtesy Handles

These are the loops that go on the B-pillars. Other than hanging dry cleaning on them, there's actually a reason that car manufacturers built them into the car's interior. Theoretically, they're for holding on to if the ride gets a little rocky or the driver takes a corner fast enough to make passengers lose their balance. However, they also make a good nonverbal communication option for passengers who'd like the driver to slow down a

Brand-new replacement seat belts are available for most VW models. Volkswagen started putting in anchor points for the Beetle with the 1965 model year but did not start installing three-point harnesses until 1968. In 1967, the lap belt became standard equipment. The first seat belts offered as a dealer option for VW were manufactured by General Motors. This is one reason all seat belt bolts are SAE, not metric.

bit. A simple grab for the loop may be all it takes to remind a driver that he or she is not, in fact, participating in an off-road rally race.

Be careful not to damage the headliner, and be careful using Loctite; it will stain fabric.

Using a #2 Phillips screwdriver, locate the mounting holes where the screws attach the handle to the B-pillar. Use Loctite on the threads of the screw and tighten firmly. Next, attach the handle and plastic cover.

Rear Kick Panels

These are installed with the heater port, usually as one assembly. Loosen or remove the rear seat's lower support frame to complete this installation if needed. Be patient. Losing your cool feels good in the moment, but one thrown wrench can do a surprising amount of damage.

Loosen the backseat's lower seat frame, then slide the panels into the kick panel channels. Make sure the heater vents line up with the heater holes in the kick panels. Tighten the lower seat frame using a 10-mm wrench or socket.

Visors

Of course you'll drive your Beetle while wearing cool shades. But it doesn't hurt to also have sun visors installed. You can either buy them new from a Volkswagen parts house or refurbish the old ones and reinstall them.

Be very careful not to damage the headliner. Use a #2 Phillips screwdriver to locate the sun visor holes through your headliner by prodding. Once they are found, hold the visor in place against the headliner. Double-check that the holes are lined up on the backside of the headliner and the hold for the visor bracket.

> **Bolt Tightening**
>
> Be careful not to tighten the fasteners too tightly. They can break rather easily.
>
> Be super careful with the headliner. It's easy to damage and heartbreaking to have to reinstall.

Use a razor blade and make a slight incision where the holes are on the roof for the visor holes. Install the two Phillips screws, pushing them through the slits in the headliner.

Rearview Mirror

Beetle owners joke about their lack of horsepower if they have a stock engine. Unless you're running a racing engine, you'll probably see a whole lot of vehicles passing you. With a rearview mirror, at least you can see them coming in hot behind you and veering into the other lane to pass. You can buy a rearview mirror from a VW parts house.

Check local laws before deciding not to install a rearview mirror. Some areas require them.

In early models, if holes were not cut for a rearview mirror when the headliner was installed, a razor blade, the rearview mirror, and a #2 Phillips screwdriver will be needed.

In later models, the header on top of the windshield has a keyed slot for the rearview mirror. Find this spot, and make sure there is a slit for installation. The mirror is installed by inserting it into the slot and turning it clockwise roughly a quarter turn.

Seats

When it comes to the Beetle's seats, there are many choices. There's the style, color, and perhaps even a pattern. You can also choose more or less ergonomic designs, and even seats that were built for completely different makes and models of automobiles.

There is also an important decision to make about whether to restore the old seats or simply purchase new ones. Seats can be found from a Volkswagen parts house or online automotive retailer. To install new seats, bolt them in.

If restoring old seats, they will need to be stripped down first. Then, send them out to blast. Repair any broken springs by welding them back into shape. Spray the frame with spray paint to protect it from rust. Then, wrap the frame with heavy felt to prevent the springs from popping through the padding and upholstery. Finally, add foam cushioning and seat covers.

After the seat frames have been cleaned, blasted, and repainted, it's time to recover them. Attach the jute to the seat frames with a hog ring. The jute is a protective layer that sits between the foam and the springs. Put the foam on top of the jute. Wrap the foam with packing wrap or plastic wrap.

Replace the cloth hold-down on the new covers with baling wire. Slip

Once the cover is removed, what you find will most likely be nasty, old, and smelly. This is where your old car smell comes from.

CHAPTER 12

Seat Recovering

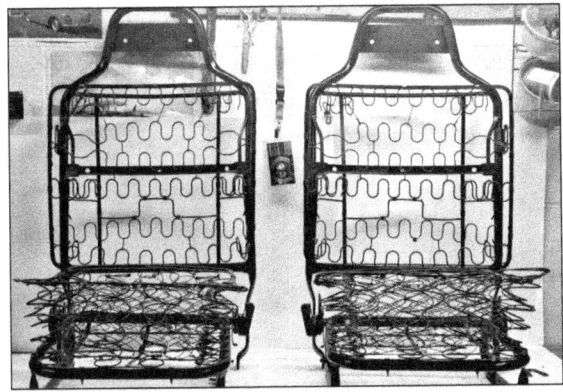

1 Here is a set of front seats ready to build. After we blast, we paint the frames to protect them from rust. Save the headrests if you can; as of the writing of this book, they are not currently readily available from any supplier.

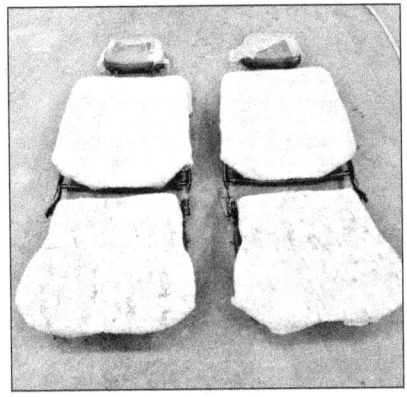

2 We suggest attaching a jute pad to each frame before you install the foam. It will help make the interior nice and comfortable. Originally, this step was done with burlap.

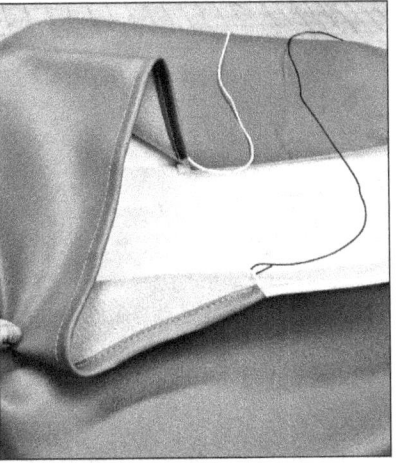

3 The original VW seat had a retaining wire in certain areas. The recovering replacement off-the-shelf seat covers have a cloth hold-down. Replace it with a length of baling wire. Your hog rings will thank you.

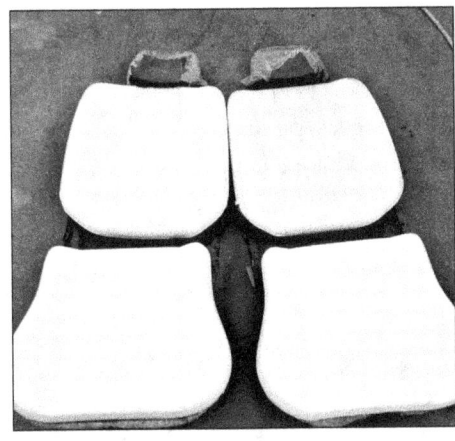

4 Once the foam (available at most VW parts houses) is installed, wrap a layer of plastic around it. If you don't have access to packing wrap, you can use kitchen plastic wrap.

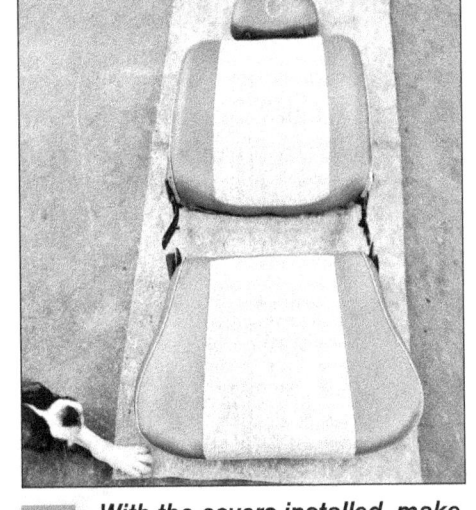

5 With the covers installed, make sure that the lines are straight before hog ringing the covers. A bit of hot air from a hair dryer will help to get the covers just right.

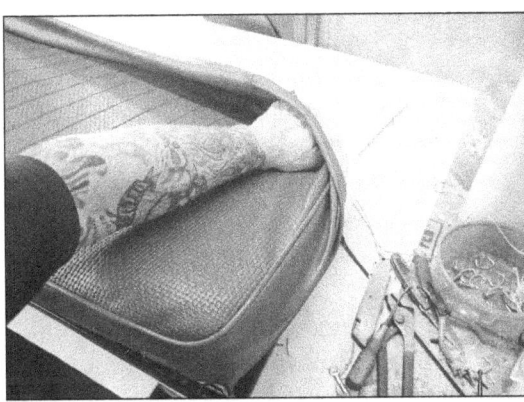

6 The easiest way to loosen the covers to make installation smoother is to set them out in the sun for a few hours first. If it's not sunny, just put them in a warm environment.

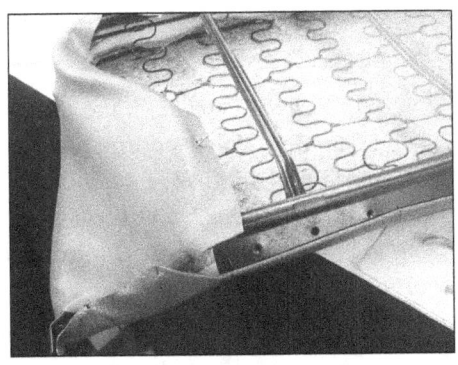

7 Do a preliminary fit with the cover. There is piping along the top and side edges, and they need to be lined up correctly. Adjust as needed.

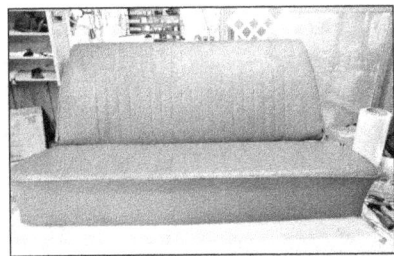

8 Here's a fully assembled lower and upper backseat for a 1968 Beetle. Note how the piping and 90-degree edges are crisp and straight, and the cover is tight.

YOUR BEETLE'S INTERIOR

Seat Cover Install

Use a length of plastic wrap to compress the seat's foam. This will help hold the foam in place and also helps the seat cover slide over the seat more easily.

Recruit a buddy to help. They get the easy part: standing on the back side of the seat frame to compress the cushion. This will allow you to pull the material tight. ■

the new covers on, starting in the front and working toward the back. Make sure the lines line up and your seams are where they should be, then start pulling the seat cover down onto the lower frame.

Flip the seat base over. Starting at the front, pull the hem up and around the lower frame, attaching it to the spikes. Hammer the tabs down so the edges are flat.

Now that your cover is on the seat, simply reassemble the seat. Apply a thin layer of grease on the seat rails and the track. Slide the seat into place.

Complete the Trunk

There are many options to spruce up the trunk area. One option is to go with a stock look and order the original-style cardboard cover. Or go all out and buy a carpet kit. It's all up to you. One suggestion we make to our clients is a wire cover. This is used to cover all the wires that are coming in from your fuse-block area.

Installing the Dash Pad

The process of installing a Beetle dash pad is completely different for a Standard Beetle versus a Super Beetle. Most Standards have a dash pad. Most Supers have an integrated dash pad and board. Earlier Standard models feature plain steel dashes. Most likely, you're going to need to replace your dash pad. They are year-specific, so be sure to order exactly what you need from a VW parts house.

Since this book focuses on a 1968 Euro Beetle project car, there is no dash pad. It is painted steel. But if you have a US 1968 or later, you will be installing a dash pad. Restoration is not typically an option because the pad is made of closed-cell foam covered with integrated vinyl, and this combination will probably be too cracked from age and UV exposure to bother with restoring.

The only oddity you're likely to encounter is that the replacement dash pad will have plastic retaining nuts instead of the metal ones you'd expect to see. This is not unique to replacement components; the Volkswagen factory used plastic here as well.

Install the glove box next. Reinstall the glove box hinges first. Then, install the glove box door using two Phillips-head screws per side. Check fit and alignment, making adjustments as needed.

Then, install the grab bar. It bolts into the dash from the interior compartment. You'll need to reach the bolts from inside the trunk.

Next, go to the driver's side to install the grilles on either side of the speedometer. Use a knife to cut the

Tools Needed

- Ashtray
- Cigarette lighter
- Emergency flasher
- Flat-head screwdriver
- Glove box
- Grab bar
- Grilles
- Headlights
- Knobs
- Pliers
- Radio
- Socket set
- Speedometer
- Utility knife
- Vents for ductwork
- Wipers

Dashboard

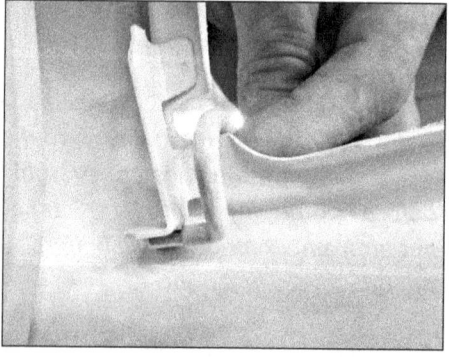

1 *Hinges for the glove box are surprisingly simple to work with. There is a metal loop with a machine pin that goes into it. A little bit of grease will lubricate the joint.*

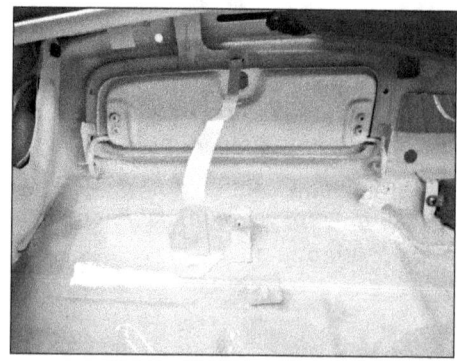

2 *The easiest way to make the final adjustment for the glove box and to make the lines even is to hand-tighten all four hinge screws from inside the trunk area. Check your work from the inside of the car. Once you like it, lock the screws down.*

Dashboard Continued

3 The grab bar was added by interior designers in the mid-1960s to make it easy for passengers to get in and out of the vehicle. Nervous passengers like to grab hold of them as a means of backseat driving.

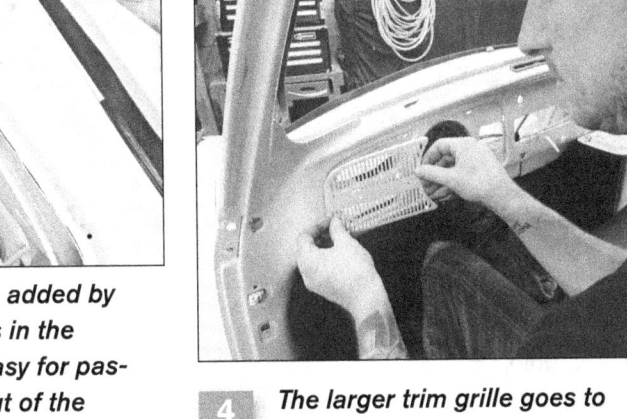

4 The larger trim grille goes to the left of the speedometer opening. Some models have a chrome trim piece going down the center of the grille.

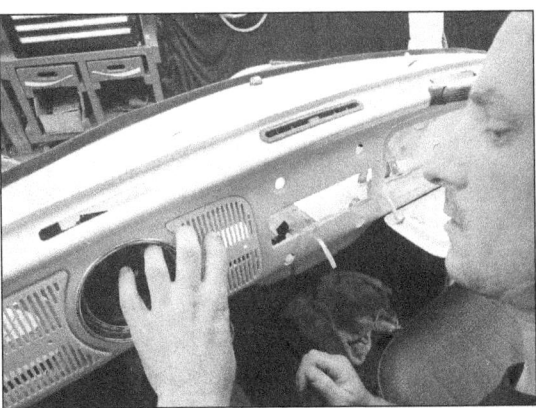

5 Once the grille is set in place, the four metal tabs will need to be bent over in the back of the dash to keep it in place. Put a little seam sealer on each tab to help keep air from coming up out of the dash.

6 When reinstalling the speedometer, it pays to have it completely rebuilt by a professional, showing zero miles. After all, your brand-new old car now has zero miles on it too.

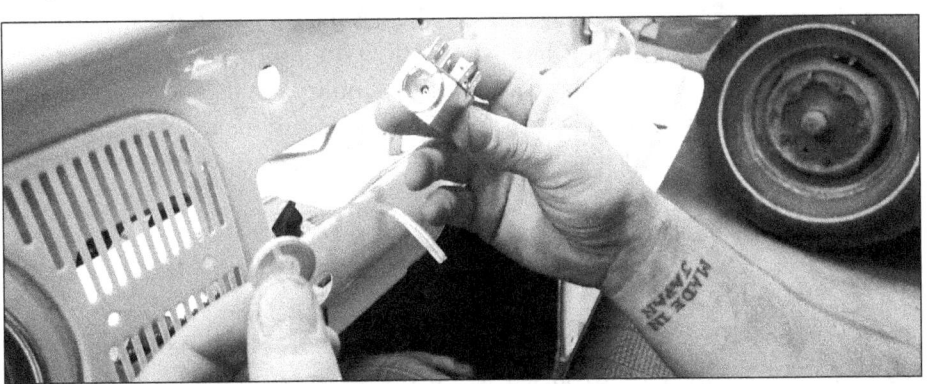

7 Line the switch up from the back using the finished trim ring. It doubles as a locking mechanism to attach the switch to the trim ring.

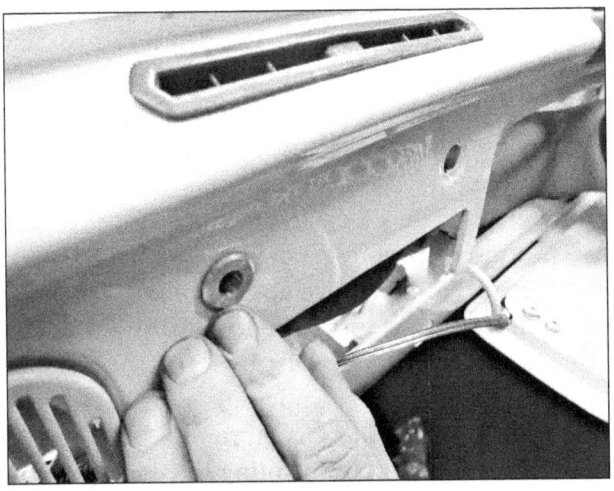

8 There are two indentations in the trim ring. They're for tightening. There is a special tool you can buy to do this, but a large screwdriver will work just fine.

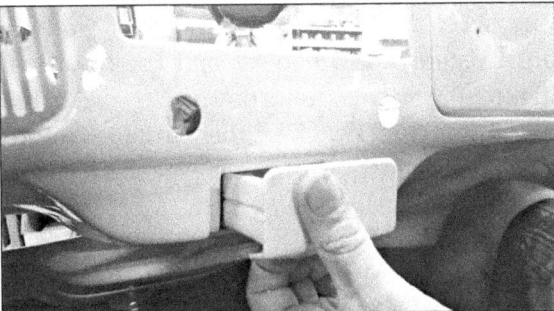

9 The ashtray lines up in the groove and is held in by a spring-tensioned set of wheels on either side of the ashtray housing. In this model, it is a two-piece unit with the face-cover painted to match the dash.

10 The dash can be cut to fit an aftermarket radio, or the original radio can be restored. In this project car, we are using a made-to-fit modular radio with Bluetooth.

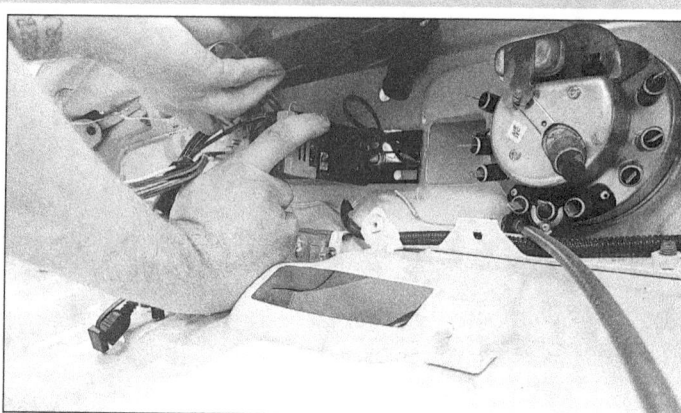

11 Installing radios isn't a difficult task. Just make sure the front faceplate is secured and the rear is supported by its ground strap.

Steering Wheel Alignment

Take a test drive to make sure the steering wheel is straight. While driving straight, the steering wheel should also be straight. If it is off-center, take the steering wheel off and readjust it.

Tools Needed

- 2 10-mm wrenches
- Flat-head screwdriver
- Hammer
- Needle-nose pliers

slots in. They have a metal tab that slides in. Twist the tabs to lock the grilles into place. Install the chrome trim ring in the speedometer opening. Install the speedometer from under the hood by sliding the speedometer in, twisting until it locks, and then tightening its two screws down.

Install the switches, then install the headlights, wipers, emergency flasher, and cigarette lighter. Most likely, there are already holes in the dashboard for these components. Use an escutcheon tool and work with a buddy. One of you will hold the component from inside the trunk area and line it up. The other will tighten it from inside the car. Install the knobs on the switches. Slide the ashtray in.

Install the radio last. Some dashes have a hole for the radio already. With others, the hole will have to be cut. The dashboard may have an embossed outline to follow as a guide. Use a sharp utility knife and work slowly. Test the fit and make small cuts as you go. Install the radio from the inside of the car.

Steering Wheel Installation

There are many options when it's time to choose a steering wheel: refurbish and reuse the one that came in the Beetle, order a stock or aftermarket steering wheel, or even use one from an entirely different make and model of car. Popular options include Bakelite, leather-wrapped, or wood steering wheels.

Make sure the Beetle's front wheels are absolutely straight. The new steering wheel should just slide on. Attach the horn ring next. The safety washer goes on first. The nut goes on next. Tighten it all down. Plug the horn wire into the horn button. The horn button should snap into place.

If using an aftermarket steering wheel, there may be extra pieces and adapters. Follow the manufacturer's instructions in this case.

Emergency Brake

When you need to stop, you really need to stop. Should the brakes ever fail, or if parked on a slope, you'll be glad an emergency brake was installed. You can refurbish and reuse the one that came with your car, or you can purchase new from a Volkswagen parts house.

Chock the wheels before starting. Use a jack and jack stands for testing the emergency brake.

Remove at least one of the front seats so there is room to work. The emergency brake can be installed without removing a seat, but it's easier if there is more room. Make sure the rod and spring are in the handle

CHAPTER 12

Emergency Brake Reinstallation

1 From the factory, VW emergency brakes were painted black. Another option is to custom match yours to go with your interior or exterior.

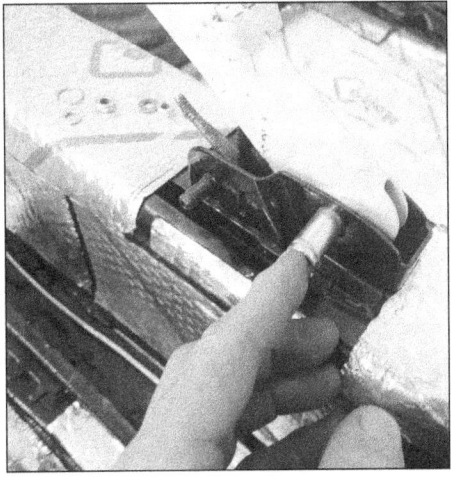

2 A little dab of grease on the emergency brake pin helps ease installation. Make sure the cables are not tight when doing this. Put one C-clip on the side you're pushing.

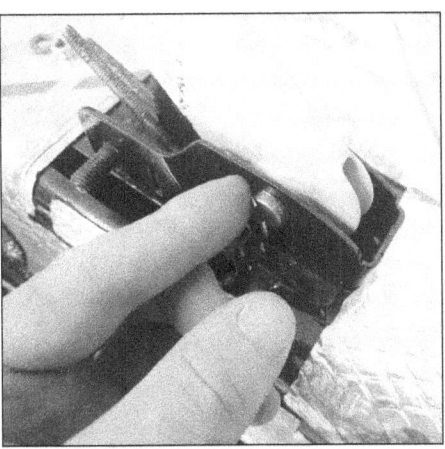

3 Once the pin is pushed all the way home, double-check the C-clips to make sure they are in the groove on both sides. There is a left side and a right side.

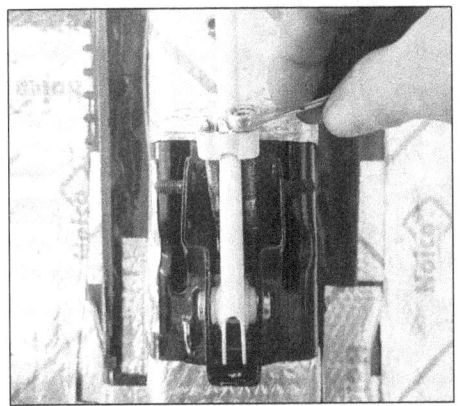

4 Route the cables through their guides on the emergency brake handle (bottom). Tighten the cables until they have fully locked up at three to five clicks.

5 Here's how the emergency brake is supposed to look after installation before adding the boot. Double-check the cable routing, retaining clip placement, and lubrication, and make adjustments as necessary.

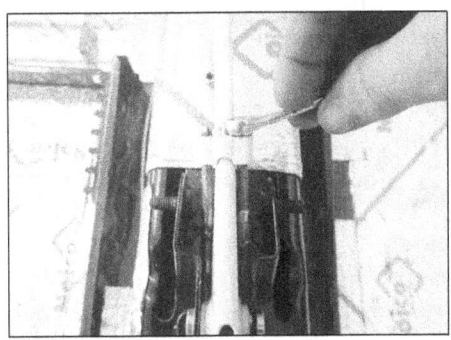

6 Final adjustments on the emergency brake cable are made by the re-tensioning nut on either side of the brake. Left is left; right is right.

and that they function as they're supposed to; they should engage the gears properly.

Pull the cables up through the tunnel. Make sure the cables are under the bottom side of the handle, in the guides. There are two cables, one for each side. Loosely put the jam nuts through the stops. Slide the handle assembly back into position. Push the large pin that goes through the handle.

There's a C-clip for each side of the pin to keep it in place. Use pliers and a screwdriver to snap the C-clips into place. Pull the cables through each side of the handle. There's a place for them.

There is one 10-mm nut on each side. Tighten those down until there are three to five clicks when the handle is pulled up. Tighten more than that and the whole apparatus will come loose and you will have to start it again. Once adjusted, work on the second 10-mm nut on each side.

Then, tighten the two nuts together so they don't work themselves out of adjustment. If there are not enough clicks, loosen it up. Jack the car up to make sure the emergency brake functions properly. The wheels should not turn when it's pulled up but should turn freely when it is released.

CHAPTER 13

TRIM AND FINISH

A Beetle restoration is not complete until all of the shiny, glassy, and plastic bits are installed. Purists will insist on refurbishing these parts and putting them back on, no matter how hopelessly worn out they look, even restored. For the rest of us, the better option is to buy new parts from a Volkswagen parts house or another aftermarket vendor.

Refurbishing Recommendations

You might decide to refurbish if you're a purist or if your wallet just can't take any more of the strenuous exercise it's had during this project. Here are our recommendations on refurbishing chrome, glass, plastic, and rubber pieces, parts, and trim.

Chrome

Get a bottle of metal polish from the local auto parts store. Or go old school with a buffing wheel and polishing compound (can be found online). If the chrome has deep dents and scratches, hammer them out then sand the same way you sanded your car body. It's tedious.

Underneath the chrome, there is chrome, nickel, aluminum, stainless steel, or pot metal (a bunch of metals melted together in a mold, then cleaned and chromed). Re-chroming is a very costly process. Most chrome bits for a Beetle are readily available for sale, or stainless steel versions can be ordered.

Original brightwork will take a beating over the years. But it is possible to bring shine back on most OEM parts.

Stainless steel bumpers are a great alternative to aftermarket chrome. We have found that a few companies make very high-quality parts. Do your homework before buying.

Buffing Safety

When using a buffing wheel, be sure to tie loose hair back (if applicable), don't wear loose-fitting clothing, and skip the jewelry. You don't want anything getting caught in the buffer. Also, be sure to wear gloves. The metal gets hot! Don't forget safety glasses, because nothing hurts quite like getting debris in the eye. ■

HOW TO RESTORE YOUR VOLKSWAGEN BEETLE

CHAPTER 13

Tools Needed

- All-purpose cleaner
- Buffer
- Clean rags
- Polish
- Sandpaper in various grits

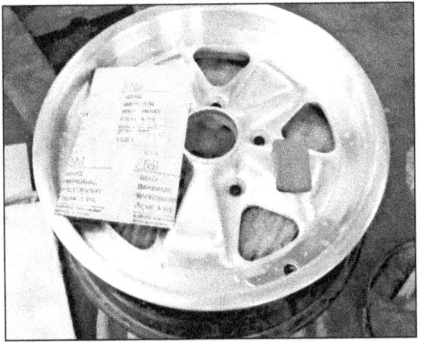

Polished aluminum is always a good look. Deeper scratches will require more time to remove. Remember, you are removing material and then refining the scratches until they can no longer be seen.

Using the Buffing Wheel

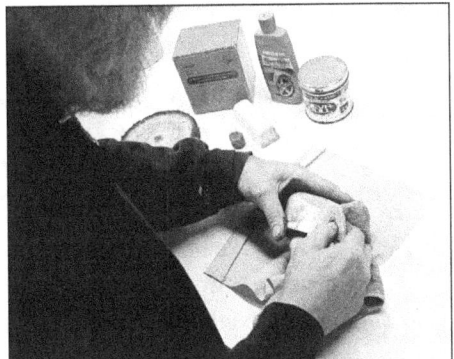

1 Remove heavy grime with a solvent-based cleaner.

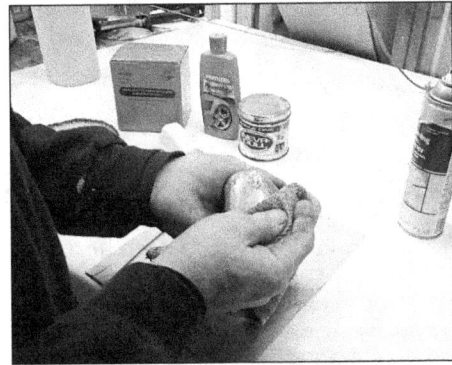

2 Use an old towel and solvent-based cleaner to wipe as much of the grime away as possible.

3 Use a little bit of foaming glass cleaner to remove any remaining oil or grease.

4 Wipe off the glass cleaner completely.

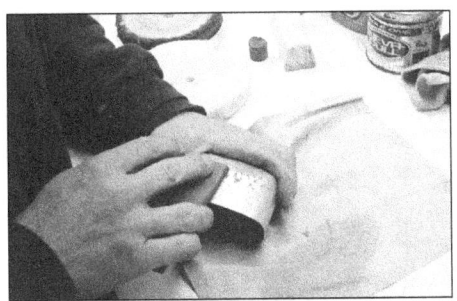

5 Start the leveling process. Depending on how badly pitted the metal is, start with either 800 or 2000 grit.

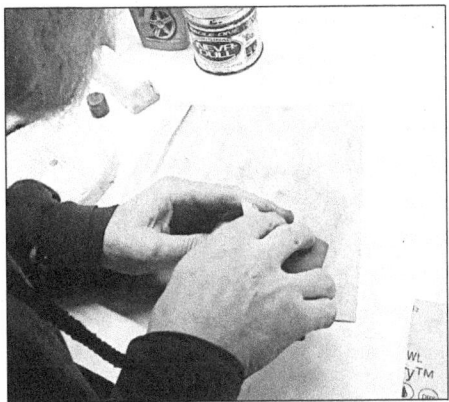

6 Sand gently in one direction with a little bit of soap and water for lubrication.

7 Prime the buffing wheel with buffing wheel compound.

HOW TO RESTORE YOUR VOLKSWAGEN BEETLE

TRIM AND FINISH

Using the Buffing Wheel *Continued*

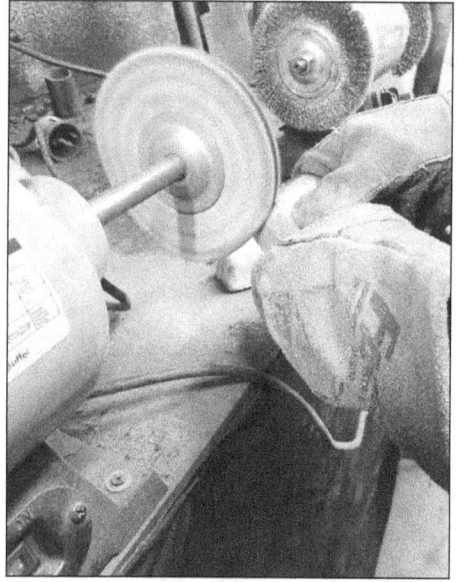

8 Start the first pass on the item being polished (in this case, a wiper motor cover). Make consecutive back-and-forth passes, overlapping by 1/2 to 1 inch until you're satisfied.

9 Move to the next area and repeat as necessary.

10 Always make sure to use safety equipment. Metal does get hot and slings off the wheel.

11 Move to the other side of the buffing wheel to remove any remaining polish compound.

12 An alternative method to the buffing wheel would be to apply polish by hand. Eagle One Nevr-Dull is a good choice.

13 Wipe off any residue from the polish.

Glass

Glass can be polished with glass polish kit, which comes with the appropriate buffing wheels and compounds needed to make a dent in decades of grime. Glass can be made to look like new if the scratches aren't too deep. However, watch the heat and don't get too aggressive or the glass will break.

Plastic

Buy a plastic polish kit (or just a bottle of plastic polish if you already have a glass polishing kit). If you have colored plastic parts (your turn signals, for example) and the plastic has faded too much, you'll need to replace it. Clear plastic pieces can be polished pretty easily with a buffer, clean rags, and polish.

CHAPTER 13

Installing Chrome Trim

No special tools are needed. Make sure all of the clips and rubber receivers have been gathered. For safety, it's best to buy new clips rather than trying to reuse originals. Be sure to buy rubber boots to go on the clips. A pair of pliers is useful to help you put the clips in place.

Separate which clips and receivers go on which side. Double-check that the chrome is free of dents and twists. Put rubber receivers into the holes and put the clips onto each piece of trim. There is no specific sequence to follow, but we find it easiest to work from left to right.

For older cars, the clips go onto the back of the trim first. For later models (1968 and newer), put the clips into the body first, then snap the trim on. Start at the door opening and work toward the back of the vehicle. On the door, start with the leading edge so it doesn't get snagged on anything as you work. Be patient and firm but gentle. The trim can dent if hit too hard with a hammer or even a hand.

Floating Beetle

Most older Beetles were built nearly airtight. The Beetle's precise level of engineering actually allows it to float briefly before sinking into a body of water, as long as the pans aren't rusted out and all seals are in good shape. ■

Installing Glass and Seals

Unlike modern cars, where the glass is held on with a rubberized adhesive, Beetles and many other older cars are different. Windows are set into an *H*-shaped rubber seal that connects the glass to the pinch welds to create a water-tight seal. It's an old-school method, so don't count on a local automotive glass repair shop to do this task.

If you are keeping the traditional window trim, that trim should be installed into the rubber before the glass is installed into the trim. It won't work the other way around because you won't be able to get the trim in. If you go with a California look, it's easier because you don't have to worry about installing the original trim.

When reinstalling glass, find the seam on the rubber seal first. That will be the bottom center of the glass. Push the rubber seal up onto the glass, working around it until the glass is completely set in the inner channel of the seal. It can be frustrating to work on because the rubber may not cooperate going around the tight corners. Just take your time to work all the way around until the glass is set in the channel.

Patience is crucial during this process. If you break the glass, you

Tools Needed

- 1/4-inch diameter cord or rope that is long enough to go all the way around the window
- A buddy or two
- Clean hands free of any jewelry
- Liquid dish soap (Dawn works the best)
- Plastic trim removal kit

Seal and Glass Installation

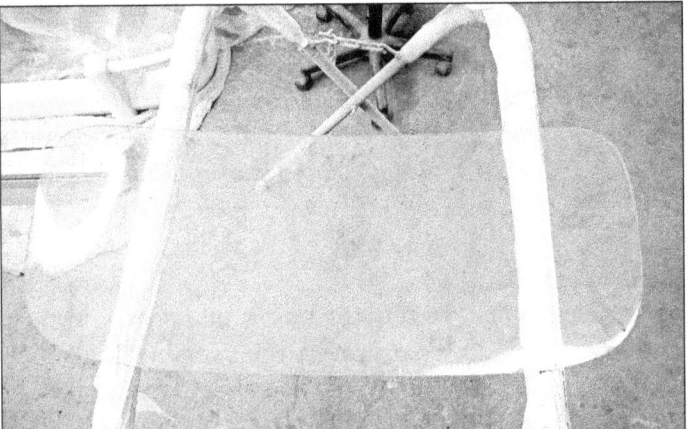

1 *Put the seal onto the glass. Make sure the seam is at the bottom of the glass. If it comes apart at the top, water will seep into the car. If the seam is on the bottom, the water will just drain out.*

2 *Put dish soap onto the window seal where it goes onto the car. This works as lube, so be generous with it. Soap the window opening too. It will be much easier if you work soapy.*

Seal and Glass Installation *Continued*

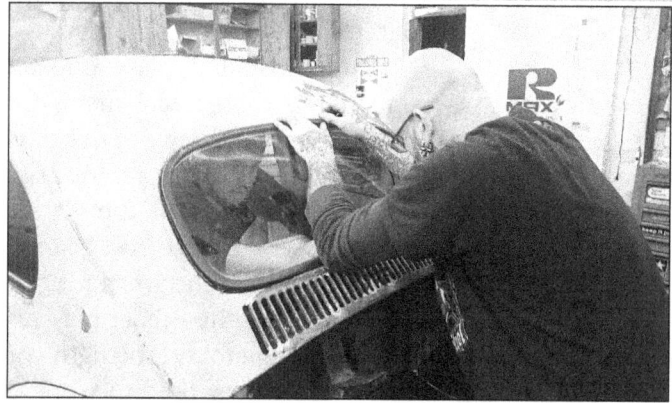

3 Put the rope or cord into the bottom of the window channel. Leave 6 to 8 inches hanging out. Now grab a friend. Put the window into the opening with the cord on the inside of the vehicle. Place the glass in the window opening. Have the friend apply steady pressure to the outside of the glass.

4 Curved front windscreens will require some help to install correctly. Always set the bottom channel first. With enough lubrication, it should slide right in.

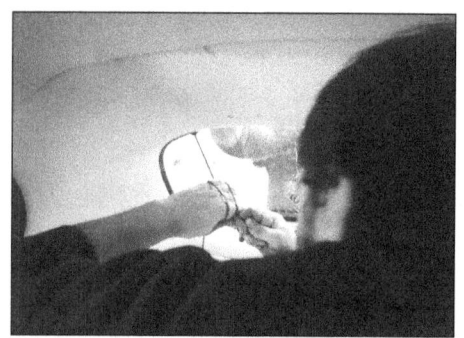

5 Go inside the car and pull the cord toward you, slow and steady. Work all the way around the window. Start from the bottom, go to the top on one side. Then, start again from the other side of the bottom and work to the top. The window will suck itself into place (pretty cool).

6 Use the plastic tool on the inside lip and make sure the seal is set right.

7 Use the heel of your hand to hit the glass around the seal, and it'll go right in. Then, do it to the outside. Make sure the seal is not folded under. Pay attention to the corners. If there are any folds or twists, dig the seal out with the plastic tool and it will flatten itself out. Clean the window with glass cleaner.

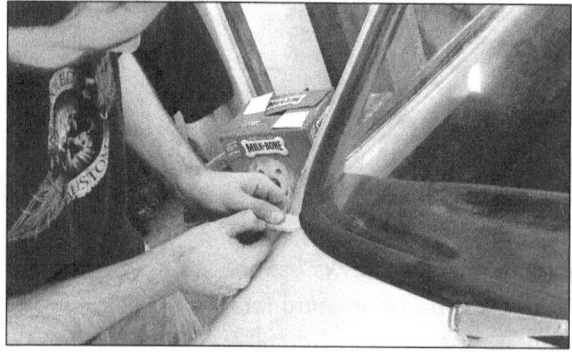

8 Using a semi-rigid trim tool, go around the outside of the rubber lip to get any tucked areas untucked. The seals will leak if they are tucked in. Also, run the tool around the inside of the seal (between the glass and seal) and on the inside of the car.

get to go buy a new one and do it again. Even the pros break glass, so don't feel bad; but don't make the same mistake again.

Also, as always, buy the best you can. Some inferior glass products break easily, fog between layers, get hazy, and leak around the seal.

Install Door Seals

Door seals will also need to be installed. To do this, get door seals, a plastic trim removal kit, black weatherstrip adhesive, and professional automotive masking tape. Cheaper tape tends to break down through atmospheric contamination and UV degradation to create a sticky residue. Some can even damage a freshly painted ride.

There are left and right door seals, and they are mirror opposites of each other. Sometimes they are marked; sometimes they are not. It's best to lay them out to determine which side is which.

Remove the door check rod if it is installed so it is out of the way. Start with the driver-side door seal at the upper rear corner of the door. Press that corner lightly into the seal's channel. Install the seal loosely all the way around, moving clockwise. The seals are molded to the shape of the door, so any angles and bends in the door should match up with angles and bends in the seal. Make sure it all fits.

Once you are happy with the overall fit of the seal, pull it out of the channel, one corner at a time. Dab a little adhesive into the channel and a little bit onto the seal to keep it in place. Continue adding adhesive, working on the A-pillar area by the front of the door. Then, continue with the center sections of each part of the seal. Finally, push the seal on so it is set and relaxed, not stretched.

Shut and latch the door. Leave it alone for at least 24 hours to allow the sealant to set. Repeat with the passenger's side.

Install Hood and Decklid Seals

Before ordering seals, measure the hood and decklid edges.

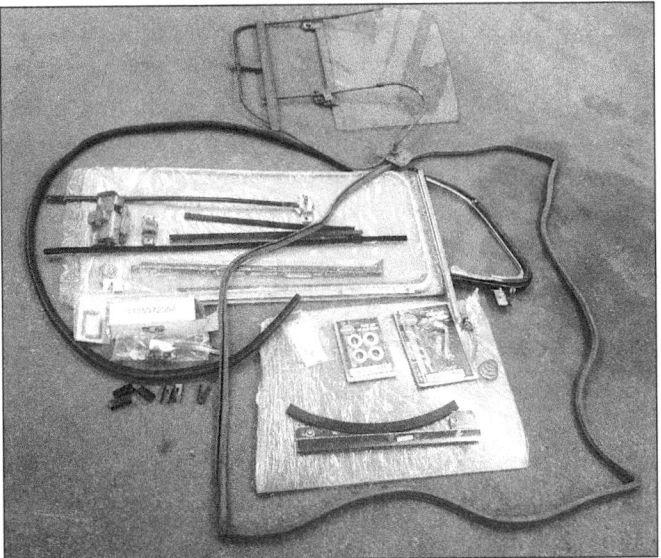
Lay out all of the door-seal components to be sure everything is there and that any parts being reused are in good working order. There's nothing more frustrating than getting halfway through only to find parts are missing or broken.

Here's a bare door frame that's ready for the installation of vent wings, glass, a window winder, seals, and latch mechanisms. All of this can be installed with the door in place or flat on a work surface.

Starting with the upper corner of the door, do a dry fit of the rubber seal into the receiving channel. After you're happy with the fit, lift it up in sections and dab a little adhesive onto the seal to keep it in place.

Now that the seal is installed and glued into place, close and latch the door. Let it sit for 24 hours until the adhesive is 100 percent cured before opening it again.

We recommend Trim-Lok 3/8-inch closed-cell sponge bulb seal (also called Mexi-Seal) for the top and hood seal or deck seal for the bottom. Use the trim removal kit, weatherstrip adhesive, masking tape, and a rubber or nylon hammer.

There are two types of these seals. You can use either type or a combination of both. Follow the same process on the hood and the engine seal installations. On the top, you'll be attaching the seal to the pinch weld. On the bottom, you'll be installing it into a C-channel.

To install seals on the hood and engine seal pinch welds, first look for the C-channel in the seal, which will go over the pinch weld. Measure the hood and decklids to get the length needed for the Trim-Lok seal.

Once cut to length, start at the top edge of the hood on the driver's side. Use a little dab of contact adhesive to hold it in place until it molds. Press the channel all the way around the pinch seal. Smack lightly with a rubber hammer to get the contour to fit correctly.

Now, it's time to install the lower hood seal, which is a slightly different process. It's helpful to lay the lower seal out in the sun for a little while to warm it up and make it more pliable. Start at the edges closest to the windshield. Use the trim-removal tool to work the seal into the C-channel, moving toward the front of the hood. It may be helpful to use some liquid dish soap to coax the seal into the channel.

At the front of the hood, trim the seal to fit. Use a little bit of adhesive to join the two ends to create one solid seal. On the rear engine decklid, it is much the same process. The only difference is that when working on the lower seal, you will start at the driver's side and work around to the passenger's side rather than working both sides at the same time. Make any adjustments to ensure it has the same amount of tension all the way around.

Running Board

All Beetles have them, and they run from the front to rear fender, connecting to the body along the rocker. While they look like they might serve as a step (although unless you have somehow raised your Beetle to monster-truck heights, you probably don't need a boost to get in), they are not strong enough to support a person's full body weight. Running boards help keep water from the roads from splashing up on the car. Some folks use them as a mud scraper; in fact, a chrome boot scraper accessory can be purchased. New running boards can be purchased from any Volkswagen parts house. Options include stock (with the rubber coating—and some years even come in different colors), plain steel (with no coating), aluminum, and fiberglass.

When installing running boards, work on one side at a time. Line the running board up along the rocker. Put bolts loosely in the front fender first to hold it as you work.

Tools Needed

- 10-mm wrench and socket
- 13-mm wrench and socket
- Awl
- Running boards

While it is tempting to not install the washers because of limited space, you will be glad you did. It helps spread the load and keeps it from rattling later.

Install the back the same way. Line up the rocker-panel holes. There should be five bolts. Tighten the bolts, making sure there is a big enough gap between the bottom edge of the door and the top of the running board, so the door doesn't scrape the running board when opened. Put those bolts in first and then tighten.

Running boards don't have to be boring. Several companies manufacture an aluminum running board that is a direct bolt-in piece. They can even be painted to match your ride.

CHAPTER 13

Stock running boards are available in the aftermarket. Do a test fit or mockup before doing the final installation. Always check the lower-door gaps for interference. The mounting lip can be adjusted for more clearance.

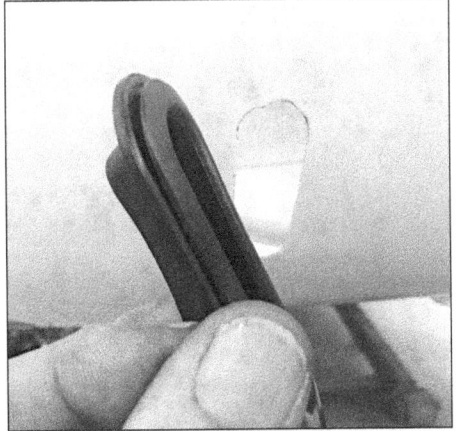

The bumper grommets have a channel that fits snugly on the body. Start by tucking one edge in and working the inner lip around the hole. This must be installed before the bumper brackets go in.

Protect Your Paint

Use rags on the ends of the bumpers to protect your paint. It's also a good idea to have a buddy help match both sides at once because it's kind of wide. Make sure the bumper is lined up straight and level.

Bumpers

The bumpers are the horizontal chrome bits on the front and back of the car that help protect the main car body in case of a low-impact accident. All Beetles rolled off the factory assembly-line with bumpers, but some owners remove them (a style called *shaved*) to achieve a different look. The original bumpers varied from year to year. There are three or four styles that are stock throughout the years. Some states require bumpers, but not all do. New bumpers can be purchased from any VW parts house, or they can be fabricated if you have advanced metalwork skills.

When installing bumpers, first insert the bumper grommet into the hole for the bumper. There's a lip that connects to the back, so get this in first to seal the bumper bracket into the body.

Slide the bumper in with the brackets attached.

Line the holes up and put the bumper bolts in loosely. Be careful not to ding the paint with the bumper. To avoid hurting the paint, wrap the bumper ends with a rag. Make sure the bumper is the same distance from the body on both sides; it's adjustable. Make sure it's straight and square before tightening. Tighten all the bolts.

Turn Signals

Turn signals are required by all states. Purchase a new turn signal kit through a Volkswagen parts house or

OEM parts may be a bit discolored from decades of use but can be cleaned and polished. Not only does it look better, but it will work better than having a good electrical ground. Don't neglect the inside of the bulb holder.

We suggest mounting the bumper brackets before installing the bumper. Leave everything finger tight until it is all together.

Tools Needed

- 13-mm wrench and socket
- Bumpers
- Screwdriver

TRIM AND FINISH

We normally pre-build subassemblies such as headlights. There are times that mocking these parts up feels tedious, but it sure beats having to completely disassemble and fix the fit.

Headlight Tips

Make sure your seal is all the way around the lens evenly and that it's not tucked under.

Make sure the wires are in the correct order and properly grounded to the body (that's what the bolts are for). Check that the left and right signals are sorted out.

---

have a set custom built for a unique look. You will need a Phillips screwdriver and an 8-mm wrench and socket.

First, install the rubber seal. Pull the wires through the seal. Mount the base to the seal and bolt it to the body. Hook up the wires, put the light bulb in, then put the lens with the chrome on top. Just screw the lens in, and installation is done.

Headlights

Headlights are also required equipment. You'll be overwhelmed by how many options are available. Choose from a sealed-beam style, H4

LED headlights are a popular upgrade for any classic Dub. Although they are a little pricey compared with the stock version, they offer a safer, brighter, and cleaner light.

The headlight is secured and adjusted via the headlight bucket framework. A simple Phillips screwdriver does the trick.

style with removable bulb, and LEDs. Prices range from $20 for a bulb to $150 apiece for LEDs. They come in different colors and styles. You can buy them from Volkswagen parts houses or a local auto parts store.

Do a little research to determine the proper height setting for your Beetle. This setting depends on the height of the car, which can vary greatly from ground scraping to sky scraping. A quick search online will determine exactly how your setup should be. With that information, park the car in front of a solid surface, turn the headlights on, and adjust accordingly.

Taillights

Again, taillights are required equipment in all states. However, unlike modern cars, antique cars are not required to have the third brake light. Taillights can be purchased from Volkswagen parts houses or local auto parts stores.

Installing Taillights

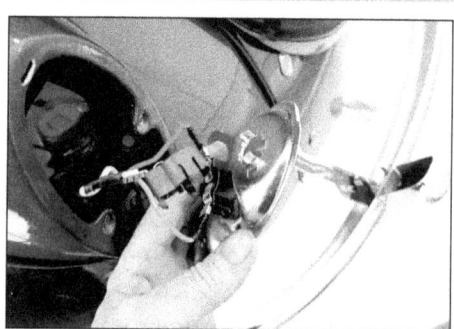

1 *Connect wires to the bulb holder.*

2 *Put the bulbs in the proper sockets.*

CHAPTER 13

Installing Taillights Continued

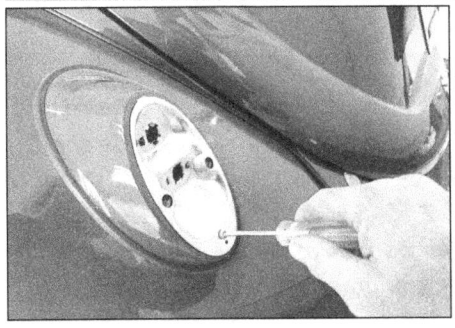

3 Mount the bulb holder to the taillight vessel.

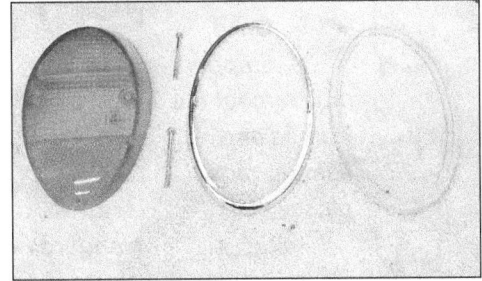

4 The lens goes on top of the bulb holder.

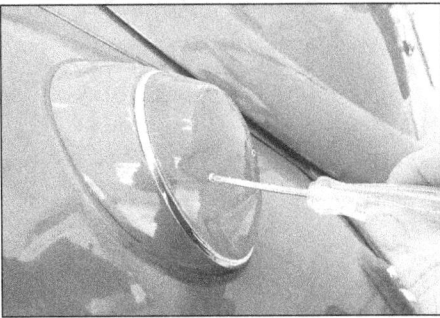

5 Install the two screws to hold the lens to the taillight base.

Miscellaneous Shiny Bits

Now you're scraping the bottom of the barrel for doodads to install on your Beetle. They're all pretty easy and typically have installation instructions on the packaging. Other than door handles, the rest of these parts are optional: gravel guards on your front and rear fenders, horn rings, and a Volkswagen emblem.

Windshield Wiper Mechanism

Sure, new ones are available, but for the purists, that is unthinkable. If you'd rather restore than replace but don't want to do it yourself, West Coast Wipers is the only specialist we know and trust. The shop takes the wiper assembly all the way apart, just the way we like it. Every nut, bolt, and wire is taken off and reassembled into a brand-new, very old wiper assembly.

> **Tools Needed**
>
> - Blast cabinet
> - Bushings, clips, grommets, ground strip, nuts, washers
> - Car battery
> - High-temperature synthetic wheel-bearing grease
> - Linkage rods
> - New brushes and springs
> - Powdercoat kit
> - Pivot shafts
> - Round file
> - Sandpaper
> - Superglue
> - Vise

Restoring the Wiper Mechanism

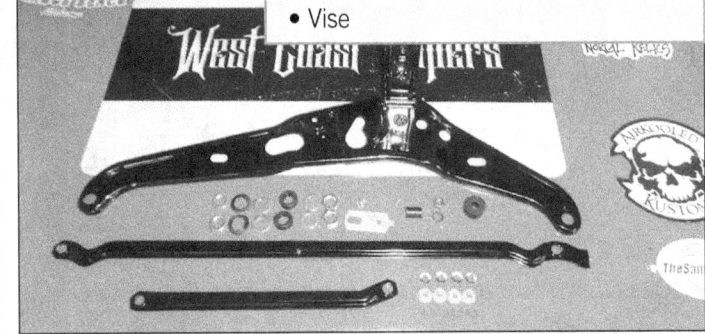

1 Start by taking the wiper assembly completely apart, laying out all of the components, and noting if anything is missing. The metal parts need to go through blast. Send them out or buy a blast tank from a pawn shop or hardware store.

2 Visually inspect the pivot arms for wear, corrosion, or stripped threads. At this juncture, decide if they can be restored or if they need to be replaced.

Restoring the Wiper Mechanism *Continued*

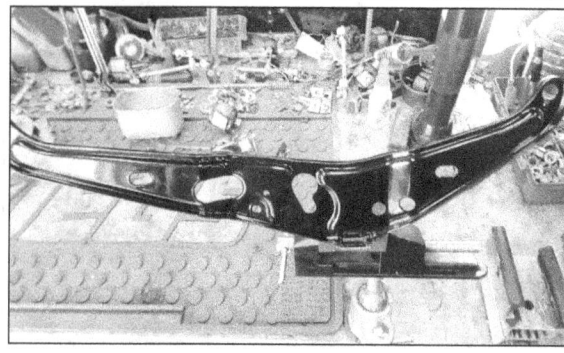

3 Once stripped, powdercoat the frames and linkage rods glossy black.

4 Pressing the shaft bushings in with a standard bench vise will make the installation a bit easier. Add a bit of grease too. Use a round file to ream them to fit.

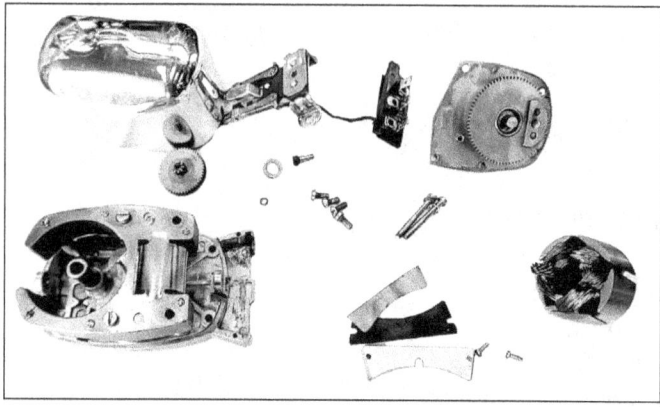

5 Clean all of the electrical contacts and gears. This motor assembly is ready to go back together and a new armature is set to be installed.

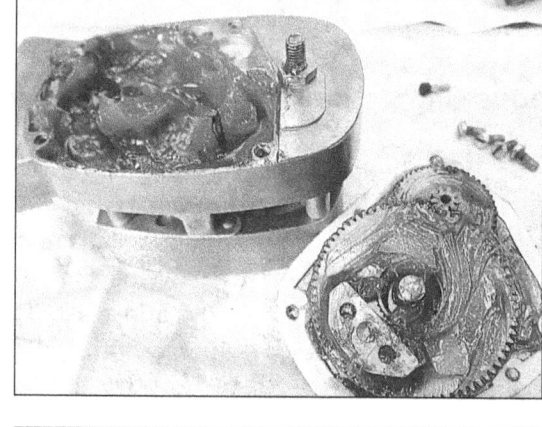

6 Packing the gear box full of grease is the best way to get a long, trouble-free life out of windshield wipers.

7 Bench test the assembly by hooking it up to a car battery. Let it run for an hour to be sure it is working properly before mounting it to the frame.

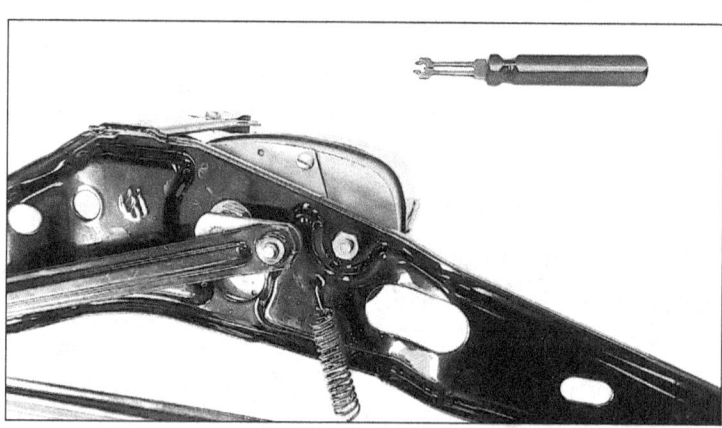

8 Service the gear case with new parts, grease, gasket contact terminals, and points.

9 While the wiper assembly is still on the bench, run it for a few minutes. Look for smooth operation. If there is anything that doesn't seem correct, now is the time to fix it.

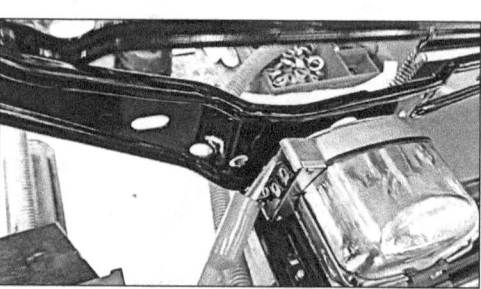

10 Use a car battery that has a 12-volt power supply with shielded alligator clips for testing. You don't want to short out your newly rebuilt wiper motor.

When taking a wiper assembly apart, it is a good idea to lay all of the components out in order; then, inspect and clean them. With all of the subcomponents cleaned, painted, or otherwise refurbished, reassembly should be fairly straightforward.

The pivot arms on the wiper assembly are where the real work takes place. Make sure they are free of marring and pits. The plastic bushings can wear out prematurely otherwise.

We like powdercoating for the frames. The coating provides many decades of protection. While paint is acceptable, it is not as durable. Replace all the hardware to install with OEM parts, including the nuts, washers, clips, grommets, ground strip, linkage rods, bushings, and pivot shafts. Take the engine apart, cleaning and inspecting all components. You will need to replace any defective parts.

You can rebuild the assembly in 6 volt or 12 volt by replacing the armature.

We do a final electrical check on the bench. This way we can address any problems or issues before installation. Any moving parts need to have a dab of grease, including the spring. Don't forget the ends of the pivot arms.

Wipers

This is one of the first pieces you'll install before assembling your dash.

> **Tools Needed**
> - 8-mm wrench and socket
> - 13-mm wrench and socket
> - 17-mm wrench and socket
> - 21-mm wrench and socket
> - Wiper assembly and installation kit

Wiper Installation

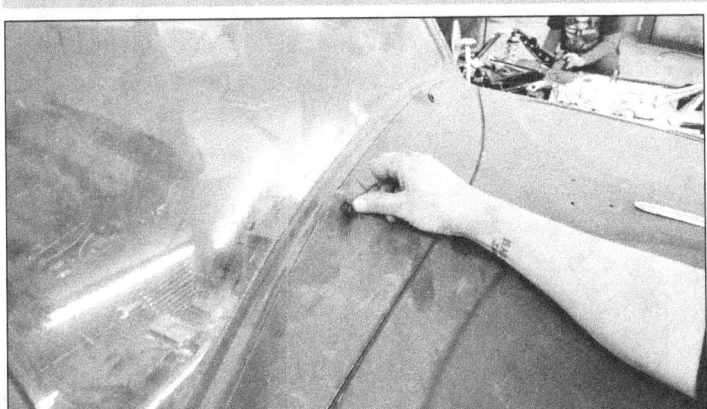

1 Install the windshield wiper arm grommets.

2 Slide the two wiper poles up through the grommets.

3 Install the anchor attachment point and ground that attaches to the wiper-motor assembly housing.

TRIM AND FINISH

Wiper Installation *Continued*

4 After the housing is installed, there is a set of brass locking nuts that go on the outside of the assembly units to press to the grommets. Attach them and tighten down.

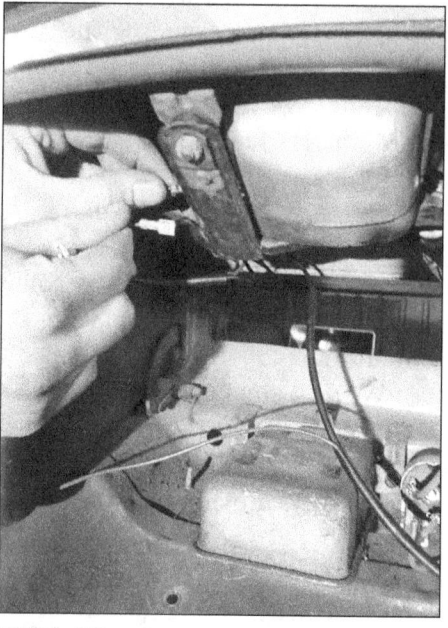

5 Wire the wiper arms per factory specifications for the Beetle's year.

6 Attach the black plastic trim sleeve that goes over the wiper poles.

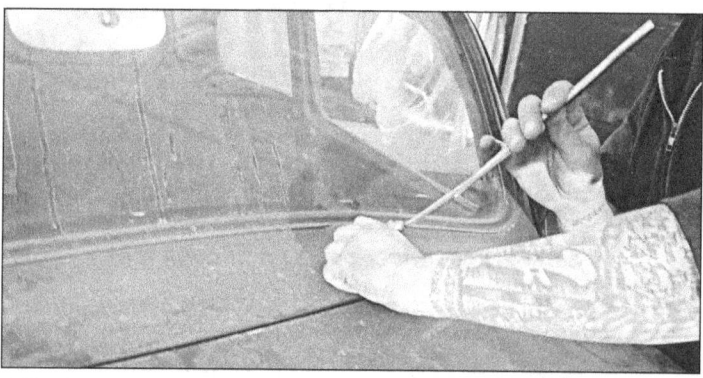

7 Attach the wiper arms (there are different attachment points, depending on the car).

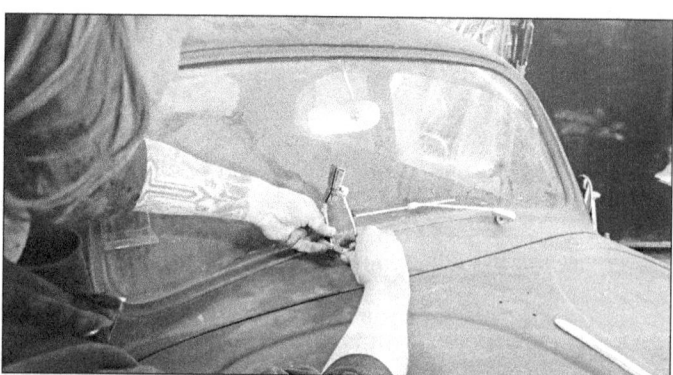

8 Install the wiper blades.

9 Install the squirt assembly by inserting it into place and twisting to lock it down. Run the hose down to the washer reservoir's fluid dispenser. Follow the manufacturer's installation instructions for the specific model of washer-fluid reservoir.

HOW TO RESTORE YOUR VOLKSWAGEN BEETLE

CHAPTER 14

EXHAUST, CARBURETOR, AND DISTRIBUTOR

At this point, you've got a great body, a practically brand-new chassis, and an engine that purrs. But if you want more than eye candy, it's time to work on everything that makes your car start, run properly, go, and stop. After all, you didn't come this far into the project just to stand there and admire the car while it's parked.

This phase of the restoration includes adding important fluids, bleeding the brakes again, installing the exhaust system, taking care of the carburetor, and working on the distributor. You will be working with harsh chemicals, so eye and hand protection is a must. It is also a good idea to equip your work space with hand cleaner and an eye-wash station. Some of these chemicals are flammable and/or corrosive. Some are drying agents, which are dangerous if they come in contact with your skin or eyes. Store all chemicals in a dry, clean area with their lids fastened. Protect yourself!

Fluid Levels

Depending on the project, it is time to either fill or check the following fluids: engine oil, brake fluid, transmission gear oil (or automatic fluid), and wiper fluid.

Your car is a piece of automotive art at this point. It's time to turn it into kinetic art. The next phase of the project will put your fine art in motion.

In an air-cooled engine, motor oil plays two main roles: lubricating the internals and keeping the engine within operating-temperature parameters. With just a 2.5-quart capacity, it is critical to keep the oil topped up.

EXHAUST, CARBURETOR, AND DISTRIBUTOR

Tools Needed

- Brake fluid (we recommend Dot3 brake fluid)
- Clean rags
- Funnel
- Oil (we recommend Lucas hot rod classic, high zinc 20/50)
- Transmission gear oil

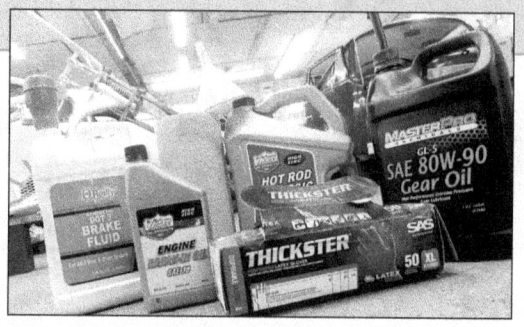

A local auto parts store should have all the products needed to lubricate your ride. Gear oil for the transmission, DOT3 or better for the brakes, and engine oil. These fluids are critical to giving your classic Bug a long life.

The pneumatic bleeder is by far one of the best ways to remove the air from the brake lines. It will also keep the brakes free from atmospheric contamination. The best part is that you can use one to do this part of your project by yourself.

Engine Oil

Be sure your engine is cold. If it has been running, let it cool for a few minutes so the oil will settle back to the bottom rather than running through the engine. Then, check to ensure that the oil level comes up to the top notch on the dipstick.

Brake Fluid

Find the brake reservoir and fill to the max line. Using a turkey baster makes this task easy and mess-free. Note: Brake fluid is hydroscopic and will absorb ambient moisture from the air and become contaminated. Also, brake fluid eats paint, so be careful.

Transmission Gear Oil

Pull the side inspection plug from the transmission case. Stick the tip of your pinky into the hole. If you can see some transmission gear oil on your pinky, you are good to go.

If you have an automatic, run the engine until it's hot, leaving the transmission in neutral. Once the engine is hot, use a dipstick to check the automatic transmission fluid level.

Wiper Fluid

Open the lid, pour the fluid in, and fill it to the top.

Brake Lines

The brake lines will need to be bled once more before taking the Beetle out on the road. Follow the same process as you did on the initial bleed (on page 91).

Brake fluid is highly corrosive and will eat anything it touches. Do not use old brake fluid that has been sitting around. Its hydroscopic nature means it will absorb moisture from the air and become contaminated. Once contaminated, the brake fluid can't contract and expand as needed, which means the brakes are not likely to work reliably.

Fill the reservoir, then start with the back passenger's side. Using a pneumatic bleeder or the buddy system, bleed the line while moving closer to the reservoir.

Pneumatic Bleeder Checklist

1. Place the hose on the pneumatic bleeder.
2. Pressurize the canister.
3. Open the bleeder valve.
4. Let the air bubbles out.
5. Close the valve.
6. Repeat this sequence until no air bubbles come out.

Buddy System

1. Have a buddy pump the brakes three times, then hold the brake to the floor.
2. While the buddy has the pedal pushed down to the floor, crack open the brake bleeder and look for air. You want to see a steady flow of fluid, not spurts from air bubbles.

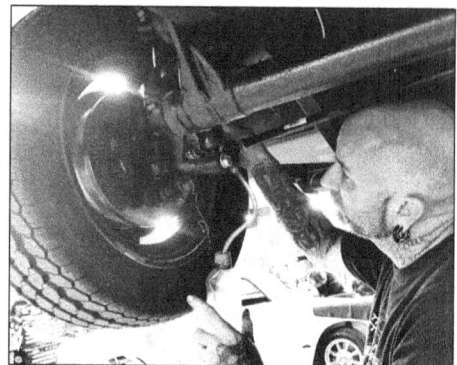

Have a buddy put pressure on the brake pedal, open the valve to move the fluid down the brake line, then close the valve and tell your buddy to release the pedal. Repeat the process until you have clear brake fluid and no air coming through. Remember to keep the reservoir topped up.

3. Repeat this sequence until all air is out of the system and the brake fluid is clean.

Exhaust System

When it comes to the exhaust system, there are a lot of options, mostly dependent on how loud or quiet you want your Beetle to be when it's running. If you built the engine, you'll probably feel comfortable building the exhaust system as well. If purchasing the engine from an engine builder, pay a little extra to have them include an exhaust system. The exhaust system can also be purchased separately from an aftermarket supplier online. The exhaust system needs to coordinate with the engine in respect to whether or not it has heater boxes.

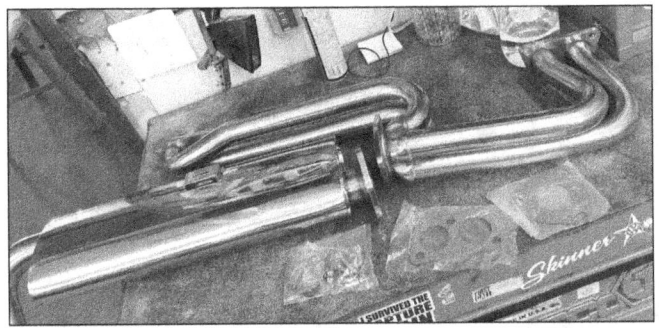

Stainless steel performance exhaust systems are in a class by themselves. They last three times as long as the less-expensive options, and as a bonus, they have equal-length primary tubes to increase performance of the engine.

There are many options for the exhaust system. A single quiet pack tucks up nicely under the body and will give a nice, throaty note for not too much money.

Tools Needed

- Anti-seize brass nuts
- Heater boxes
- J-Tubes (can have heater boxes built onto them)
- Muffler
- Tubing

Exhaust Checklist

- ☐ Level the face of the exhaust. All mating surfaces should be flat and level all the way around.
- ☐ Inspect the head studs and make sure that they are clean and that the threads are in good shape.
- ☐ Inspect the gaskets, making sure they're in good shape with no nicks and they're the right size and fit for the system.

While finishing the tin install on the engine, take the time to mock up the exhaust and carburetor. Some parts will not line up correctly and will require a bit of massaging. It is easier to do it now than when it's in the car.

Facing the exhaust flanges with a flat file before installation is a must. If the machining is off, you could have an issue with post-ignition (backfiring). Any air leaks will cause issues with a smooth-running car.

You may discover that you'll have to make what you cannot buy. If you want heater boxes on an upright Type 4 conversion, some custom fabrication will be necessary. Don't let it scare you. There is always the option of taking it to a local muffler shop.

A pair of dual Weber IDF, IDA, or ITC carburetors is a very popular and easy way to get a bit more scoot out of your ride. Very few carburetors are ready to go out of the box. Some adjustments and maybe some jet changes will be needed to make an engine perform up to its potential.

A basic set of tools is required to install a carburetor. Besides the air and fuel jets and a synchometer, you will need your flathead screwdriver and a 13-mm wrench.

- Install the metal gaskets over the studs.
- Install the newly faced exhaust flanges to the head.
- Make sure the metal donut (if using) is new and is not ripped, torn, or deformed.
- Use proper clamps to hold in place.
- Tighten according to factory specs.

Remove High Spots

This is not a hard task, but it is time consuming. Be patient and work cleanly and carefully. It will be easier to do this part of the project with the Beetle up on a lift or on jack stands so you can get under the vehicle.

While holding the exhaust flanges in a vise, file them to get the high spots down. Some areas will be shiny and some will be black. Keep filing until they are all shiny and the surface is smooth. Apply the gasket. This leads to better engine performance. ■

Carburetor

A carburetor provides the proper air-to-fuel mixture ratio to create combustion within the cylinders. It is controlled by idle air jets and main jets. Idle air jets control how the car idles. Main jets control acceleration. Proper jet sizing is essential to tuning and engine performance. For example, if the idle jets are too small, there will be popping and spitting followed by the engine dying. Another telltale sign is that the engine may hesitate when you try to accelerate.

Most carburetor manufacturers offer a setup and tuning guide with their products or on their website. We suggest printing them out and adding these instructions to your build book for easy reference.

With a set of performance dual carburetors, a synchometer is invaluable for tuning the intake airflow. These can be purchased through a local VW parts shop or online.

CHAPTER 14

You can run single or dual carburetors. That choice will impact your car's performance and its aesthetics. There are many stock and custom options available. A few brands that have earned good reputations include Solex, Dellorto, and Weber. Be sure to consider your engine's specifications to figure out which carburetor will work best for your Beetle.

Carburetor Safety

Be aware of fire hazards. The carburetor contains a mixture of fuel and air. If there is a spark nearby, you could quickly have a fireball on your hands.

Never run a foam air cleaner. Over time, it will become brittle, deteriorate, and crumble into the carburetor. If that happens and the carburetor backfires, the foam will catch fire easily. Instead, use a paper element or a high-performance air cleaner.

For dual carburetors, a synchrometer will be needed to measure air velocity coming in as the carburetors are synced to each other. With dual carburetors, you will also need a linkage assembly. Check the manufacturer's specifications because every setup is different.

Carburetor Checklist

❏ Perform a preliminary bench tune. Read and understand the manufacturer's recommendations. The carburetor will be tuned again after installation. The precise process for this bench tune varies from manufacturer to manufacturer.
❏ Install the carburetor according to the manufacturer's instructions.
❏ Make sure all mating surfaces are clean and level.
❏ Look into the intake valves to make sure no shipping materials are lodged inside. If you stuffed rags into the valves while you were doing other parts of your project, remember to remove them so they don't get sucked down into the engine, which may cause catastrophic engine failure.
❏ Use the proper gaskets and/or manifold spacers (optional) for the exhaust system. These gaskets or spacers slow the heat transfer down as it moves from the intake to the carburetor. This makes it less likely for the fuel to boil. Always follow the manufacturer's specifications.
❏ Install the gaskets.
❏ Install the carburetor, being careful not to drop any parts or debris into it.
❏ Torque the nuts to manufacturer's specifications.
❏ For a single-carburetor setup, simply follow the manufacturer's specifications for startup. Then, conduct the preliminary tuning.
❏ For a dual-carburetor setup, install the linkage, making sure it does not bind. Follow the manufacturer's recommendations for tuning.

Distributor

The distributor is one of the main controls that enables an engine to fire. It produces a spark, which controls the ignition. The distributor can run old-fashioned points or go with electronic ignition. Both options have pros and cons. With points, the biggest drawback is that they can go out while on the road. It's a good idea to carry extras in the glove box. An electronic ignition is less likely to go

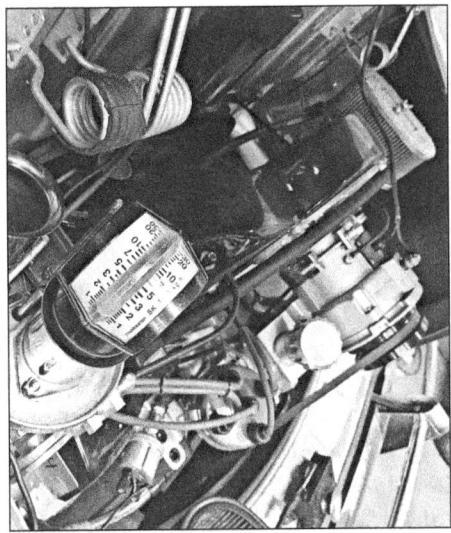

Distributors regulate the spark in an engine. You can get fancy with this or go stock. The better the sparks, the better the engine runs.

Mechanical-advance distributors work fairly well. The 009 Bosch unit was originally designed for drag racing with a very steep advance curve. It does very well at idle and at wide-open throttle. But it will have a slight hesitation as the timing curve advances.

out, but it can still happen. An electronic ignition gives a more efficient spark ratio, and it costs a bit more.

Another choice is a vacuum advance distributor or a mechanical advance. Do some research to determine which is the best match for your engine.

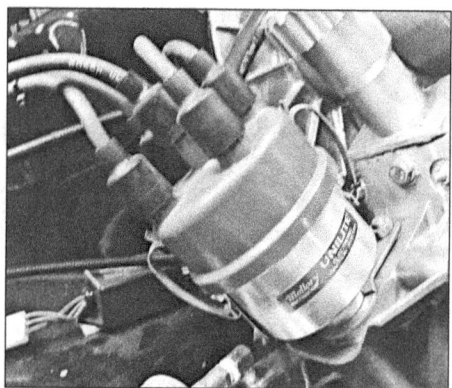

Top dead center (TDC) refers to when the number-1 cylinder is at its farthest point of travel. If your engine is at TDC, then your number-1 intake, number-1 exhaust, and number-2 intake valves will be at rest or all the way closed. This configuration only happens at TDC.

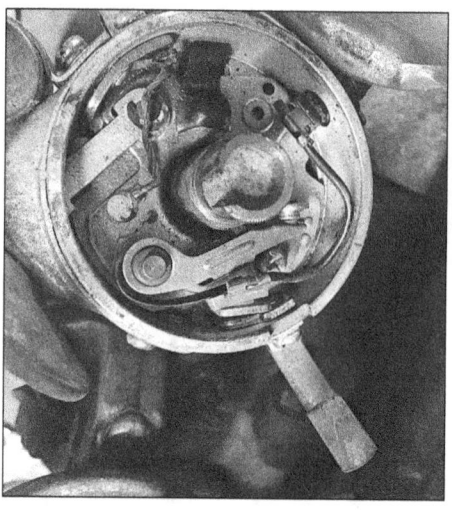

Tried and true, nothing beats a set of points for reliability as long as the gap is set correctly (0.016 inch/0.4 mm). They will provide long and stable ignition spark for your Dub.

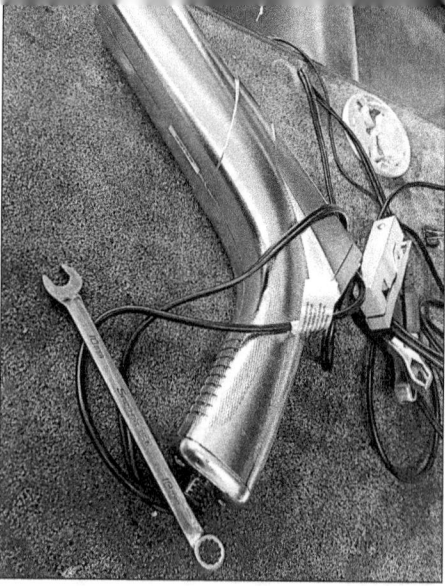

If you are going outside the box with your exhaust, there will be fabrication required. Putting a VW bus engine into a Bug with stock heater boxes was a configuration never offered by Volkswagen, so you will need to make what you can't buy to make it work.

A ceramic-coated header and Fat Boy is a very popular upgrade to mid-performance engines. They look good and perform well for many years.

Distributor Checklist

- Make sure the engine is set at top dead center (TDC) on the number-1 cylinder.
- When installing the distributor, make sure the engine is pointing to the number-1 cylinder so it's not 180 degrees out. If it's out of alignment, the engine either will not start or will not run right, and you'll have to pull the distributor out and start again.
- Once the distributor is positioned properly, double-check the rotor button and install the cap.

Timing can be done at idle. But we suggest setting the base timing at 2,200 rpm to 28–32 degrees. At that run speed, the distributor is at full advance and under load.

- Make sure spark-plug wires and spark plugs are installed properly.
- Snug down the distributor, but make sure you can still spin it.
- Start the engine and let it warm up.
- Adjust the distributor so that it runs.
- For a vacuum advance, the most common setting is 28 degrees advanced. For a mechanical advance, the setting is 32 degrees.
- With your timing light at idle, make sure the advancement is set to 0 so TDC is directly on the line.
- Rev the engine to 2,000 to 2,500 rpms.
- Set the timing light to the appropriate advancement. Note these settings are not set in stone. Your engine may require higher or lower advancements. Use your best judgment based on how the engine runs.
- Adjust the distributor to the appropriate advancement for your type.
- Tighten it all down, being careful not to change the settings in the process.

Timing Tip

It's easier to work on the distributor if you have a buddy to help. Otherwise, you will need to control your throttle, hold the timing light, and adjust the distributor all at the same time.

CHAPTER 15

BEFORE THE FIRST 1,000 MILES

Before putting that Bug on the road, there are a few more matters that need your attention.

License Plate, Registration, and Insurance

With as much work as you've put into your new and improved Beetle, the last sight you want to see is it being towed away to an impound because it's not street legal. Just like with any modern car, register and insure your Bug. However, there are more options with a classic car than with a more modern ride. It all varies from state to state, but here are some options to consider if they're available.

License Plate

There are some options here. One option is a year-of-manufacture (YOM) plate for your state, which you can find online with a little bit of hunting. Do some comparison shopping to find a plate that's in good condition at a good price. You may even find a plate that comes from your specific county.

Other options are a plain, old regular plate; an antique vehicle plate; or a vanity plate if you prefer. The historic or antique plates requirements range from 10 to 25 years to qualify.

Registration

Registering the car is a simple matter of figuring out what your local Department of Motor Vehicles requires. The registration process varies from state to state. You may or may not need a title to register the Beetle, and that requirement may differ depending on whether you bought the Beetle in your state or elsewhere. Some states will not issue a title for older cars; they count them as personal property instead. It's better to call ahead or research online so you don't make a wasted trip to somewhere nobody wants to go.

Insurance

Insuring your restored Beetle is different from insuring your late-model daily driver. There are insurance companies out there that specialize in insuring antique cars (Hagerty and Grundy are a couple that we use), and some large auto insurance companies even have specialty divisions that offer classic car coverage. Check with your local agent and be prepared to shop around.

What's crucial to remember is that you don't want to insure your car for what they say it is worth according to Kelley Blue Book evaluation. Instead, get replacement-value coverage. By insuring your car as an antique vehicle, you can get much higher coverage amounts for the replacement value. You'll have to provide receipts and photographic proof of the parts and labor you've put into restoring your car to show the company that the car is worth its replacement value.

You may need to have your vehicle appraised to prove its value. Appraisers can be found online, or your insurance company may provide a list of approved appraisers. Check with your local Volkswagen club; they usually have a list of resources they'll be happy to share.

The only hitch is that to get antique car coverage, the Beetle cannot be your daily driver. In fact, if you say the words "daily driver" to the insurance company representative, the conversation will pretty much be over immediately. Your antique car insurance policy may stipulate that the car will only be driven less than 100 miles per month, say to go out for ice cream now and then.

Gently Breaking In the Beetle

Unlike buying a brand-new car from a dealership, your Beetle is not ready for a wild ride right out of the gate. For the first 500 miles of its resurrected life, it requires some babying. You wouldn't buy new shoes and wear them on a day-long walk through Las Vegas. That's a guaranteed way to get blisters so painful that you'd spend the next week with your feet propped up. It's the same concept with your engine.

Engine parts need to get used to each other. The parts are mating themselves to each other so that they'll function in the most efficient pattern possible. All that rubbing and grinding creates a bit of debris, which is carried from the engine components into the oil. The bits of metal in the oil during this break-in period might shock you.

With this in mind, it's best not to rev an engine above 3,500 rpm during the break-in phase. This will help keep the engine's oil contamination as minimal as possible, decrease the amount of stress on your engine and transmission, and help prevent serious problems. After that 500 miles, knock yourself out.

During this break-in period, pay special attention to how the car runs. Be on the lookout for anything that doesn't feel, sound, or look right. Gather feedback from your hands, feet, and your butt in the seat. If anything seems strange, check it out.

There are more than 30,000 individual parts and components on the Beetle, which have just been taken apart and put back together. You want to catch any small irregularities and fix them before they become big problems.

Troubleshooting

Track down any gremlins that show up during the 500-mile break-in. The best way to do this without getting stranded is to take the first test drive close to home. When you return, compile a list of anything that needs to be checked, fixed, adjusted, or straightened. Now is the time to address these. Then, take your Beetle on a drive that's a bit farther from home and repeat the process. Get those 500 miles in, with each trip going a bit farther from home.

Once one problem is taken care of, it will seem like four more crop up in its place. The reality is, the bigger problems mask the smaller ones. Once a bigger problem is cleared up, the smaller ones become more obvious. Just keep at it, and remember that a vintage Beetle is a project that's never truly finished.

If you run into any problems that leave you stumped, look online for resources. Forums, social media groups, and VW-enthusiast sites offer a wealth of advice on fixing almost any problem. The people there have been where you are and are happy to share their experiences. If that doesn't work, find a reputable VW repair shop that is experienced with old air-cooled Dubs.

With your Beetle, you'll need to inspect it before driving anywhere. Keep a close eye on all its systems to make sure everything is operating properly. As mentioned, driving a decades-old vehicle is not like driving a car you just bought from a dealership. With a new car, you can just hop in and go. With the older Beetle, you have to pay attention to how it is running as you drive.

Mechanical Standards

If the Beetle was in a shop for a checkup, the mechanic would inspect it from bumper to bumper, making sure every system is operational. You can and should do the same, not only to ensure the car is roadworthy but also to catch any concerns while they are small.

75-Point, 500-Mile Inspection Checklist

Pre-Road Test
❏ Decklid is functioning properly
❏ Brake-fluid reservoir is filled
❏ Washer-fluid reservoir is filled

When doing the initial tune, make sure the timing is set to specifications. If you have carburetors, make sure they are set up right. It will run like a tractor until those carburetors are in sync.

CHAPTER 15

- ☐ Battery condition is good
- ☐ Charging system is operational
- ☐ Throttle linkage is operational
- ☐ Check oil level

Operational Checks
- ☐ Doors, decklid, and hood latches are functioning
- ☐ Seat adjustors are secure
- ☐ Steering column is functioning
- ☐ Check ignition switch
- ☐ Check indicator warning lamps
- ☐ Turn signals and hazard lamps are functioning

It might not seem like a big deal, but always check to be sure the latches are working. There's nothing worse than getting stuck on the outside of your car with it unlocked but not able to open the door.

Those little red and green lights are not just warning lights; they are also system-check lights. They should illuminate and then go out when the car is started.

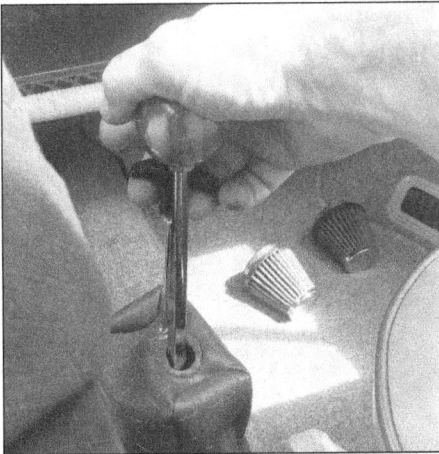

Before starting the car, put your foot on the clutch. Do a quick run through the gears to make sure the gates are functioning properly. If not, adjust the shifter base.

- ☐ Horn works
- ☐ Brake lights illuminate when brake is depressed
- ☐ Headlamps, including high beams and low beams, work
- ☐ Interior lights work
- ☐ Door locks function
- ☐ Windows open and close
- ☐ Parking brake functions and releases
- ☐ Windshield wiper is operational
- ☐ Wiper blades are in good condition
- ☐ Rearview mirror is in working order
- ☐ Side mirrors are adjusted properly
- ☐ Seat belts are in working order
- ☐ Convertible top opens, closes, and latches (if applicable)
- ☐ Sunroof opens, closes, and latches (if applicable)
- ☐ Shifter is working

Road Test
- ☐ Starts easily
- ☐ Cold-idle quality is good
- ☐ Gear selection quality is good

Steering Performance
- ☐ Steering wheel is aligned to center
- ☐ Vehicle tracking performance is good

Equipment Operation
- ☐ Instrument panel and all gauges are functioning
- ☐ Sound system in working order

Can you see all of the gauges clearly? Are they all functioning correctly? Test the headlights before driving as well. They will help you to see and be seen.

Powertrain Performance
- ☐ Check acceleration performance
- ☐ Check clutch operation (manual transmission)
- ☐ Check upshifting and downshifting performance
- ☐ Check steady throttle performance
- ☐ Check hot idle performance

Braking Performance
- ☐ Check vehicle tracking
- ☐ Check overall stopping performance

Post-Road Test
- ☐ Check for fluid leaks (visible inspection)
- ☐ Check all fluid levels
- ☐ Check hot restart performance

BEFORE THE FIRST 1,000 MILES

It's a good idea to check the oil level after the first road run. Let it sit for a few minutes so all the oil will settle. Otherwise, you will get an inaccurate reading.

While inspecting the tires, use a penny. To do a quick tread check, make sure Old Abe's face is covered to the top of his head. That's 4/32ths of an inch. If it doesn't cover, it's time for new tires.

Fluid Inspections and/or Changes
- ❏ Change engine oil, and oil filter (if installed)
- ❏ Check air filter
- ❏ Check automatic transmission fluid and filter (if applicable)
- ❏ Check manual transmission fluid
- ❏ Ensure front brakes have 50 percent or more material left and that components are in good working condition
- ❏ Ensure rear brakes have 50 percent or more material left and that and components are in good working condition
- ❏ Tires match, are properly inflated, and are in good working order
- ❏ Wheels match and are correct size and offset
- ❏ Tread depth has 4/32 inch remaining
- ❏ Tire sidewall condition is good
- ❏ Brake line condition is good
- ❏ Shocks and struts condition is good
- ❏ CV joints boot condition is good
- ❏ Check exhaust system
- ❏ Check front suspension
- ❏ Check rear suspension
- ❏ Check steering components
- ❏ Check wheel bolts torqued to specifications
- ❏ Check tire-changing equipment (including start, if applicable)
- ❏ Fan belt is tight and not damaged

Remote oil filters are readily available but not that common. If yours has one, this is the time to change it out.

Clean airflow requires good filters. Don't skimp on this. You have already spent a pretty penny on your engine, and it's wise to protect it.

HOW TO RESTORE YOUR VOLKSWAGEN BEETLE

CHAPTER 15

Appearance Standards
- ❏ Check body panels
- ❏ Check bumpers
- ❏ Check decals, emblems, and trim pieces are in place
- ❏ Check glass and lamp covers

Interior Condition
- ❏ Check instrument panel
- ❏ Check door panels
- ❏ Check seats
- ❏ Check headliner and package tray (if applicable)
- ❏ Check carpet, mats, and floor mats

The Volkswagen factory fan belt is designed to have a little bit of looseness. To check deflection, push on the center between the two pulleys. There should be no more than 3/8 inch in play.

There are six bolts on each side of the CV. It never hurts to go back to double-check that they are tight and not about to come off.

While inspecting the rear suspension and its components, go ahead and jack that corner of the car up. Remove the tire to get a clear view of everything.

It's always nicer to get into a clean ride than a dirty ride. If this is your pride and joy, keep it clean.

CHAPTER 16

CARE AND MAINTENANCE

One of the best perks of getting your ride finished is just looking at what you built, driving it, and enjoying your Dub. But why stop there? Attending an enthusiast event will let others see what you have done and give them inspiration on their builds too.

You've come a long way, baby! Hopefully you've taken a ton of photos throughout your restoration project. There's a certain sense of satisfaction that comes from being able to look at what you started with and see how far your Beetle has come to reach this point. You've learned a lot along the way too. Now, it's time to enjoy the fruits of your labor.

After pouring all of that blood, sweat, and tears into your project, you'll want to protect and care for your Beetle. You'll also enjoy showing it off to people who will appreciate all that went into the project.

Protecting Your Baby

You love your Beetle. Others lust after it. Even fully insured, you'd face a whole new level of heartbreak if someone decided to steal it. Fortunately, your Bug comes equipped with a highly effective theft deterrent, at least where most folks under the age of 50 are concerned. Driving a stick shift is a dying art form. One look at that rather mysterious third pedal and weird metal stick between the front seats might be enough to send thieves looking for another ride home.

However, some thieves do know how to drive stick. If they are determined enough, they will take it to strip it for parts or go for a joy ride. So take some measures to protect the car you have worked so hard to restore.

Park Smart

Half the battle is keeping your ride out of view from people who want to steal it. If at all possible, park it in a garage you can lock. Some classic car

The mysterious third pedal is nothing more than a lever and cable, but it can increase your driving pleasure as well as protect your ride. When was the last time you bought a manual car? And how long has it been since you learned to drive one?

owners rent storage space so they can park in a covered, locked structure if they don't have one at home.

It's a good idea to park in a covered area even if theft is not likely in your area. That's because of damage from the environment. Assuming you have waxed, sealed, or ceramic coated your ride, it should be able to withstand the sun's UV rays and other environmental elements. However, the finish will fare better under cover than out in the weather. Other options include building a carport, building a temporary garage (essentially, a metal surround with a heavy-duty tarp over the top), or using a custom cover. If you opt for a cover, be sure to get one specifically made for Beetles.

When away from home, pay close attention to your surroundings before parking. Dark alleys, run-down parking garages, or poorly lit parking lots with shady characters walking around are clear signs that you should keep looking for a better spot. Leave as much room between your Beetle and surrounding cars as possible, but don't be obnoxious about it.

Sometimes people are tempted to key or otherwise vandalize cars of owners they perceive to be offensive. While it's not recommended, if you plan to take up more than one parking spot, do it in the far corner of the lot so you don't occupy multiple desirable spots.

Make Your Beetle Hard(er) to Steal

You might want to consider equipping your Beetle with a global positioning system (GPS) tracker. Make sure to install it in a spot that is not obvious and where it is not likely to fall off during normal driving conditions. You'd hate to find out, after tracking your stolen car, that the geo-locator is transmitting from the spot where you usually park at your local grocery store.

A car alarm is not a viable strategy, although some owners still install them. Because of the age of these cars, there is no computer onboard, so an alarm would require a major upgrade to the wiring. Sensors would also need to be installed, which would quickly become a drain on the battery.

We recommend mechanical anti-theft measures. We will cover kill switches, fuel cutoffs, and battery shutoffs. Years ago, there was also a mechanism called a shift lock, which created a lockout in the shifter so a car would not be drivable. While the idea sounds like a good one, the mechanism received mixed reviews from the VW community. They are available from some aftermarket parts vendors.

Kill Switch

This handy mechanism interrupts the electrical circuit needed to start the car. Hidden in plain sight, it could be a hidden switch or button on the floor, in the glove box, or on the dash. It could even be installed

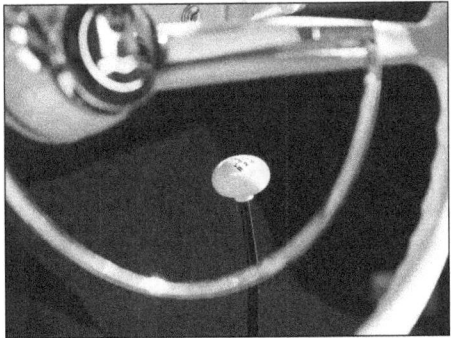

The stock 4-speed shifter is a tried-and-true choice. It also has a unique reverse lockout that only works correctly if you are in the know.

All of the time invested to bring your ride to this point is worth protecting. The blood, sweat, and tears you have shed makes it more precious.

Aftermarket car alarms are an option but not recommended. You would have to perform extensive modifications on the wiring harness to make an alarm work.

CARE AND MAINTENANCE

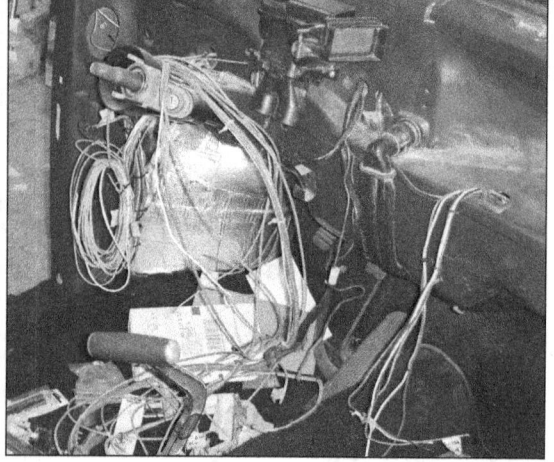

The way the alarm and disabling systems work is by adding sensors that control the flow of electricity to the electrical system.

While you can buy individual bits and pieces for a kill switch from the local auto parts store, we recommend buying a selection of wire-end connectors. If you make your own wiring harness, you should have this already. It is a less expensive way to go than buying individual ends.

in the spot for the rear window defroster control if you don't have a defroster. This spot is under the dash to the right of the steering wheel.

Kill switches are usually wired into the ignition system so the car can't be started, even with the key, if the switch is turned off. You can buy them at a local auto parts store.

Disconnect the battery before working on any part of the electrical system.

Tools Needed

- Correct-gauge wire
- Crimpers
- Drill and bits
- Kill switch
- Wire connectors

To install a kill switch, you will need a cordless drill, wire strippers and crimpers, a pair of needle-nose pliers, the switch, and various electrical connectors.

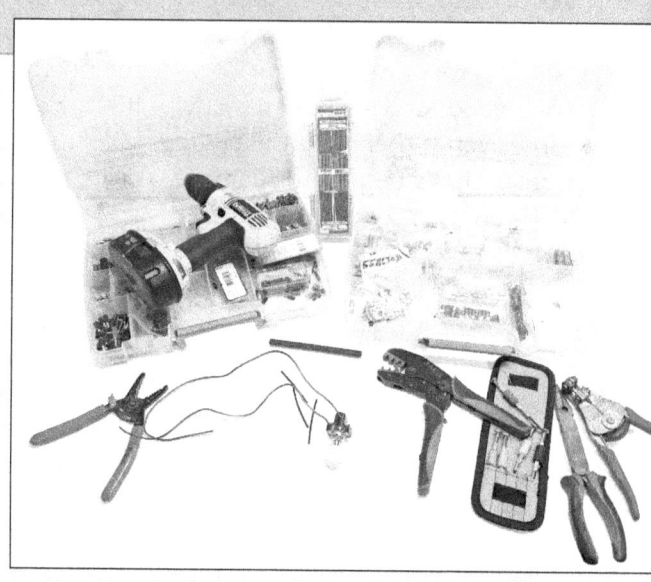

Kill Switch Installation

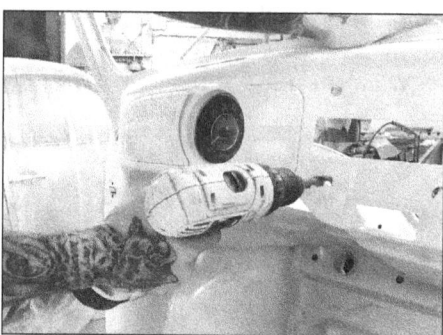

1 To install a hidden kill switch, sometimes it's best to hide it in plain sight, making it look as factory-correct as possible. It doesn't get any more factory-looking than being one of the dash switches.

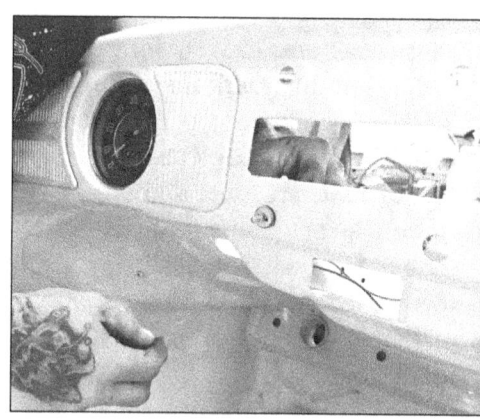

2 After drilling the hole to the correct size, we've converted a factory light switch into a kill switch. It sure looks like it came from the factory that way.

3 One of the finishing touches that makes this kill switch so stealthy is that we've installed a factory knob onto a factory switch in a factory location. That's how we got a factory look.

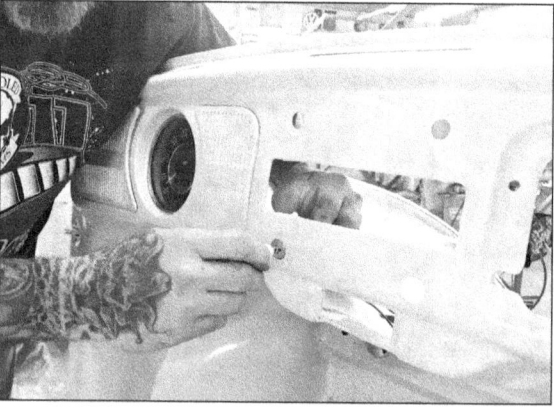

HOW TO RESTORE YOUR VOLKSWAGEN BEETLE

CHAPTER 16

Drilling Tips

Work neat. Measure twice, drill once. Put a piece of tape over the drill-hole location to help protect the finish. Drill slowly. Remember, it's not a race, and it's worth taking the time to do it right.

Tools Needed

- Fuel line
- Hose clamps
- Kit (Note: none are made specifically for Volkswagens, so you'll have to modify it to make it fit your needs)
- Screwdrivers
- Valve and/or remote control

You can add a secret switch that looks like a factory switch. Sometimes the best place to hide something valuable is in plain sight.

Drill the hole where you want to install the kill switch. You could pick somewhere it won't be seen, or you could make it blend in on the dash. Install the switch, interrupting the starter relay wire (likely, a 22-gauge red wire with a black tracer). Screw the capture nut on and you're all set.

Fuel Cutoff Switch

This mechanism shuts off the supply of fuel from the tank to the carburetor. The main fuel line runs inside the tunnel, and that's what you'll be working on. If the fuel line was replaced during the restoration, add a simple on/off switch that exits the tunnel somewhere by your feet. If it was not replaced, it can go underneath the gas tank, but it's a lot harder to do because you have to reach into a really cramped spot and practically be a contortionist to do the work. So if you're going to use a fuel cutoff switch, it's best to plan ahead and install it when you've got the best access to your work area.

You can get a fuel-cutoff switch at a local auto parts store. There are also fuel-rated manual switches available from larger online suppliers in the aftermarket. Or there are remote valves, maybe even one that's Bluetooth enabled, featuring an electric solenoid that opens and closes the valve via remote control.

When working with fuel, make sure the connections are tight and

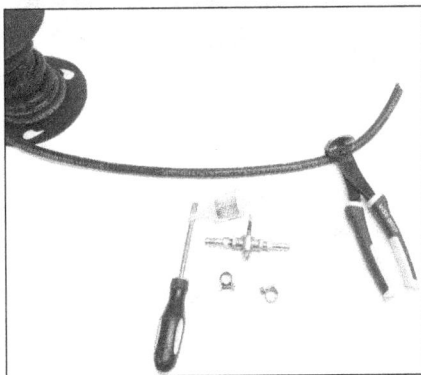

To install a fuel-cutoff switch, you will need a couple feet of SAE 1/4-inch ethanol-rated fuel line, a new fuel filter, a fuel petcock, and four fuel clamps.

the lines are clean. Stay away from open flames and have good ventilation. Keep a fire extinguisher within reach (a carbon-dioxide model is best). If you don't drain your fuel first, you may discover the joys of an armpit fill-up.

It's best to remove all fuel from the tank before installing this switch. Remove the fuel tank from the car.

Gather all the components needed to build this switch. They include an ethanol-rated fuel line, fuel filter, hose clamps, and the fuel-cutoff switch itself.

Install the fuel-cutoff switch on the bulkhead between the fuel line and the fuel tank. You may have to figure out some creative mounting strategy to make it work. It's easiest to attach to the fuel-pump bracket.

To assemble a fuel-cutoff switch, connect the rubber hose to the petcock, which connects to another rubber hose, which connects to the fuel filter. Snug it all down with the band clamps. Note, fuel filters are directional, and yours should be oriented toward the tank.

Here's what a fuel-cutoff switch will look like when it is installed. Inspect the hoses annually and replace them every 1 to 5 years, depending on your climate and fuel type.

Battery Cutoff Switch

This mechanism kills power at the source and is key-operated. The best location is usually behind the front passenger's seat in the kick panel in front of the battery. There is no kit; you'll be piecing it together like a member of the *A-Team*.

Disconnect the battery first before working on any part of the electrical system. Leave it all disconnected until it's time to test the switch after installation.

Disconnect the battery if it's not already disconnected. Pull the lower backseat out. It'll be easier to work that way. Remove the retaining bolts from both sides of your rear seat lower rail support. Take the passenger-side kick

Tools Needed

- 18-inch positive battery cable, eye end to eye end
- 48-inch positive battery cable, eye end to eye end
- Box cutter
- Dielectric grease
- Drill and bits

The battery cutoff switch is a very simple theft deterrent. Turn the key and remove it, and the battery will get no power.

There are a few types of fire extinguishers that you can buy. The carbon dioxide variety is the one to have. They are rechargeable and will not do damage by corrosion of parts and paint.

Power Side

Always run the power side on the interrupt. That will also stop any power drains in the car when the switch is not engaged. This will essentially unhook the battery. ∎

panel off. While the battery-cutoff switch can go anywhere, our preference is the passenger-side kick panel close to the tunnel. It is then within easy reach of the driver, close to the battery, and fairly well out of sight if someone doesn't know to look for it. Reinstall the kick panel and the rear seat lower rail support once the switch is installed.

Now, replace the starter-to-battery cable connection. Remove the existing positive cable from the starter. Then, replace the double-eye-end cable with the new cable, but wire it to the switch rather than the positive terminal on the battery. Take the shorter cable and attach that to the switch. The other end goes to the battery when it is reinstalled.

Keep It Shiny

There are two kinds of classic Volkswagen owners: the ones who happily spend hours washing, drying, and buffing their babies until they shine like glass, and those who dream of having a finish that would make that kind of tender loving care worthwhile.

If yours is a patina ride, it doesn't matter much how it is washed or even whether it is washed at all. If you're rolling with rust, remember that water feeds the hungry rust monster that's eating your vehicle. Keep it dry. If you wash it, dry it thoroughly as quickly as possible.

But if your Beetle is blessed with a beautiful newly painted and polished finish, are you going to go through a drive-through car wash? Would you pay the neighbor kid to hit it with the hose, some dish liquid, and a squeegee? No! Not after the time, effort, and money you just spent. The more you've invested in your vintage steel, the more careful you'll be about washing it. To *normal* folks (those who haven't been bitten by the bug) this might sound like drudgery—a dreaded task added to a weekend to-do list. But for the rest of us, doing it right and getting that gleaming finish is a project we enjoy.

Tools Needed

You will need a clean bucket that has been scrubbed out, not just emptied and air dried from the last time you used it. It's best to keep two

CHAPTER 16

Battery Disconnect Switch Installation

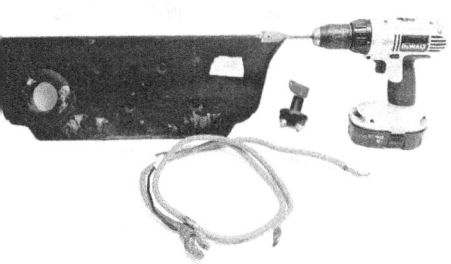

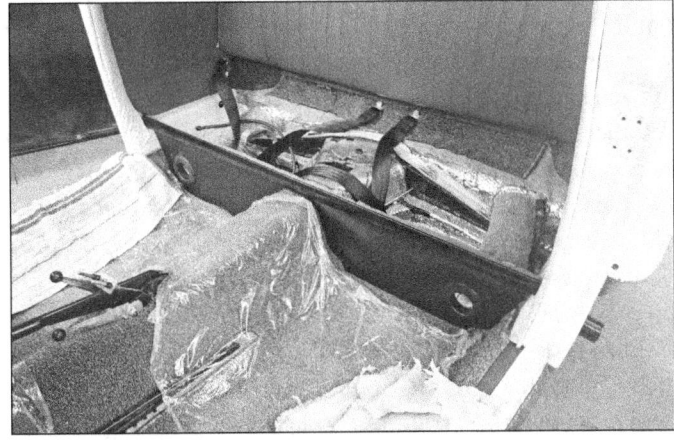

1 The battery cutoff switch will disconnect all power going from the battery to the electrical system. You will need a rear kick panel, a switch, a cordless drill with correct sized bit, and battery cables.

2 With the lower backseat removed, next you'll take off the front seat's rail support. There are two 10-mm bolts on each side. Remove them to access and remove the kick panel.

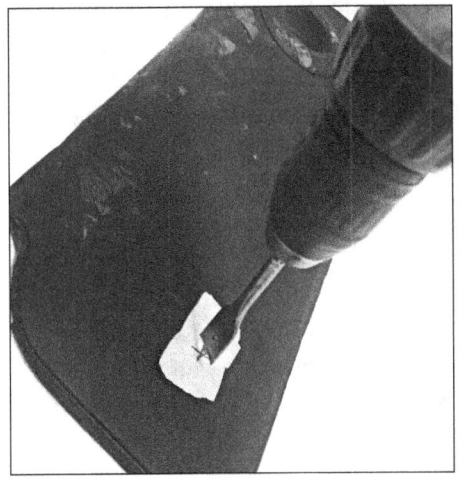

4 This battery cutoff switch was installed in a good location. This fairly inexpensive part installs easily and will keep your Beetle safe.

3 Mount the switch in the kick panel. We suggest doing it closer to the driver's side so you can reach it when you park.

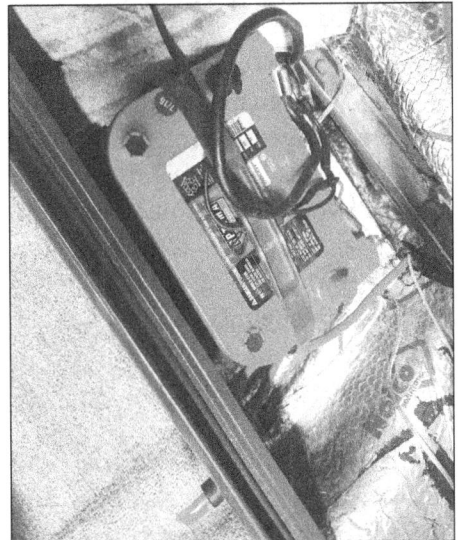

5 Hooking up the battery cutoff switch is fairly straightforward. One end goes from the starter to the switch. The other end goes to the battery.

6 Routing on the battery cables is key. While it might be tempting and easier to interrupt the ground side of the battery, we suggest installation on the positive side instead.

new buckets set aside in your garage only to ever be used to wash your Beetle.

Quality microfiber towels are a must. When you wash them, keep them separate from any other laundry. If you wash them with other cotton items, the cotton will cross-contaminate, potentially causing scratches or marring your paint finish. Always air dry because heat is microfiber's enemy.

Fill the buckets with clean water, and replace the water frequently while you work. Even if your supplies and water *look* pretty clean, they may have bits of dirt that can easily scratch your finish, deposit dirt on the finish, and leave runs and streaks. You might spend what seems like a ridiculous amount of time dumping and refilling your rinse bucket, but it will pay off with a beautiful shine.

When washing your car, always

> **Window Cleaning**
>
> • Use newspaper to get a streak-free shine on your windows. That's one of those tips you might remember your grandmother sharing. Not only does newspaper prevent streaking better than paper towels, you'll also avoid getting those tiny fibers all over the glass.
> • Wipe in one direction only. Pick side to side or up and down and stick with it. This is the best way to minimize streaks and will make them far less visible to the eye if you still manage to have some.
> • Start clean; and replace often. Everything you touch your car with needs to be clean, throughout the whole process. This means: clean rags should be used (washed in a washer, to remove lint, not just rinsed in a sink and hung to dry).

start at the top and work your way down. You don't want to scratch your finish by rubbing old dirt into your paint.

Show and Shine

Now that your baby is squeaky clean, it would be a shame not to show off your handiwork. On any given weekend, there's a car show, meet-up, Sonic Friday Cruise Night, or show and shine within driving distance. Some of the bigger regional events have been going on for well over a quarter century, bringing Dub lovers together for a good time.

Check with local shops to see if they do a show. Ask at clubs too. This is a good time to get together with new Dub buddies to see what they've been working on. You'll find that hanging out with other enthusiasts proves to be a good source of information (both good and bad). You'll meet hobbyists just like you and enjoy showing off your handiwork with someone who gets it.

Some of these shows have trophies for categories you can enter. At large regional events, there are usually classes for every category you can imagine: farthest driven, loudest sound system, most rust, lowest suspension, and more. Shows are typically either one- or two-day events, but there are a few that stack shows together to last a whole week.

Bring Your Baby to a Show

If you built it and you're comfortable and confident in your work, go ahead and drive it. If you're not sure, not comfortable, or don't want to pile on the extra miles, trailer it. Either way, it's a good idea to get tow insurance. Most plans offer free towing up to a certain distance, and it's a cheap backup plan to get you home or to your local shop just in case you need it.

Security at shows is 100 percent up to you. Of course, some shows have security guards roaming around to keep an eye on things, but in the end, the safety and security of your car is on you. It's rare, but sometimes malfeasants creep in and steal Dubs.

With that being said, here are some tips to help keep your ride safe at a show.

Got Your Keys?

Make sure you have your keys on your person. Shows can get busy when we find ourselves catching up with old acquaintances; it's easy to forget.

That Ride Won't Run!

If you're parked overnight on the show grounds; pull the coil wire or even all the wires. Disable the vehicle or at least make it hard to do the old *run and roll*. If it's hard for them to get moving quick, they will probably look for easier pickings.

Keep Your S.A. Up

Look out for your mates and their rides. Just asking a question may run off a ne'er-do-well. Situational awareness is king. If you know someone is camping close to your baby, ask them to do a spot check on your ride, even if it's on the way to the facilities or to grab a cold beer.

Open Your Mouth

Report all suspicious activity and get as many details as you can about what you saw. Don't be a hero. Contact authorities and show personnel as soon as possible if you see anything suspicious.

Keep Your Details Handy

Know your vehicle's information, including the VIN, registration, etc. Having photos helps as well. You've got a smartphone, let it make you smart. It helps during the reporting process if the car does go missing.

We've All Got *That* Friend...

Make sure it wasn't one of your mates with *that* sense of humor. We have all seen that happen and know *that* guy. Friends don't let friends have coronaries over fake stolen cars.

Maintenance

By now, you should know your Beetle inside out and be able to feel, see, and hear any problems as it runs. Do you hear a noise you haven't heard before, or one that sounds different than it used to? Check it out quickly.

Remember, these old cars aren't the same as any modern car you

Get out and enjoy the local car show scene. Check with local car clubs, current events pages, and local shops. There is usually a show or two going on every weekend within driving distance.

Sometimes the simplest things are the easiest to do. No coil-to-distributor wire? No fire. No run. Thieves are looking for the easy way out, and if you make your ride harder to steal, they may just keep looking and skip yours.

can drive off the lot and neglect for months before pulling in for a quickie oil change.

In addition to responding to your Beetle's every plea for attention, be sure to check the following regularly.

- Oil changed?
- Valves adjusted?
- Fluid levels checked?
- Checked for leaks?

Transmission Troubles

Shifting your Dub should be a breeze, but sometimes it's not. Let's look at some common transmission issues you may encounter, especially if you refurbished the transmission rather than rebuilding or replacing it.

Ailing Shift Rails

We'll start with the first-to-second and third-to-fourth shift rails. They routinely wear their respective bores in the gear carrier. Shifting movement of the steel rail in the softer magnesium carrier wears enough material in the bore to allow the rail to move, and it affects how the fork shifts. We also see many mainshaft bearing bores in the gear carriers worn too much, allowing for the bearing to slide. The gear carrier will then need to have a sleeve machined in to allow a tight bearing bore.

Fourth Gear Pop-Outs

Another common problem is the transaxle/transmission popping out of fourth gear. The makeup of the angle between the operating sleeve and synchronizer hub is really what keeps the gearbox in gear. Volkswagen factory third- and fourth-gear operating sleeves were only flank cut on the fourth gear side and only on one side of the tooth. Over time, this would allow the operating sleeve to wear, so the angle of engagement with the synchronizer hub would not properly hold it in gear.

Back-Up Abuse

Reverse gear is probably the most abused item in a Volkswagen transaxle/transmission. Reverse was made to be engaged when the vehicle is stopped. Most transaxles/transmissions that have a reverse gear problem will have the associated operating sleeve damaged. Once both are replaced, proper engagement will allow smooth operation with no grinding.

The Nose Knows

Nose cones are another item vital to the transaxle/transmission shifting correctly. Used and worn, they can allow differences that put pressure on the hockey stick and shift rails. Normal movement of the helical cut gears can cause a force that pushes on the mainshaft bearing, which in turn puts a force on the inside of the nose cone and causes internal wear.

Spot Weld Shafts May Fail

One of the most-overlooked areas on a transaxle/transmission is the clutch cross shaft. Volkswagen only spot-welded the arms from the factory. Over the years, with many types of clutch and pressure plate combinations, the welds have a tendency to weaken and the arms break off. We advise anyone who takes the engine out to either replace or strengthen the factory shaft before the engine in reinstalled.

Shifting Your Shifting Style May Help

Most of the transmission problems the driver has no control over. Others, such as the driver not stopping the vehicle before shifting into reverse, can be controlled and overcome with proper shifting techniques.

Conclusion

People either get the fascination with Beetles or they don't. It's understandable, really, given that these little cars were mass-produced to the point many considered them disposable, almost like the metal lunchboxes kids used a few generations ago. They were cool, even cute, but not obviously destined to become prized belongings.

Once Bug fever hits, it's hard to shake. It's no wonder that so many enthusiasts drag their old, rusted-out Beetles with them for years, even decades, waiting for the right time to restore them. Others carry an odd fondness for these little cars, building theirs in their imagination for years before they ever get to turn a wrench for real.

They say that about 10 minutes after the first Model-T rolled off the factory line, there were tinkerers already planning how they'd modify theirs. Make it faster, better, shinier; make it yours. The drive to mess with perfection is always there for us. That said, don't be surprised if your nearest and dearest raise an eyebrow or two as you reveal your plan to undertake a restoration project. Just as importantly, consider carefully whether you should share details (especially money-wise) about your plan with them.

While the highly desired barn find is becoming an urban legend, there are still so many Beetles out there looking for a little love. Unlike with some car makes and models, there is really no *correct* way to restore a Beetle. Of course, this means that one owner's customization dream is enough to set another's teeth on edge. We all develop personal preferences, and it doesn't take long to determine what you like and hate. A quick stroll through any Volkswagen car show will help you refine your project's punch list.

Will it all be worth it in the end? If we're talking dollars and cents on the open market, it might take a generation or two to recoup your investment. The law of supply and demand is working in your favor, though. So much depends on the year, model, condition, and even your location. In some countries, certain VW types are extraordinarily rare, where they're commonplace in others. For example, in the United States, it's unusual to see a single cab or double cab because not many were imported. We can thank the infamous Chicken Tax for that particular shortage.

For a long time, enthusiasts went wild for old Beetles while wrinkling their noses at later models, and downright snubbing Super Beetles. But as each year passes, there are fewer and fewer Beetles around, making the available ones more desirable just because they're becoming rare. All that being said, your Beetle restoration project is primarily a matter of personal preferences and desire. Build the Bug you love, consider it a work in progress, and then enjoy it to the hilt, whether that means driving it around town or across the country, or sheltering it securely in a trailer.

We hope this guide will help you through your Beetle's restoration process and wish you many years of enjoyment to come.

There's nothing more satisfying than stepping back to appreciate the result of all your toil. What you've accomplished is truly a remarkable feat, one that very few people ever tackle. Drive and enjoy your Beetle in good health!

Source Guide

3M Corporate Headquarters
3M Center
St. Paul, MN 55144-1000
888-364-3577
3m.com

Aircooled Werk
456 Peachtree Circle
Ringgold, GA 30736
423-364-4669
aircooledwerk.com

Aircooled Net
379 West 6500 South
Murray, UT 84107
801-453-1906
Aircooled.net

Aircooled Accessories
The Old Slaughterhouse
Shipley Gate
Eastwood
Nottingham
NG16 3JE
UK
aircooledaccessories.com

Airhead Parts
1604 Morse Ave.
Ventura, CA 93001
805-650-2050
airheadparts.com

Albrights Supply
2102 S Tate St.
Corinth, MS 38834
662-287-1451
albrightssupply.com

Auto Atlanta
505 S. Marietta Pkwy.
Marietta, GA 30060
800-792-4944
autoatlanta.com

Barrett Jackson Auctions
7400 E. Monte Cristo Ave.
Scottsdale, AZ 85260
480-421-6694
barrett-jackson.com

Bus Depot
4801 Gravel Pike
Perkiomenville, PA 18074
866-BUS-DEPOT
busdepot.com

Busware
C/O Thomas A Buese
922 Southern Bay Rd.
Penobscot, ME 04476
801-521-3335
busware.biz

Buttys Bits
buttysbits.com

Calfornia Pacific-Jbugs
1338 Rocky Point Dr.
Oceanside, CA 92056
800-231-1784
jbugs.com

California Imports
1124 Fir Ave. PMB #108
Blaine, WA 98230
800-313-3811
cip1.com

CB Performance
1715 N. Farmersville Blvd.
Farmersville, CA 93223
800-274-8337
cbperformance.com

Ceramic Pro
5745 Kearny Villa Rd., Suite 107
San Diego, CA 92123
800-280-6856
ceramicpro.com

Chirco
9101 E 22nd St.
Tucson, AZ 85710
800-955-9795
chirco.com

Chucks Convertible Parts
866-673-5123
chucksconvertibleparts.com

Ed's Foreign Car Parts
535 Locust St.
Gadsden, AL 35901
256-546-9279

Farrar Hazel Green Tire Center
14153 Hwy. 231 431 N
Hazel Green, AL 35750
256-693-8030
farrartire.com

Finishmaster
115 West Washington St., Suite 700 S
Indianapolis, IN 46204
888-311-3678
finishmaster.com

Goodspeed Motoring
5404 Pirrone Rd.
Salida, CA 95368
209-577-1133
goodspeedmotoring.com

Griot's Garage
3333 South 38th St.
Tacoma, WA 98409
800-345-5789
griotsgarage.com

Grumpy's Metal
15924 Manufacture Lane
Huntington Beach, CA 92649
714-869-1028
grumpysmetal.com

Huntsville Mobile Blasting
256-424-2406
hsvsandblasting.com

It's Not Paint
856 Nick Fitchard Rd.
Huntsville, AL 35806
256-726-9009
itsnotpaint.com

Johnson Foreign Auto Inc.
1215 Putnam Dr.
Huntsville, AL 35816
256-830-0620
johnsonforeignauto.com

Line-X Decatur Customs
301 James Record Rd., Suite 250
Huntsville, AL 35824
877-330-1331
linex.com

Mid-America Motorworks
17082 N. US Hwy. 45
Effingham, IL 62401
800-428-2200
mamotorworks.com

Retro Sound
7470 Commercial Way
Henderson, NV 89011
888-325-1555
retromanufacturing.com

Rochford Supply
7624 Boone Ave. N., Suite 200
Brooklyn Park, MN 55428
866-681-7401
rochfordsupply.com

Rusty Bottom Garage
219 Bellaire Dr.
Smyrna, TN 37167
615-400-2059
rustybottomgarage.com

The Samba
thesamba.com

Summit Racing Mail
800-230-3030
summitracing.com

T & T Soda Blasting
28 Snow Rd.
Flintville, TN 37335

Tire Rack
7101 Vorden Pkwy.
South Bend, IN 46628
888-541-1777
tirerack.com

Wagenwerks
12127 Mall Blvd., #263
Victorville, CA 92392
760-949-2494
wagen-werks.com

Wawak
1059 Powers Rd.
Conklin, NY 13748-1400
800-654-2235
wawak.com

Wolfsburg West
2850 Palisades Dr.
Corona, CA 92880
888-965-3937
wolfsburgwest.com

Wolfgang International
1117 Parkview Ave.
Redding, CA 96001
530-246-4264
wolfgangint.com

www.ingramcontent.com/pod-product-compliance
Lightning Source LLC
Chambersburg PA
CBHW081448070526
44586CB00019B/2269